THE LANGUAGE OF
SHAKESPEARE'S PLAYS

THE LANGUAGE OF
SHAKESPEARE'S PLAYS

by

IFOR EVANS

Provost, University College, London
Sometime Professor of English Language and Literature
in the University of London

METHUEN & CO. LTD, LONDON
11 New Fetter Lane, E.C.4

First published February 14, 1952
Second Edition 1959
Third Edition 1964

3.1
CATALOGUE NO. 02/5375/35

PRINTED IN GREAT BRITAIN BY
JARROLD AND SONS LTD, NORWICH

CONTENTS

▼

41834

TO
SIR ALBERT STERN

INTRODUCTION

THE literature in English on Shakespeare's use of language is small when compared with the many studies of his characters, of his stage technique, and of all the bibliographical problems which surround the text of his plays. Through incidental references Dryden, Samuel Johnson and others said notable things about his language, and the way it was employed in the plays, but they did not approach the question systematically, or as a separate theme. Here they realised was something impressive and unusual, and it is clear from a number of passages, some of which are quoted in this volume, that Johnson had thought closely on the whole problem.

One of the earliest studies, as Professor F. P. Wilson has recently indicated,[1] was W. Whiter's *A Specimen of a Commentary on Shakespeare*, *1794* with, "(1) Notes on *As You Like It*, and (2) An attempt to explain and illustrate various passages on a new principle of criticism, derived from Mr. Locke's Doctrine of *The Association of Ideas*". Whiter did give a number of examples of Shakespeare's use of imagery, particularly of his repeated employment of the same cluster of images. Whiter had no uncertainty as to the importance of his own work: 'I have endeavoured to unfold the secret and subtle operations of genius from the most indubitable doctrine in the theory of metaphysics. As these powers of the imagination have never, I believe, been adequately conceived, or systematically discussed, I may perhaps be permitted, on this occasion, to adopt the language of science and to assume the merit of DISCOVERY'. Unfortunately, Whiter was left neglected both by the romantic critics and by more recent writers.

It has been one of the happy features of modern criticism, possibly following Coleridge's discussions in *Biographia Literaria*, that a new and rewarded attention has been given to these questions. Two studies appeared in the middle 'thirties, Professor Caroline Spurgeon's *Shakespeare's Imagery*[2] and Dr. Wolfgang Clemen's *Shakespeares Bilder*.[3] These two volumes gave the

[1] *Shakespeare and the Diction of Common Life* (1941).
[2] *Shakespeare's Imagery and What it tells us* (1935).
[3] *Shakespeares Bilder, ihre Entwicklung und Funktionem in dramatischen Werke* (Bonn, 1936); *The Development of Shakespeare's Imagery* (London, 1951).

general direction to recent studies of Shakespearian language. They both concentrated on exploring Shakespeare's use of imagery, which remains the most memorable single element in his language. While Clemen attempted to set his comments on imagery within the general problem of dramatic writing, Professor Spurgeon, who was using statistical methods, was concerned rather in estimating what could be discovered of Shakespeare's thought, personality and taste from the language he employed.

Apart from a lecture by Professor Ellis-Fermor, *Some Recent Research in Shakespeare's Imagery*[1] I feel that Professor Spurgeon's work has not been generously received in either England or America. It is true that she pursued her method so ruthlessly that some of her results were rather naive, and the spirit of mockery can play successfully over some passages in the study. But her work, if considered justly, must be regarded as a whole. We all use the volume, even those who have treated it with less than the respect it deserves. The work of Spurgeon and Clemen has shown that there were many further problems to be considered. Already, earlier than either of these, George Rylands in *Words and Poetry* (1928) had studied, most successfully, the development of Shakespeare's language as it was shown in his imagery. Wilson Knight in *The Wheel of Fire* (1930), *The Imperial Theme* (1931) and in other studies made imaginative speculations on the relation of the imagery, particularly what Professor Spurgeon called an 'iterative imagery' to the meaning of the tragedies as a whole. F. P. Wilson brought his great resources of knowledge of the whole problem of Shakespearian language, as far as the limits of an Academy lecture would allow, into *Shakespeare and the Diction of Common Life* (1941). More recently E. A. Armstrong in *Shakespeare's Imagination* (1946) made some interesting discoveries of the associations in Shakespeare's language worked out in a psychological method, happily and unaggressively employed. He approached the problem somewhat as Whiter had done in the eighteenth century.

There has also been a revival of a close study of Shakespeare's linguistic training and background, especially in T. W. Baldwin's *William Shakespeare's Small Latine and Lesse Greeke* (1944) and in Sister Miriam Joseph's *Shakespeare's Use of the Arts of Language* (1947). Both authors emphasise Shakespeare's knowledge and

[1] Oxford University Press (1937).

employment of the forms of rhetoric and logic regularly taught in the Latin textbooks in the Tudor grammar schools. Sister Joseph presents the general theory of composition current during the Renaissance, and illustrates Shakespeare's employment of it. The studies of Baldwin and Sister Joseph emphasise the complexity of the background of Shakespeare's language and the difficulty of distinguishing his personal contribution from patterns which were traditionally at his disposal. Sister Joseph tabulates numerous passages in Shakespeare's plays which correspond precisely with the figures of Tudor logic and rhetoric. It is not, of course, necessary to conclude that Shakespeare was conscious on all occasions in this practice, but she does emphasise that he was far more conscious than a modern audience, with a different training, would imagine. Further, he came at a time, when despite all this precision of terms, the language itself was free and unformed and ready for an adventurer. The terms of grammar, logic and rhetoric were derived from the Latin textbooks and from those who imitated them, and the freedom came from the very genius of the English language at that period. From this contrast grew Shakespeare's opportunity as George Gordon noted: 'Shakespeare was to do what he liked with English grammar, and drew beauty and power from its imperfections. In the rankness and wildness of the language he found his opportunity, and exploited it royally, sometimes tyrannically.'[1]

In the present study I have made use of these earlier studies. I have emphasised that imagery, however brilliant and original, is only one part of Shakespeare's language. Much that was most moving in his plays was written in the simplest language without any dependence on those great sources of imagery which he had always at command. I came to this study with the belief that some of my predecessors, whose work I have so much admired, thought too often of Shakespeare's language as something detached from the theatre, and separate from the problems of the dramatist.

I have followed through the plays, commenting on the problems which faced Shakespeare. As a dramatist he was always in a sort of splendid peril, for language so delighted him that he loved words for their own sake and it was as if they knew his weakness and were ever ready to overpower him. He was in danger as a

[1] *Shakespeare's English* (1928).

dramatist of being overwhelmed by the exuberance of his own verbal genius. In some of the plays he was able to release all his linguistic energies freely into his creation as he did in *Love's Labour's Lost*. At times he was analytical and self-critical in his use of language and the results are to be found in *Romeo and Juliet* and *Hamlet* and in some of the other plays. At times there seems a unity between the critical and creative elements and this leads to the linguistic triumph of *King Lear*.

I have found it necessary to make a frequent distinction between the language of simple, and direct statement where Shakespeare is so effective, though his achievement here has never been sufficiently praised, and the language of true or false persuasion where the formal embellishments of language are exploited. I have used the term *rhetorical* for this second way of writing. It is true that *rhetoric* was also used in the Elizabethan age for the formal rules and arts of language, and I have also employed the term, *rhetoric*, where necessary, in that sense. Yet I know no term, other than *rhetoric* which will define the ornate way of writing which Landor defined as the *opaque* style. I think no ambiguity exists in the text, but I felt that this amount of explanation might be necessary.

We, in this age, have been able to welcome verse back into drama on the stage. The poetic dramatist is not merely writing verse, but verse that can be employed in the theatre. This Shakespeare did supremely, but he was always tempted to do much else.

I have had to accept a certain chronological order for the plays, but there is little in my argument that depends on the precise order which I have employed. In a volume such as this, quotations must play an important part, and so, for ease of reference, I have had to fall back upon a modernised text and I have used the *Globe* edition.

In a work on Shakespeare one is always indebted to one's predecessors, both the living and the dead, and where I have failed to make an acknowledgement I would ask to be forgiven. As Dryden said in introducing a far more original piece, this is a discourse mainly drawn from the discoveries of others. I would add, less modestly, that one or two of the ideas are my own derived from a quarter of a century of study of this theme. What I have tried to emphasise throughout is that language in drama must be referred to the effect that it can make in the theatre. Far too much English criticism appeals to the reader in the study rather than the man or woman in the theatre who stood or sat around that Elizabethan stage and listened to a dramatic action.

I.E.

For some time now this volume has been out of print. In preparing this new edition I have much expanded the chapters dealing with the history plays. I have been increasingly impressed by the place which they occupy in the development of Shakespeare's writing as a dramatist.

January, 1959.   I.E.

CHAPTER I

THE BEGINNING IN WORDS:

Love's Labour's Lost

EVEN if *Love's Labour's Lost* was not the first of the plays it must have been among the earliest, and it is concerned almost wholly with words. Unlike the later comedies and romances this brilliant and original piece has no *story* plot. The King of Navarre and his three companions take an oath to keep themselves apart for three years to study, and above all 'not to see a woman'. To them come the Princess of France and her ladies and, each in turn, the men break their oath. The whole is very prettily conceived, with a regularity in all the essential concerns of the unities, but with the real charm and beauty lying in an atmosphere of sophisticated society displayed through an elegant variety of verbal entertainments.

Something Shakespeare derived from his contemporaries, and more precisely from John Lyly, and he had come to the stage when words were one of the major excitements and adventures of alert and creative minds. So he fell upon a plot, or rather an elegant device, which was cunningly and dramatically maintained, so that language might have the necessary situations for diverse and entertaining employment. It is with words, not with plot and characters that the play lives. They are words sought for their own sake, words dancing to unexpected rhythms, and twisting themselves into fantastic shapes, words robbed from the rhetoricians, and strung out, half-mockingly, into patterns borrowed from the grammarians, with images and conceits already made popular by the sonneteers, and words handled lovingly, and placed into new contexts, with a beginning of an awareness of their illimitable power.

He thinks consciously about the delight of words and compares them to costumes worn with a studied pride in their magnificence, to taffeta and silk, and velvet luxuriously woven with a triple pile:

> Taffeta phrases, silken terms precise,
>   Three-piled hyperboles, spruce affectation,
> Figures pedantical.   (v.2.406)

Even in this earliest phase he knew the difference between the pleasure derived from these elegant varieties and from 'russet yeas and honest kersey noes' (v.2.413). Already he had seen the great conflict, ever to pursue him in his employment of language: on the one hand all the temptations and opportunities of a sumptuous diction, with cohorts of proud words, and, on the other, all the dramatic strength which could be gained in simple and direct statement.

He knew that there were words and phrases which had in some strange way a power beyond their immediate context, as if the imagination were holding in reserve resources which it could not use within the present pattern. Walter Pater noticed this,[1] and quoted some of the most striking examples: 'below the many artifices of Biron's amorous speeches we may trace sometimes the "unutterable longing" and the lines in which Katharine describes the blighting through love of her younger sister are one of the most touching things in older literature.'[2] Again, how many echoes seem awakened by those strange words, actually said in jest: 'The sweet war-man [Hector of Troy] is dead and rotten; sweet chucks, beat not the bones of the buried: when he breathed, he was a man' (v.2.665).

In this early play the battle of words was thus already set, and the trial of strength between elegance, bravura, action, contemplation, discipline, extravagance and tenderness continued to the end.

His mind delighted in coloured and decorative extravagances, and his ear responded to all the commensurate devices of sound. One can see the image of this fresh and glowing creation of words in his own description of Armado:

> a most illustrious wight,
> A man of fire-new words, fashion's own knight.
>
> (i.1.178)

Despite the few phrases which explore some unplumbed depth he had not yet developed a high seriousness in employing words. In this early exercise it is the enjoyment that is supreme, the breathless playfulness, almost as if language were an intoxicating merriment. Later he was often to consider the danger of words, as in *The Merchant of Venice*:

[1] *Love's Labour's Lost* in *Appreciations*.   [2] Act V, Scene II.

> The fool hath planted in his memory
> An army of good words; and I do know
> A many fools, that stand in better place,
> Garnish'd like him, that for a tricksy word
> Defy the matter.
>
> (iii.5.71)

Here no such considerations restrain him, and 'the army of good words' makes onslaught where it will.

In *Love's Labour's Lost*, more than anywhere else, the mechanics of language, grammar, logic and rhetoric dominated his attention. It was as if he had just escaped from the class-room into the theatre. Thus the language of logic entered into the very protestations of love, as with Longaville:

> Did not the heavenly rhetoric of thine eye,
>   'Gainst whom the world cannot hold argument,
> Persuade my heart to this false perjury?
>
> (iv.3.60)

Shakespeare's training had taught him all the complex nomenclature for grammar and the figures of speech, but fortunately, he came at a period when, despite all the elaboration of the rules, language itself was in a state of flux, when grammar and spelling were both uncertain. As G. S. Gordon has written: 'One exhilarating result of the linguistic licence of the century was, in its later years at any rate, a period of almost complete freedom'.[1]

Some of the patterns which he detected in contemporary artifice he satirised, but he was fascinated even when he mocked, so that it is difficult precisely to draw the distinction between his own language and his parody of current excesses. 'They have been at a great feast of languages,' says Moth (v.1.39) of Holofernes and Nathaniel, and indeed this is true of all the characters: they have all lived long 'on the alms-basket of words' (v.1.41). Language is for them a game to be played as they might play a game of tennis. After Katharine and Rosaline have had a pretty exchange of phrases the Princess says: 'Well bandied both; a set of wit well play'd' (v.2.29). Holofernes and Nathaniel enjoy together their 'sweetly varied epithets', and when Holofernes gives his verbal portrait of Armado so memorable does Nathaniel consider it that he takes out his notebook to record the 'most singular and choice' epithet with which it concludes.

[1] *Shakespeare's English* (1928).

Out of this great welter of language, this rapier play of words, Shakespeare was later to develop his own imaginative diction highly metaphorical, and, at its best, disciplined for the service of drama. But the fascination of words themselves, their sound and shape, their music and their arrangement, remained with him to the end as a power capable in moments of danger of overwhelming any other purpose he might have in hand. The vitality in Shakespeare's language means that there is ever this struggle to retain control 'to beget a temperance in a storm of passion'. Even in the most mature plays a character can be led away on one occasion or another by the *fata morgana* of a phrase. It is as if Shakespeare were riding some spirited animal, capable of moving with beauty and swiftness, but whose power remains a problem calling for dexterity and concentration. Samuel Johnson described the temptations which beset Shakespeare in one of the most memorable of all the passages in his *Preface to Shakespeare*:

A quibble is to *Shakespeare* what luminous vapours are to the traveller! he follows it at all adventures; it is sure to lead him out of his way, sure to engulf him in the mire. It has some malignant power over his mind, and its fascinations are irresistible. Whatever be the dignity or profundity of his disquisition, whether he be enlarging knowledge or exalting affection, whether he be amusing attention with incidents, or enchaining it in suspense, let but a quibble spring up before him and he leaves his work unfinished. A quibble is the golden apple for which he will always turn aside from his career, or stoop from his elevation. A quibble, poor and barren as it is, gave him such delight, that he was content to purchase it by the sacrifice of reason, propriety, and truth. A quibble was to him the fatal Cleopatra for which he lost the world, and was content to lose it.

Some of the topical affectations and pretensions of speech are so precisely satirised that they can be easily identified. The King's opening speech is in the language of the sonneteers:

When, spite of cormorant devouring Time,
The endeavour of this present breath may buy
That honour which shall bate his scythe's keen edge
And make us heirs of all eternity.

(i.1.4)

The rhythm and imagery of the sonneteers dance in and out of the verse as if constantly to remind the audience that the mood of the whole is one of pseudo-seriousness. In the Fourth Act

Nathaniel reads a sonnet which Armado has written for Jaquenetta and later Longaville reads a sonnet of his own composition, and both of these William Jaggard seized upon for the miscellaneous collection of sonnets which in 1599 he published as 'The Passionate Pilgrim by William Shakespeare'.

As Walter Pater realised, this play with the mannerisms of the sonnet had its own half-discovered beauty: 'Such modes or fashions are, at their best, an example of the artistic predominance of form over matter; of the manner of the doing of it over the thing done; and have a beauty of their own. It is so with that old euphuism of the Elizabethan age—that pride of dainty language and curious expression, which is very easy to ridicule, which often made itself ridiculous, but which had below it a real sense of fitness and nicety; and which, as we see in this very play, and still more clearly in the Sonnets, had some fascination for the young Shakespeare himself.'

Armado's language is more pedantical and affected than that of the sonneteers:

> A man in all the world's new fashion planted,
>   That hath a mint of phrases in his brain;
> One whom the music of his own vain tongue
>   Doth ravish like enchanting harmony.
>
> (i.1.165)

In a self-conscious way he explores the remoter territories of speech seeking the 'high born words' which he considers admirable. He runs through a triple series of phrases, obeying that rhetorical principle of triplicity, employing it here satirically, though later Shakespeare used it for other purposes: 'I do affect the very ground, which is base, where her shoe, which is baser, guided by her foot, which is basest, doth tread' (i.2.172).

So self-conscious is Armado in his language that he is ever ready to add comment and explanation on his verbal procedure, and so when Moth asks why he should be called a 'tender juvenal' Armado replies: 'I spoke it, tender juvenal, as a congruent epitheton appertaining to thy young days, which we may nominate tender' (i.2.13).

Some critics, notably Frances M. Yates[1] and Miss M. C. Bradbrook[2] have, most ingeniously, discovered satiric portraits of individuals behind the various characters in the play. 'Armado',

[1] *A Study of Love's Labour's Lost* (1936).   [2] *The School of Night* (1936).

writes Miss Bradbrook, 'fits Ralegh perfectly. The fact that he is a Spaniard is such an insult to one of the sea-dogs that it also serves as positive evidence. The king gives his character at length: he is a literary man and orator, and a writer. . . . The dandy, the planter of Virginia, the spinner of travellers' tales appears at once in "fashion's own knight".' It may well be that Shakespeare was involved in the satire of Ralegh and his friends of the 'School of Night', and many of the minor characters must have meant more to the sophisticated in the contemporary audience than they can do to-day. But the real interest of the comedy lies elsewhere, for its characters are not individuals, only types, intelligible dramatically, even if one has not heard of Ralegh. Miss Bradbrook courageously admits this: 'the play is, on the whole, more concerned with theories of living than with personalities: the satire is not sustained or consistent.'

The 'congruent' side of Armado's 'epitheton' he shares with the schoolmaster, Holofernes, who also is an explorer in the lesser known continents of words. Some who would try to define the shadowy path of Shakespeare's biography would rely on Aubrey for the story said to be told by William Beeston, son of Christopher Beeston, a fellow actor with Shakespeare, that before he came to London Shakespeare was himself a country schoolmaster. T. W. Baldwin is ready to accept Aubrey on this occasion.[1] If one were to credit this theory then Holofernes might be a portrait of an extravagant, fantastic, but ultimately dull-witted pedant. If Shakespeare had been a schoolmaster then the play represents his release from the schoolroom to life and to the theatre, and it would serve as an interpretation of his extraordinary familiarity with the arts of grammar and rhetoric.

Holofernes is a critic of Armado's speech and of his pronunciation. He is different from the courtiers, for he has more of the apparatus of learning, however fantastically it may function and however defective it may be in parts. He is the pedant, displaying his Latin, his knowledge of grammar, and the dullness of his mind, but a dullness rendered comic by the fancy created out of it. Indeed the opening phrases of his criticism of Armado could well be applied to his own utterances: 'He draweth out the thread of his verbosity finer than the staple of his argument. I abhor such fanatical phantasimes, such insociable and point-devise compan-

[1] *William Shakespeare's Small Latine and Lesse Greeke.*

ions; such rackers of orthography, as to speak dout, fine, when he should say doubt; det, when he should pronounce debt—d, e, b, t, not d, e, t: he clepeth a calf, cauf; half, hauf; neighbour vocatur nebour; neigh abbreviated ne. This is abhominable—which he would call abbominable: it insinuateth me of insanie: Ne intelligis, dominie? to make frantic, lunatic' (v.1.18). Later Armado and Holofernes are to be found in a competitive exercise of their comparative skill, for when Armado comments 'the posteriors of this day, which the rude multitude call the afternoon', Holofernes replies: 'The posterior of the day, most generous sir, is liable, congruent and measurable for the afternoon: the word is well culled, chose, sweet and apt, I do assure you, sir, I do assure' (v.1.94). The deficiencies of Holofernes' scholarship are a matter open to argument. It has been asserted with some confidence that he misquotes the opening line of the first eclogue of Mantuan (iv.2.98-9), but it might be suggested that this is possibly a defect of the text rather than a defect in Holofernes' wits. If he misquotes this commonplace tag he is at the same time familiar with more complicated matters, so the jest is not wholly well-founded.

Sir Nathaniel, the curate, shares much of Holofernes' muddled enthusiasm for language. Seldom is he satisfied with a single phrase, and he piles them one upon the other until the resources of his mind are exhausted: 'Your reasons at dinner have been sharp and sententious: pleasant without scurrility, witty without affection, audacious without impudency, learned without opinion, and strange without heresy' (v.1.2). Through Nathaniel, it would seem that Shakespeare, at times, reflects precisely upon some of the linguistic idiosyncrasies of his time. For instance this excitement and ambition about words had led some writers to follow a noun or a verb derived from Anglo-Saxon sources with a synonym of French and Latin origin. It was a habit into which Lord Berners, for instance, had fallen in his introduction to Froissart when he had not the clear model of the French before him: 'for when we (being unexpert of chances), see, behold, and read the ancient acts, gests, and deeds how and with what labours, dangers and perils they were gested and done, they right greatly admonish, ensigne and teach us how we may lead forth our lives.' Nathaniel in describing Armado to Holofernes has a similar triple elegance: 'I did converse this quondam day with a companion of the king's, who is intituled, nominated, or called, Don Adriano de Armado' (v.1.7).

When Armado himself plays this game, a triplicity of words is not enough for him and so he addresses Costard: 'By my sweet soul, I mean setting thee at liberty, enfreedoming thy person: thou wert *immured, restrained, captivated, bound*' (iii.1.124). Even as late as *Hamlet* Shakespeare was to allow the Gravedigger to play with a triple movement, though glancing at the same time at a legal quibble: 'if I drown myself wittingly, it argues an act: and an act hath three branches; it is, to act, to do, and to perform' (v.1.10).

The texture of the play, with its single main incident of plot and its loose episodes, gives leisure for the exploration of all these verbal devices. Of many of them the meaning has now been lost, and the game is no longer as entertaining as it was in that early, Elizabethan period, when the expanding possibilities of English were such an excitement to men of imagination. The humour has dropped out of 'honorificabilitudinitatibus', one of the longest words which late Latin produced.

Even the game of punning has lost much of the amusement which it had for Shakespeare and his contemporaries. In none of his plays are there so many puns and word plays, and one sober critic, approaching the problem statistically, found that there were two hundred and fifty puns divided among the sixteen characters.[1]

The king's opening speech begins with a play on words—'And then *grace* us in the *disgrace* of death' (i.1.3)—and the game continues to the years of Shakespeare's maturity. Some of this is only an exercise of that delight which the Elizabethan mind, above all others, discovered in an identity of sound in words that had a different meaning. Beyond this there was a verbal elegance making its own appeal. At the same time the play of the meaning often half-conceals a merry exercise in bawdry which has, on occasion, been left undetected by some of Shakespeare's editors. If anyone doubts the sexual second meaning of the exchange between Costard and Boyet at the beginning of the fourth act, he must assess his wits as less keen than those of Maria, who protests: 'Come, come, you talk greasily; your lips grow foul' (iv.1.139).

The place of the pun in Shakespeare's artistic development has often been a theme of comment and there is a danger that too elaborate a position may be given to its importance. So much of

[1] T. R. Price, *Shakespeariana*, vol. vi, p. 292, 1889.

the punning is merely the stock-in-trade of the dramatists whose audiences had lively minds and would follow the niceties of word-play as a modern crowd might watch with discrimination a game of football or baseball.

There remains the fact that a reasonable case can be made out that for Shakespeare and his contemporaries the pun had a dignity and importance which it no longer possesses. To this Sister Joseph draws attention:[1] 'to play upon the various meanings of a word represented an intellectual exercise, a witty analysis commended and relished by Aristotle, practised by Plato, and by the great dramatists of Greece, esteemed and used by Cicero, employed by medieval and Renaissance preachers in their sermons, regarded as rhetorical ornament by the Elizabethans, but frequently despised as false or degenerate wit from the eighteenth century to the present day'. Shakespeare was to use puns even in moments of tragedy as when the dying Gaunt in *Richard II* plays on his own name:

> Gaunt am I for the grave, gaunt as a grave (ii.1.82)

This enlarged and most important function of the pun is well defined by Professor F. P. Wilson: 'To an Elizabethan the play upon words was not merely an elegance of style and a display of wit; it was also a means of emphasis and an instrument of persuasion. An argument might be conducted from step to step—and in the pamphleteers it often is—by a series of puns.'[2]

The boundary between the pun and more genuinely imaginative language cannot be precisely defined. The element of verbal identity is carried over into the metaphorical language. In fact it could be urged that the type of ambiguity on which puns are based is also to be discovered in the most imaginative language in the plays. Metellus in *Julius Caesar* urging the inclusion of Cicero in the plot says:

> O, let us have him, for his *silver* hairs
> Will *purchase* us a good opinion. (ii.1.144)

Here the sense of *silver* as a precious metal or as coinage is added to the context of the first line so that the metaphorical suggestion of *purchase* can be exploited in the next.[3]

William Whiter in his work, to which reference has already

---

[1] *Shakespeare's Use of the Arts of Language* (1947).
[2] *Shakespeare and The Diction of Common Life* (1941).
[3] E. E. Kellett comments on this example in *Suggestions* (1923).

been made,[1] furnishes further examples of the way in which a
cluster of images is derived from a play upon words. All this may
be said to have its origin in the type of ambiguity which rests in
a pun, so whether regarded as a solemn or a despised figure, it
is still an element which cannot be detached from Shakespeare's
imaginative language as a whole. One of Whiter's most interesting
examples is based on a speech in *Coriolanus*: 'In the following
passage', he writes, '*weed* in the sense of *dress* is connected with
the word *suit* in the sense of *petition* and there is likewise a new
notion annexed, which relates to a peculiar meaning of the equi-
vocal word *suit*.

> Besides, forget not
> With what contempt he wore the humble *weed*,
> How in his *suit* he scorn'd you: but your loves,
> Thinking upon his *services*, took from you
> The apprehension of his present portance,
> Which most gibingly, ungravely, he did *fashion*
> After the inveterate hate he bears you.

In the foregoing passage the remarkable words are *weed—suit—
services—fashion*, and the reader will not imagine that I refine too
much, when I inform him that the word *services* is to be referred
to the same association; and that it was suggested to the Poet by
another signification which *suit* sometimes bears of *livery*—the
peculiar dress by which the servants and retainers of one family
were distinguished from those of another.'

All metaphorical language is seeking out towards a unity. At
its highest imagery, and in a supreme way, metaphor, by drawing
together widely separated objects and experiences into a brief and
unbelaboured expression, asserts the unity of human life.

So, more philosophically, it may be maintained that behind
the conflict of contrasting appearances, there is a single life of the
spirit. Thus metaphor might be called the applied metaphysics
of poetry. What began as wit has gone beyond wit. Imagery, in
its purest form, can become an empirical mysticism made manifest
by sources that depend on ordinary experience. Shakespeare, who
had the most complete control of these nobler and more imaginative identities in language, delighted in exercising his verbal talent
unceasingly in the pun and the quibble where in its simplest forms
the identity is merely verbal.

[1] *A Specimen of a Commentary on Shakespeare* (1794).

— play of court

Surprise has often been expressed that Shakespeare could have
discovered so much of the atmosphere of the Court in a play
which must have been written soon after his coming to London,
while parts may indeed already have been conceived and composed
in his Stratford days. But there is little technical knowledge of a
Court in the play. The graces of manner and movement must be
left to the gestures of the players, and the elegance of their words.
The dramatist has supplied them with an imaginary language of
courtly life with other types of diction given for contrast and
entertainment. *Love's Labour's Lost* is the idealised conception
of magnificence expressed by the only instrument that the young
dramatist had available, namely these beruffed and elegant verbal
courtiers. The great feasts are 'feasts of language'; the fine
clothes are phrases of taffeta, and hyperboles of three-piled velvet,
and the only courtly manners are the spruce affectations of phrase.

At first sight it may seem difficult to find elements in the diction
which are personal. Yet the strange thing is that closer examination shews the play to be full not only of the verbal elegances of
London, but of an imagery drawn directly from country life. It is
as if the memories of Stratford were still strong and competing
with the new-found and sophisticated excitements of courtly
circles. The king in the first scene describes Biron as:

> like an envious sneaping frost
> That bites the first-born infants of the spring.

> (i.1.100)

Moth, in describing to Armado how to 'win your love with a
French brawl', is more obviously rustic: 'With your arms crossed
on your thin-belly doublet like a rabbit on a spit' (iii.1.19). It is
a rural imagery that Biron uses in describing the soft and 'sensible'
feeling of love:

> Love's feeling is more soft and sensible
> Than are the tender horns of cockled snails.

> (iv.3.337)

and Biron again, in describing Boyet, turns to a rustic imagery:

> This fellow pecks up wit as pigeons pease,
> And utters it again when God doth please:
> He is wit's pedler, and retails his wares
> At wakes and wassails, meetings, markets, fairs.

> (v.2.315)

It is true that the comparison of pecking up wit 'as pigeons pease' is claimed as proverbial, but as all the proverbs quoted are later than Shakespeare he may well have been the inventor of the phrase.

The proverb, either traditional or invented, was, as Professor F. P. Wilson has noted,[1] to play an important part in his work, both here and later. They were to enter even into the most moving moments in the tragedies. Among the examples quoted by Wilson are the proverbs 'mingled with folk-tale and ballad in the snatches of half-sense and half-nothing, spoken by the mad Ophelia: "They say the owl was a baker's daughter. Lord, we know what we are, but know not what we may be." In *King Lear* Shakespeare puts into the mouth of the Fool the silliest catch-phrase—"Cry you mercy, I took you for a joint-stool"—with poignant effect, and the Fool's last speech is a reference to the homely, ironical proverb: "You would make me go to bed at noon".'

Love's Labour's Lost, which has so much deliberate affectation and mock pedantry, ends with a lyric, the only one in the play which is constructed out of simple and realistic country scenes:

> When icicles hang by the wall
>   And Dick the shepherd blows his nail
> And Tom bears logs into the hall
>   And milk comes frozen home in pail,
> When blood is nipp'd and ways be foul,
> Then nightly sings the staring owl,
>   Tu-whit;
> Tu-who, a merry note,
> While greasy Joan doth keel the pot.
>
> When all aloud the wind doth blow
>   And coughing drowns the parson's saw
> And birds sit brooding in the snow
>   And Marian's nose looks red and raw,
> When roasted crabs hiss in the bowl,
> Then nightly sings the staring owl,
>   Tu-whit;
> Tu-who, a merry note,
> While greasy Joan doth keel the pot.

(v.2.922)

[1] *Shakespeare and the Diction of Common Life* (1941).

The interest in nature which comes so compellingly into the comedy was to remain a permanent element in Shakespeare's language. In a number of the early plays nature seemed almost to force itself into the action and into the speeches of unlikely characters such as Petruchio and Richard III. Its influence diminished in the middle period and then returned in the last romances with an added elaboration, with a rustic elegance rather than a 'russet yea and honest kersey no'. As I have suggested it is sometimes difficult to distinguish the phrases which are proverbial and the images belonging to the common fund of Elizabethan blank verse, from the new experience and the observed scene. But however any individual example may be interpreted nature is present in sufficient detail and frequency for one to have no doubt as to its importance to Shakespeare.

Apart from the references to nature it is difficult to discover much in the language of the play that belongs more intimately to Shakespeare's mind. Nor is there any continuing image, related to the major action, as in so many of the later plays. Stated in most general terms the theme is the contrast of the atmosphere of fantasy and of the realities of life. The major part of the action presents the fantasy, particularly a verbal fantasy, from which all real action has been excluded. At the very close there is a suggestion that this mood of poetical playfulness is over: 'The words of Mercury', Armado says, 'are harsh after the songs of Apollo. You that way; we this way' (v.2.940). Those last six compact and expressive monosyllabic words have a compression and directness which no-one in the play had previously attempted.

The word 'world' itself, in a number of interesting passages, illustrates this contrast between reality and the oasis of carefree entertainment in which *Love's Labour's Lost* is played out. This expressive 'world' appears first in the king's opening speech:

> for so you are,
> That war against your own affections
> And the huge army of the *world*'s desires.

> (i.1.8)

It recurs in the description of Armado:

> In high-born words the worth of many a knight
> From tawny Spain lost in the *world*'s debate.

> (i.1.173)

Similarly, though with less emphasis, Rosaline in describing Biron distinguishes the 'world' from the gentle entertainment of the play:

> and the *world*'s large tongue
> Proclaims you for a man replete with mocks,
> Full of comparisons and wounding flouts.   (v.2.852)

Some have found a satire of Chapman's way of writing in the comedy and Miss M. C. Bradbrook discovers this in the opening speeches of the king and his followers[1] which recall Chapman's symbolism of conflict.   Whether the satire be present or not I find a genuine quality of poetic imagination in the line, 'and the huge army of the world's desires', which does not occur elsewhere in *Love's Labour's Lost,* and is the beginning of that cunning combination of concrete and abstract description imaging out a single idea which Shakespeare was to employ so frequently.   Cleopatra was later to greet Antony:

> O infinite virtue, comest thou smiling from
> The world's great snare uncaught?
>   (*Antony and Cleopatra,* iv.8.17)

The most compressed and imaginative phrase in the play is 'the world's debate' which is presumably a description of the Crusades where Christendom and the heathen were joined in an issue of universal import.

The most sustained speech is Biron's famous address to the king and his friends in Act iv, which opens with the lines:

> Have at you, then, affection's men-at-arms.
> Consider what you first did swear unto,
> To fast, to study, and to see no woman;
> Flat treason 'gainst the kingly state of youth.   (iv.111.290)

The speech has a structure built out of formal rhetorical figures with imagination and a lyrical quality ever breaking through.

In much of the play Shakespeare is a commentator on language and literary theory with verbal comedy as his instrument.   So Holofernes commenting on Armado's sonnet: 'Here are only numbers ratified; but, for the elegancy, facility, and golden cadence of poesy, caret. Ovidius Naso was the man: and why, indeed, Naso, but for smelling out the odoriferous flowers of fancy, the jerks of invention? Imitari is nothing: so doth the

---

[1] *The School of Night* (1936).

hound his master, the ape his keeper, the tired horse his rider'
(iv.2.125).

Of the early plays, *Love's Labour's Lost* demonstrates most
clearly Shakespeare's lively awareness of language, for it is as if
nothing of linguistic significance in the atmosphere of his time
escaped him. For the moment he is a light-hearted critic, and is
not yet employing language for the more profound purposes which
are to follow. Indeed some of the characters are less characters
than examples of verbal clowning. So as Miss G. D. Willcock
writes, 'Dull, Costard, and Jaquenetta are foils to both Armado
and Holofernes. Costard excellently illustrates the almost purely
verbal nature of the early fooling. It is a mistake to try to unify
the mental processes of a Costard into a consistent character.
Such clowns are walking word-games.'[1]

Holofernes's reference to *imitari* is one of many pieces of evidence to show that Shakespeare knew of the classical literary
discussion. Holofernes is armed with much of the new vocabulary
of that literary criticism which was only in those years coming to
have an independent existence. While Shakespeare seems interested and entertained by the neo-classical discussions on the
drama he is already reaching out towards the conception of invention, and to the 'poem unlimited'.

On more than one occasion in the comedy he discusses whether
the resources of imaginative language are to be discovered in
experience or in books:

> Study is like the heaven's glorious sun
>   That will not be deep-search'd with saucy looks:
> Small have continual plodders ever won
>   Save base authority from others' books.
>
> (i.1.84)

One would more readily determine that this is a piece of personal
experience if this image were not to be found so frequently in the
sonneteers. It might be urged that Shakespeare's return on more
than one occasion to this comparison is some evidence that he
had considered the matter in relationship to his own composition.
Not only does Moth tell the audience that,

> They have been at a great feast of languages, and stolen
> the scraps. (v.1.38)

[1] G. D. Willcock, *Shakespeare as a Critic of Language* (1934).

but Biron returning to the very term 'plodding' says:

> Why, universal plodding poisons up
> The nimble spirits in the arteries,
> As motion and long-during action tires
> The sinewy vigour of the traveller.

(iv.3.305)

On one occasion Holofernes speaks of his own gift: 'a foolish extravagant spirit, full of forms, figures, shapes, objects, ideas, apprehensions, motions, revolutions: these are begot in the ventricle of memory, nourished in the womb of *pia mater*, and delivered upon the mellowing of *occasion*. But the gift is good in those in whom it is acute, and I am thankful for it' (iv.2.68).

In such words Shakespeare might well have described his own power over words in this first period, and as the future was to show, 'the gift is good in those in whom it is acute'. Words were to be the instrument, and in words was to lie the ultimate triumph, but these restless tumultuous symbols were to be unceasingly a torment as well as a joy. They were not dull 'mechanicals' whose duties could be prescribed, but the instruments of nature herself, for whose successful employment all the combined resources of genius and will were imperative.

Here he had wantoned with words, exercised his wit amid their 'fopperies', to use Pater's term, but already, as has been suggested, he knew that direct speech has its power, and that in a moment of action or of emotional crisis it may be the only language: 'Honest plain words', as Biron says, 'best pierce the ear of grief' (v.2.763). The only moment of real action was told simply enough:

> MERCADE. The king your father—
> PRINCESS. Dead, for my life!
> MERCADE. Even so; my tale is told.

(v.2.728)

CHAPTER II

FROM WORDS TO ACTION AND FROM WORDS TO PEOPLE:

The Comedy of Errors; *The Two Gentlemen of Verona*;
The Taming of the Shrew

THE exact order of the early comedies before *A Midsummer Night's Dream* cannot be precisely determined, nor for the purpose of the present study is it necessary to resort to conjecture. For the conclusions set out in this chapter remain the same whatever order be given to the three plays mentioned in the chapter-heading. It would be unwise to judge the order of composition from any theory of an alleged maturing of style, for a creative writer, working as Shakespeare did at great speed, does not develop in a mechanical or regular way. Memories of an earlier manner will always remain in the more mature work, apart from all those instances, which Samuel Johnson recognised, of a temporary weariness or mis-direction of the creative impulse.

What is clear is that, leaving the world of words of *Love's Labour's Lost*, he came to the problem of incidents and stories and people. Conceivably the order may be reversed, and that while writing these plays, Shakespeare took an excursion into *Love's Labour's Lost* and into purely verbal entertainments. To my mind that is less likely. Rather I see the new problem of adjusting dramatic verse to an ample narrative action as disrupting temporarily the brilliance of style of *Love's Labour's Lost*, so that, for a time, verbal dexterity and poetry become subdued. Apart from the problems of these comedies of action he had also in these years the far sterner task of adjusting language to the histories. Adjusting poetry to dramatic action, even when that action was only a romantic tale, proved difficult, and the verse in these comedies is sometimes disappointing. As so often in a period of development in the comedies the prose is livelier than the verse. To the student of Shakespeare's poetry this road through the early comedies is one which it is essential to explore in order to study Shakespeare's development, but one, in itself, among the least interesting.

The Comedy of Errors depends almost entirely on plot, with little characterisation, and still less poetry. Incident and coincidence dominate, not sentiment and imagination. For this very reason Shakespeare has few opportunities for poetic liveliness. In the comic passages there is some verbal dexterity and a play of ideas, but the cleverness and gaiety of *Love's Labour's Lost* seem drained away. The Dromio of Syracuse's description to Antipholus of Syracuse of the woman he is about to meet makes a gesture towards verbal wit: 'I warrant, her rags and the tallow in them will burn a Poland winter' (iii.2.99). The whole of the passage that follows is long drawn out, descending sometimes to bawdiness, and using the method of comparison in a dull and mechanical way:

ANTIPHOLUS OF SYRACUSE. What complexion is she of?
DROMIO OF SYRACUSE. Swart, like my shoe, but her face nothing like
  so clean kept: for why, she sweats; a man may go over shoes in
  the grime of it.

(iii.2.103)

In all this little can compare with *Love's Labour's Lost*, and, as has been suggested, much of what is present has slipped out of the verse into the prose. Similarly, as the play has few passages of genuine sentiment, or even of strong affectation of sentiment, the resources of poetry are seldom called upon. It can be argued that the only moving and direct passage of verse is the speech of Aegeon when he is denied by Antipholus of Ephesus:

Not know my voice! O time's extremity,
Hast thou so crack'd and splitted my poor tongue
In seven short years, that here my only son
Knows not my feeble key of untuned cares?
Though now this grained face of mine be hid
In sap-consuming winter's drizzled snow
And all the conduits of my blood froze up,
Yet hath my night of life some memory,
My wasting lamps some fading glimmer left,
My dull deaf ears a little use to hear.

(v.1.306)

Shakespeare was writing the early historical plays in the same years as these comedies, and it is remarkable how distinct he keeps the style of the two types of drama. This passage just quoted is exceptional in that its style is reminiscent of the manner of the histories and could well be incorporated into *Richard II*, for instance, without incongruity.

There are some instances of narrative imagery but these are argued out in a slow and plodding manner, as different as is possible from the later, compressed and imaginative language. So Adriana speaks:

> Thou art an elm, my husband, I a vine,
> Whose weakness married to thy stronger state
> Makes me with thy strength to communicate:
> If aught possess thee from me, it is dross,
> Usurping ivy, brier, or idle moss;
> Who, all for want of pruning, with intrusion
> Infect thy sap and live on thy confusion.

(ii.2.176)

This narrative imagery is common in the early plays and is continued even after the language has become more mature. Sometimes Shakespeare seems fascinated by an image, and continues with its detail even when the imaginative aspect of the comparison has been fully exploited. Often this worrying of an image occurs when the poetic imagination is not working at a mood of high stimulation. On the other hand language such as this is sometimes written consciously as a heavy-moving diction appropriate to the duller characters, and such is its purpose, increasingly, in the more mature plays.

Another and similar example of this slow, meditative development of description and comparison can be found in Luciana's speech to Adriana:

> There's nothing situate under heaven's eye
> But hath his bound, in earth, in sea, in sky:
> The beasts, the fishes and the winged fowls
> Are their males' subjects and at their controls:
> Men, more divine, the masters of all these,
> Lords of the wide world and wild watery seas,
> Indued with intellectual sense and souls,
> Of more pre-eminence than fish and fowls,
> Are masters to their females, and their lords.

(ii.1.16)

The sparing use of imaginative language in *The Comedy of Errors* is Shakespeare's developing recognition that words are the servants of drama. Seen on the stage, the action is the major part

of the entertainment, and, with its aid, the audience is presented
with a dramatic pleasure achieved in *Love's Labour's Lost*, in
another way, by language alone,

As on occasion in the later plays, Shakespeare has some lines
and even passages which seem independent of the mood of the
action, belonging rather to a personal experience. In the early
plays this more personal language frequently arises from memories
of nature. So Antipholus of Syracuse speaks:

> When the sun shines let foolish gnats make sport,
> But creep in crannies when he hides his beams.
>
> (ii.2.30)

and later Adriana has her moving line on the lapwing:

> Ah, but I think him better than I say,
> And yet would herein others' eyes were worse.
> *Far from her nest the lapwing cries away:*
> My heart prays for him, though my tongue do curse.
>
> (iv.2.25)

One passage looks towards the later language for in it the
abstract and the concrete seem to join together in that formidable
imaginative combination which Shakespeare could use so powerfully. It is to be found in the Lady Abbess's description of

> moody and dull melancholy,
> Kinsman to grim and comfortless despair,
> And at her heels a huge infectious troop
> Of pale distemperatures and foes to life?
>
> (v.1.79)

It is a phrase of such imaginative amplitude that it shows up the
thinness of much of the language.

With *The Two Gentlemen of Verona* he came to a comedy
which had not only a plot, however far-fetched, but a world of
sentiment though romantically fantastic. The range of language
is far more varied than in *The Comedy of Errors* though more
restricted than in *Love's Labour's Lost*. However strong may be
his personal interest in words, he has here a story to maintain,
and this has its inevitable linguistic consequences. The satire of
current verbal fashions he has abandoned, and, while some of his
characters employ decorative devices he has ceased, for the time
being, to be a critic of words, and is content only to employ them.
The game of words remained, though played less frequently, but

the characters are still connoisseurs of language as well as of sentiment. After Valentine and Thurio have had an interchange of
verbal playfulness Silvia comments: 'A fine volley of words,
gentlemen, and quickly shot off' (ii.4.32). This is almost identical
with the Princess's comment in *Love's Labour's Lost* to Katharine
and Rosaline: 'Well bandied both; a set of wit well play'd'
(v.2.29).

It is interesting, though no excessive emphasis must be attached,
that in this play where Shakespeare turns from words to people,
there are, as Professor Spurgeon noted, an array of 'characters'
employed as one of the favourite themes for simile, including a
child, a baby, a muse, a physician, a beggar, a pilgrim, a bankrupt,
a beadsman, a soldier, a swarthy Ethiope, a herald, a mighty lord,
as well as prisoners, slaves, bastards and messengers.[1]

The influence of some contemporary writers and fashions are
allowed to enter. Speed is made to adapt a phrase from Lyly:
'though the chameleon Love can feed on the air, I am one that
am nourished by my victuals and would fain have meat' (ii.1.178).
The temptation of triplicity in phrasing which dogged Shakespeare
with such persistence is also present here:

> Some to the wars, to try their fortune there;
> Some to discover islands far away;
> Some to the studious universities. (i.3.8)

Nor can one escape the impression that in this period Shakespeare's
mind was filled with memories of Spenser, and there remained in
the unhurried movement of some of the verses a number of those
compound adjectives, found so frequently in the *Faerie Queene*,
and used by Shakespeare more liberally here than in any other
play: 'O sweet-suggesting Love' (ii.6.7); 'with twenty thousand
soul-confirming oaths' (ii.6.16); and 'a true-devoted pilgrim is not
weary' (ii.7.9).

In a play which gathers up moods very like those of the sonneteers, and whose characters share the affections and sentiments
of the sonneteering lovers, it is only natural that the language of
Elizabethan sonneteering should again hold a firm place. Proteus
for instance tells Thurio:

> You must lay lime to tangle her desires
> By wailful sonnets, whose composed rhymes
> Should be full-fraught with serviceable vows. (iii.2.68)

[1] Caroline F. Spurgeon, *Shakespeare's Imagery* (1935).

2

To this the Duke replies that 'much is the force of heaven-bred poesy'.

The dramatic movement permits the use of a number of passages of loosely textured verses in which the sentiments of these young romantic lovers can be displayed in the imagery and the classical reference which contemporary taste enjoyed:

> Say that upon the altar of her beauty
> You sacrifice your tears, your sighs, your heart:
> Write till your ink be dry, and with your tears
> Moist it again, and frame some feeling line
> That may discover such integrity:
> For Orpheus' lute was strung with poets' sinews,
> Whose golden touch could soften steel and stones,
> Make tigers tame and huge leviathans
> Forsake unsounded deeps to dance on sands.
> After your dire-lamenting elegies,
> Visit by night your lady's chamber-window
> With some sweet concert; to their instruments
> Tune a deploring dump: the night's dead silence
> Will well become such sweet-complaining grievance.
> This, or else nothing, will inherit her.
>
> (iii.2.73)

One dominant theme emerges from this language of sentiment, and here, for the first time, Shakespeare gives to a single comparison a continuing associative value. The vow of love he compares to the vow made in the dedication of a life to the Church, as if thus symbolising the sacredness of passion as conceived by a romantic lover. In both *Love's Labour's Lost* and in *The Two Gentlemen of Verona* the action depends upon a vow. In *Love's Labour's Lost* it is an artificial one made by the king and his companions to study and celibacy, while in *The Two Gentlemen of Verona* it is the vow of Proteus and Valentine to be faithful in friendship and love. Holofernes in *Love's Labour's Lost* speaks of Biron as 'one of the votaries' of the king, and in *The Two Gentlemen of Verona* Valentine describes Proteus as 'a votary to fond desire' (i.1.52). Armado had already used very similar language in *Love's Labour's Lost*: 'I will kiss thy royal finger, and take leave. I am a votary; I have vowed to Jaquenetta to hold the plough for her sweet love three years' (v.2.891). This association of ideas develops in *The Two Gentlemen of Verona* and so the Duke says to Proteus:

And, Proteus, we dare trust you in this kind,
Because we know, on Valentine's report,
You are already Love's firm votary
And cannot soon revolt and change your mind.

(iii.2.56)

while Julia has already used a similar imagery in speaking to Proteus:

PROTEUS. Why, then, we'll make exchange; here, take you this.
JULIA.   And seal the bargain with a holy kiss.
PROTEUS. Here is my hand for my true constancy.

(ii.2.6)

Meanwhile the association of prayer and holiness, of duty and penance with love is naturally a part of a romantic conception. In an early speech Proteus says to Valentine:

Commend thy grievance to my holy prayers,
For I will be thy beadsman, Valentine.

(i.1.17)

and Valentine in a later speech to Proteus says:

Ay, Proteus, but that life is alter'd now:
I have done penance for contemning Love,
Whose high imperious thoughts have punish'd me
With bitter fasts, with penitential groans,
With nightly tears and daily heart-sore sighs.

(ii.4.128)

Julia in two of the more successful lines in the play returns to a similar comparison:

A true-devoted pilgrim is not weary
To measure kingdoms with his feeble steps.

(ii.7.9)

This association of love and holiness which remains as long as the theme of romantic love is employed, is to reappear notably in the conversations of Romeo and Juliet.

Much of the language is easy in its movement, rather like the rippling of slow waves, though at times, one can see here the beginning of words and phrases which are to be used later in a more imaginative and concentrated form. Proteus, for instance, used the fawning persistence of the spaniel to describe his own love for Sylvia:

> She bids me think how I have been forsworn
> In breaking faith with Julia whom I loved:
> And notwithstanding all her sudden quips,
> The least whereof would quell a lover's hope,
> Yet, spaniel-like, the more she spurns my love,
> The more it grows and fawneth on her still.
>
> (iv.2.10)

By *Antony and Cleopatra* instead of this slow descriptive movement 'spaniel' has become a verb and the whole phrase gains a commanding compression: 'The hearts that spaniel'd me at heels' (iv.12.20).

Some words appearing in their ordinary meaning are already on their way towards transmutation into that metaphorical language which is later Shakespeare's outstanding power. For instance Valentine says:

> She shall be dignified with this high honour—
> To bear my lady's train, lest the base earth
> Should from her vesture chance to steal a kiss.
>
> (ii.4.158)

By *The Merchant of Venice* the transition over into metaphor has been made, and we hear human life described as this 'muddy vesture of decay' (v.1.64), and even more powerfully in *Othello* as 'the essential vesture of creation' (ii.1.64).

Shakespeare uses again here the comparison of 'crystal' with eyes, which he had used already in *Love's Labour's Lost*. This was one of the more common decorative indulgences of the sonneteers. Boyet in *Love's Labour's Lost* had said:

> Methought all his senses were lock'd in his eye,
> As jewels in crystal for some prince to buy.
>
> (ii.1.242)

and Valentine in *The Two Gentlemen of Verona* might have been reciting two lines of a sonnet when he commented:

> his mistress
> Did hold his eyes lock'd in her crystal looks.
>
> (ii.4.89)

When one proceeds forward to *A Midsummer Night's Dream*, Shakespeare, as if tired of the comparison in its common form, stretches out beyond it, and Demetrius is made to say:

> To what, my love, shall I compare thine eyne?
> Crystal is muddy.   (iii.2.138)

and by *Henry V* the identity of eyes and crystals is so complete
that Pistol is able to say to the Hostess:

> Go, clear thy crystals. (ii.3.56)

Of outstanding poetry the play has little to offer, and, with the
removal of the critical satire on language, the general effect is less
exciting than in *Love's Labour's Lost*, though, as has been suggested
the romantic sentiment offers opportunities which *The Comedy of
Errors* did not permit.

There are few phrases which have any suggestion of the compression and power of the more mature language.

An interesting line such as the Second Outlaw's 'To make a
virtue of necessity' (iv.1.62) comes direct from Chaucer's *Knightes
Tale*, 'To maken vertu of necessitee', and is, anyway, a proverbial
phrase. Rather, as has been suggested, the impression is of an
unhurried gentleness, and while there is far less nature imagery
than in *Love's Labour's Lost* one of the best remembered passages
is found in Proteus's four lines:

> O, how this spring of love resembleth
>   The uncertain glory of an April day,
> Which now shows all the beauty of the sun,
>   And by and by a cloud takes all away!
>
> (i.3.84)

We may begrudge these beautiful lines to Proteus, a false perjured
man. They seem to belong to the wash of fine words to be discovered in many of the comedies, as if Shakespeare were using a
lyricism and making a gift of his own mind and thoughts to any
character who might be available.

There is one passage of outstanding interest where the association is with nature, and the claim can be made that the background
is based on personal experience. Lucetta has been telling Julia
that she does not wish to quench her 'love's hot fire', but only so
to qualify it 'lest it should burn above the bounds of reason'. To
this Julia replies:

> The more thou damm'st it up, the more it burns.
> The current that with gentle murmur glides,
> Thou know'st, being stopp'd, impatiently doth rage;
> But when his fair course is not hindered,
> He makes sweet music with the enamell'd stones,

> Giving a gentle kiss to every sedge
> He overtaketh in his pilgrimage,
> And so by many winding nooks he strays
> With willing sport to the wild ocean.
>
> (ii.7.24)

A memorable passage in *The Rape of Lucrece* has this same memory of the 'rage' of a current that is checked in its course:

> As through an arch the violent roaring tide
> Outruns the eye that doth behold his haste,
> Yet in the eddy boundeth in his pride
> Back to the strait that forced him on so fast;
> In rage sent out, recall'd in rage, being past:
> Even so his sighs, his sorrows, make a saw,
> To push grief on, and back the same grief draw.
>
> (*Luc.* 1667)

It was Professor Spurgeon[1] who found in this passage the very movement of the current as Shakespeare must have seen it at Old Clopton Bridge at Stratford. Her description of her visit to the Bridge with Captain Jaggard to watch the current being forced beneath the narrow eighteenth-century arch is one of the most memorable in her Shakespearian studies. The passage in *The Two Gentlemen of Verona* though less circumstantial would seem obviously to derive from the same source.

Few lines surpass in concentration the comment by Valentine, 'and feed upon the shadow of perfection' (iii.1.177), and it is here, in the combination of the abstract and the concrete, of the idea and of the experience, that Shakespeare's language is to develop. Similarly one finds the beginning, in a very tentative way, of that mounting imagery where one idea is rejected before it is developed but made the basis of a new association and comparison. So in Proteus's speech:

> That I did love, for now my love is thaw'd;
> Which, like a waxen image 'gainst a fire,
> Bears no impression of the thing it was.
>
> (ii.4.200)

Somewhere among these early comedies is *The Taming of the Shrew*, depending like *The Comedy of Errors* upon incident, though not in such a mechanical way. All the excitement is captured by the theme which makes no demand on a continued

---

[1] See Caroline F. Spurgeon, *Shakespeare's Imagery* (1935).

illumination by poetry, while the under-plots are conceived and written in an enervated manner. Much of the verse is straightforward and informative, but unadorned and undistinguished. Such are the lines in which Petruchio addresses Signior Gremio:

> You wrong me, Signior Gremio: give me leave.
> I am a gentleman of Verona, sir,
> That, hearing of her beauty and her wit,
> Her affability and bashful modesty,
> Her wondrous qualities and mild behaviour,
> Am bold to show myself a forward guest
> Within your house, to make mine eye the witness
> Of that report which I so oft have heard.
>
> (ii.1.46)

This is clear without being lively.

On the other hand the direct language can develop in the play to a realistic dialogue such as is to be used strongly and effectively in the later plays. It is in such language that Petruchio addresses Kate in one of the later scenes:

> They shall go forward, Kate, at thy command.
> Obey the bride, you that attend on her;
> Go to the feast, revel and domineer,
> Carouse full measure to her maidenhead,
> Be mad and merry, or go hang yourselves:
> But for my bonny Kate, she must with me.
> Nay, look not big, nor stamp, nor stare, nor fret;
> I will be master of what is mine own:
> She is my goods, my chattels; she is my house,
> My household stuff, my field, my barn,
> My horse, my ox, my ass, my any thing.
>
> (iii.2.224)

While only intermittently illuminated with poetry the play does at the same time give the impression that Shakespeare was holding poetical powers in reserve and some of the qualities which later appear, make their first appearance here. As frequently in the comedies the prose seems to have outstepped the verse both in imagery and in a free and flexible use of syntax. For instance Biondello in a passage of prose describes the appearance of Petruchio and of his horse:

Why, Petruchio is coming in a new hat and an old jerkin, a pair of old breeches thrice turned, a pair of boots that have been candle-cases, one buckled, another laced, an old rusty sword ta'en out of the town-armoury, with a broken hilt, and chapeless; with two broken points: his horse hipped with an old mothy saddle and stirrups of no kindred; besides, possessed with the glanders and like to mose in the chine; troubled with the lampass, infected with the fashions, full of windgalls, sped with spavins, rayed with the yellows, past cure of the fives, stark spoiled with the staggers, begnawn with the bots, swayed in the back and shoulder-shotten; near-legged before and with a half-cheeked bit and a head-stall of sheep's leather which, being restrained to keep him from stumbling, hath been often burst and now repaired with knots; one girth six times pieced and a woman's crupper of velure, which hath two letters for her name fairly set down in studs, and here and there pieced with pack-thread.

(iii.2.43)

The words came tumbling out as if they had been imprisoned, and had escaped while the custodian was asleep. One feels that here is a rich imaginative store, employed by a writer who has felt the need of denying himself his resources of words for the sake of the dramatic action.

Petruchio's language is the most poetical in the play and the most interesting. Some of it belongs to that comic and sardonic tradition, very appropriate to his temperament, and somewhat allied to the language of Faulconbridge in *King John*, and leading on ultimately to one aspect of the language of *Hamlet*. This element of comedy and satire is of frequent occurrence, but perhaps best illustrated when the Haberdasher hands Petruchio a cap for Katharina, and he replies:

> Why, this was moulded on a porringer;
> A velvet dish: fie, fie! 'tis lewd and filthy:
> Why, 'tis a cockle or a walnut-shell,
> A knack, a toy, a trick, a baby's cap:
> Away with it! come, let me have a bigger.   (iv.3.64)

It is to Petruchio that Shakespeare gives most of the nature imagery which constitutes one of the play's most poetical elements. Some of it is conventional as when he says of Katherine:

> For I will board her, though she chide as loud
> As thunder when the clouds in autumn crack.   (i.2.95)

or again:

> She sings as sweetly as a nightingale:
> Say that she frown; I'll say she looks as clear
> As morning roses newly wash'd with dew.   (ii.1.172)

Others seem to derive from a genuine rustic experience; or if not
a direct experience then a proverb, based on rustic observation:

> And do you tell me of a woman's tongue,
> That gives not half so great a blow to hear
> As will a chestnut in a farmer's fire?

(i.2.208)

A similar detailed and authentic description seems to accompany
Petruchio's account of Katharina:

> Kate like the hazel-twig
> Is straight and slender and as brown in hue
> As hazel nuts and sweeter than the kernels.

(ii.1.255)

Closely allied to this rustic imagery is Petruchio's long narrative
image derived from falconry:

> My falcon now is sharp and passing empty;
> And till she stoop she must not be full-gorged,
> For then she never looks upon her lure.
> Another way I have to man my haggard,
> To make her come and know her keeper's call,
> That is, to watch her, as we watch these kites
> That bate and beat and will not be obedient.

(iv.1.193)

It would seem that here, as in *Love's Labour's Lost*, autobio-
graphical experience intruded, and into places where its presence
could not have been anticipated. The life of the neighbourhood
of Stratford is remembered in Christopher Sly's Induction to the
play:

Am not I Christopher Sly, old Sly's son of Burtonheath, by birth a
pedlar, by education a cardmaker, by transmutation a bear-herd, and
now by present profession a tinker?   Ask Marian Hacket, the fat ale-
wife of Wincot, if she know me not: if she say I am not fourteen pence
on the score for sheer ale, score me up for the lyingest knave in
Christendom.

(Induction, 2.18)

and the rustic element remains in Petruchio's language as a genial
contrast to the harshness of the action.

The self-consciousness about language, which gave *Love's
Labour's Lost* its brilliance, is not present here. The only comment
on language is that of Tranio in the opening scene, where his

master seems determined to follow a regimen like that of a noble's
in *Love's Labour's Lost*: 'I pray', Tranio says,

> Or so devote to Aristotle's checks
> As Ovid be an outcast quite abjured:
> Balk logic with acquaintance that you have
> And practise rhetoric in your common talk;
> Music and poesy use to quicken you;
> The mathematics and the metaphysics,
> Fall to them as you find your stomach serves you.

(i.1.31)

Language presented no formidable problem to Shakespeare in
The Taming of the Shrew for he does not feel the language competing for its own liberties against the interests of the theme.
Later he was to discipline both 'rhetoric' and 'common talk' for
his dramatic purposes.

CHAPTER III

THE EARLY HISTORIES
Henry VI (Parts I, II and III)

A T some stage in Shakespeare's early work subject suddenly intervened. Instead of the 'taffeta phrases' and 'the silken terms precise' people and events so crowded in that they took possession of the medium. To some extent this had occurred in the early comedies but it was the epic material of the history plays, beginning with the most unmanageable material of all in *Henry VI*, Parts I, II, III that faced Shakespeare with all the problems of dramatic language and stretched his resources. In the early comedies language had first been a dalliance, and then a medium whose employment presented new but not strenuous problems. It may be compared to the contrast of speaking prettily in a foreign language the phrases one knows, and of struggling with the vocabulary which the situation demands. In the history plays language became a discipline. The untractable mass of events had somehow to be turned into verse and managed in the succession of scenes. Action became the taskmaster of language. So York in *Henry VI*, Part II.

> Then thus:
> Edward the Third, my lords, had seven sons:
> The first, Edward the Black Prince, Prince of Wales;
> The second, William of Hatfield, and the third,
> Lionel, Duke of Clarence; next to whom
> Was John of Gaunt, the Duke of Lancaster;
> The fifth was Edmund Langley, Duke of York;
> The sixth was Thomas of Woodstock, Duke of Gloucester;
> William of Windsor was the seventh and last.
>
> (ii.2.9.)

Nor does the explanation end there, but continues in a passage where the blank verse becomes increasingly refractory. Even when the matter was not so unaccommodating the continual pressure of circumstance in the history plays remained, so that the verse could no longer be developed in the leisurely way of *The Two Gentlemen of Verona*. As Mowbray says in another context in *Richard II*, the issue cannot be settled by 'cold words' alone:

> 'Tis not the trial of a woman's war,
> The bitter clamour of two eager tongues,
> Can arbitrate this cause betwixt us twain.

Even in that festival of words, *Love's Labour's Lost*, Shakespeare had found that when action intervened a direct manner of writing was helpful. Now action and not the dance of words is dominant. The only reference to language in the *Henry VI* plays has an emphasis on the virtues of simple expression. In 1 *Henry VI* Vernon addressing the king complains that Basset did 'seem with forged quaint conceit To set a gloss upon his bold intent' (iv.1.102). In the same play the Bishop of Winchester had challenged the Duke of Gloucester:

> If thou canst accuse
> Or aught intend'st to lay unto my charge,
> Do it without *invention*, suddenly;
> As I, with *sudden and extemporal speech*
> Purpose to answer what thou canst object.

> (1 *Henry VI*, iii.1.3)

He had already used *extemporal* twice in comic moments in *Love's Labour's Lost*, but now the word is employed with urgency. Holofernes had asked Sir Nathaniel to hear 'an *extemporal* epitaph on the death of a deer', and Armado had pleaded for the assistance of 'some *extemporal* god of rhyme, for I am sure I shall turn sonnet'. Now, after this single use in a serious passage Shakespeare discards the word which does not appear in his work again.

In exploring the language of the early histories it is difficult to use the material of *Henry VI*, Parts I, II and III as the controversy over the authorship remains. Yet even the most disintegrating and cautious critic would admit that Shakespeare had a great part in Parts II and III and composed some of the scenes in Part I. In my view he did more but for the purpose of the present argument it is enough to agree that he had a share in the authorship. Stylistic evidence, in any case, must not be assigned too important a place in determining authorship. On the whole 1 *Henry VI* is *flatter* in style than Parts II and III, as if the poet's energies were wholly occupied with the problem of containing the material within the medium. Yet flat passages, used dramatically, as a language deliberately assigned to the duller characters are to be found even in the most mature plays, and there also recur throughout Shakespeare's plays some elements of flatness that arise from moments of creative exhaustion. But there is not present elsewhere the accumulative effect of flat passages which 1 *Henry VI* presents. So that all concessions having been made, one has the sense that the language of Part I is the least exciting in the plays.

Many of the passages develop a thin or pedestrian movement without lively imagery or any emphasis or power. Yet it is clear from an examination of the whole of *Henry VI* that whoever wrote the Second and Third Parts was aware of the language of Part I and sufficiently approved of it to recall some of its phrases. So, to quote only a single example, the word *corrosive* is found in the First Part:

> Care is no cure, but rather corrosive,
>
> (iii.3.3)

and again in Part II in a very similar image:

> Away! though parting be a fretful *corrosive*
> It is applied to a deathful wound.
>
> (iii.2.403)

The word is not employed elsewhere in any of the plays.

He has for the first time a source which he must follow closely. In *Love's Labour's Lost* he had reduced his obligations to plot to a minimum; in the early comedies he has no over-riding loyalty to the story if wit and invention tempt him. But now the historical theme and one known at least in outline to many of his audience requires him to regard events with respect. A number of sources were open to him, but in the main he was to rely on the *Chronicles* of Hall and Holinshed. Much about Shakespeare's work as a dramatist is uncertain but this, at least, can be safely asserted: while in the act of composition he spent more hours in the close study of the *Chronicles* of Edward Hall and of Raphael Holinshed than of any other two books. Though the chronicler gave him the narrative, and Hall, more particularly, his concept of the whole dynastic theme of the history plays they were but little support in style and language. He could not rely on them as later he was to rely on the very phrases of North's translation of Plutarch.

As a result his control of language in these plays is far from complete, and yet in the development of his use of language in drama they are of first importance. The discipline required in rejecting the verbal delights of the early comedies was of a major order. Rarely a passage of playfulness is allowed to intrude, and the pun, though common to the comedies and the histories, is often now used with a gravity that excludes all comic effect.

He had to employ a line often unillumined by imagery, though this enforced directness and simplicity have seldom the strength which can adorn them in their all too occasional appearances in the mature plays. Whatever may be said later of the passages in the two plays where a heightened style is in the ascendant the main texture is illustrated by a passage such as Henry's speech to York:

> I here entail
> The crown to thee and to thine heirs for ever;
> Conditionally, that here thou take an oath
> To cease this civil war, and, whilst I live,
> To honour me as thy king and sovereign,
> And neither by treason nor hostility
> To seek to put me down and reign thyself.
>
> (3 *Henry VI*, i.1.194)

Statement follows statement, with clarity and unerring precision, but one seems to hear the dull thud of innumerable prisoners walking in unending line: and indeed the material is holding the poet prisoner.

Such is his difficulty with these new linguistic requirements of his epical material that sometimes when the action is most effective the language gives only a dull support. Thus one of the most moving scenes is in 3 *Henry VI*, ii.5 when Henry standing alone sees a son bringing in the body of his father whom he has killed, and a little later a father bringing in the dead body of a son. The interpretation of the historical action is effectively reduced to the simplicity of a symbol showing the blind and insensate cruelty of civil war. The strength of the scene is in its conception, in its reduction of the whole intractable complexity of historical incident to a single and enduring vision of the effect of the strife on human lives. But the language does not rise to the imaginative vision. In this scene much of the language follows the same dull and even step, familiar in both these plays. So the son who brings in the body of his father:

Ill blows the wind that profits nobody.
This man, whom hand to hand I slew in fight
May be possessed with some store of crowns,
And I that haply take them from him now,
May yet ere night yield both my life and them
To some man else, as this dead man doth me.

Where in this scene Shakespeare departs from this plainness it is still to employ the schemes and tropes of the schoolroom rhetoric, which he played with so effectively in *Love's Labour's Lost*. So the king introduces this original and imaginative scene with a speech replete with the conventional figures of rhetoric:

This battle fares like to the morning's war,
When dying clouds contend with growing light,
What time the shepherd, blowing of his nails,
Can neither call it perfect day nor night.
Now sways it this way; like a mighty sea
Forc'd by the tide to combat with the wind;
Now sways it that way, like the self-same sea
Forc'd to retire by fury of the wind.

(3 *Henry VI*, ii.5.1)

F. P. Wilson has commented that any grammar-school boy could have picked out the figures in this speech, although perhaps he would not have observed how the speech is redeemed by the lyricism which cuts across the formalism of the rhetoric. But if the boy had been confronted with *Hamlet* or *King Lear* his task would have been more difficult. There is a development in Shakespeare similar to that which Professor Manly noticed in Chaucer: 'a process of general release from the astonishingly artificial and sophisticated art with which he began and the gradual replacement of formal rhetorical devises by methods of composition based upon close observation of life and the exercise of the creative imagination'.

Conventional language is again employed to conclude the speech. Here a pastoral setting is used, though again the set formulae of rhetorical language are shot through with a certain lyricism:

Methinks it were a happy life,
To be no better than a homely swain;
To sit upon a hill, as I do now,
To carve out dials quaintly, point by point,

> Thereby to see the minutes how they run,
> How many makes the hour full complete;
> How many hours brings about the day;
> How many days will finish up the year;
> How many years a mortal man may live.
>
> (3 *Henry VI*, ii.5.21)

Sometimes the imagery is so feeble that it seems an anti-climax to a vivid direct description. Thus Warwick is given a passage of powerfully conceived realistic description to portray the dead Gloucester. Not a detail is missed; eyeballs, hair, nostrils, all have a reference, and then the *summer corn* is dragged in with the odd comparison:

> His well-proportioned beard made rough and rugged,
> Like to the summer's corn by tempest lodged.
>
> (2 *Henry VI*, iii.2.175)

Shakespeare's ultimate success was to bring language and action together in a completely united service of drama. Here they live apart. Either the plain language dominates and the action proceeds, or Shakespeare seems suddenly to recollect that he has powers of rhetoric unused. For a passage he unleashes the puissant but dangerous rhetoric he has restrained, and then when the bout is over the play again proceeds at its own pedestrian level. One of the most effective of these detached 'purple patches' is given to the Lieutenant who has Suffolk as a prisoner in Part II *Henry VI*, iv.1:

> The gaudy, blabbing and remorseful day
> Is crept into the bosom of the sea;
> And now loud-howling wolves arouse the jades
> That drag the tragic melancholy night,
> Who with their drowsy, slow and flagging wings
> Clip men's graves, and from their misty jaws
> Breathe foul contagious darkness in the air.
> Therefore bring forth the soldiers of our prize.
>
> (II.iv.1.1)

It can be argued, as Johnson did, that Shakespeare wished to emphasise that night was the appropriate time for the destruction of the prisoners: 'Guilt, if afraid of light', he wrote, 'considers darkness as a natural shelter, and makes night the confidant of those actions which cannot be entrusted to the *tell-tale* day.' Logically, this is sound enough, but emotionally the passage remains detached, and there is certainly no other reference to *night* in the rest of the scene. Taken by itself the passage is among the most brilliant in the two plays.

The memory of it remains and is transfigured in the passage in *Macbeth*:

> Now o'er the one half-world
> Nature seems dead, and wicked dreams abuse
> The curtain'd sleep; witchcraft celebrates
> Pale Hecate's offerings, and wither'd murder,
> Alarum'd by his sentinel, the wolf,
> Whose howl's his watch, thus with his stealthy pace
> With Tarquin's ravishing strides, toward his design
> Moves like a ghost.

(ii.1.49)

The presence of the 'wolf' in the two passages seems to suggest that somewhere in Shakespeare's mind he recalled the earlier passage when he wrote the later and most imaginative and sustained symbolical pageantry. Apart from the contrasting merits of the two passages in themselves there is this further vital difference. In the *Macbeth* passage the *night* passage creates a dread image of murder at the very hour of the performance of the deed, and this by the murderer himself. In the 2 *Henry VI* despite all Johnson's analysis the Lieutenant has his 'purple patch' on night and then goes on to deal with his prisoners. The passage of rhetoric is a detachable ornament, indifferent to the dramatic action.

Throughout, the more highly coloured language is introduced intermittently, as if almost as an afterthought, or as if the poet became aware from time to time of the modest, serviceable, but plodding verse that he was using and felt that he should do something to enliven it. Thus classical imagery is used liberally in both plays, indeed the examples are more frequent than anywhere else in Shakespeare. But they seem class-room examples, caught, as it were, out of some anthology of classical mythology. Ovid, remembered from the Stratford class-room, and obviously much read and enjoyed after those days for his own sake, is ever readily at hand, though with varying effectiveness. One of the most impressive of such passages is Young Clifford's speech on seeing his dead father:

> O, let the vile world end,
> And the premised flames of the last day
> Knit earth and heaven together.
>
> (2 *Henry VI*, v.2.40)

So Ovid in the *Metamorphoses* had written of how Jove 'remembered
also that 'twas *in the fates* that a time would come when *sea* and
land, the unkindled palace of the *sky* and the beleaguered structure
of the universe should be destroyed by fire'.[1]

At times the classical allusions seem forced into the texture of
the speeches. So Margaret when she rails at Henry in 2 *Henry VI*,
iii.2:

> How often have I tempted Suffolk's tongue,
> The agent of thy foul inconstancy,
> To sit and witch me as Ascanius did
> When he to madding Dido would unfold
> His father's acts, commenced in burning Troy!
> Am I not witched like her? Or thou not false like him?
>
> (2 *Henry VI*, iii.2.114)

Here it may be a memory of Chaucer's *Legend of Good Women*
rather than a classical reference for Chaucer made Ascanius
responsible while in the Aeneid it had been Cupid disguised as
Ascanius.

Very little in the more coloured language of the play seems to
arise from direct experience, yet when it does it is very effective.
So in this same scene where Margaret is deploring Henry's
grief at Gloucester's death she finds an utterance far more effective
than the belaboured classical passage, in 'an ale house sign'
reference which seems to arise naturally from contemporary
recollection:

> Erect his (i.e. Gloucester's) statue, and worship it,
> And make my image but an alehouse sign.

Out of these immediate experiences what would seem to come
most vividly is the image of the *slaughter-house*. Henry uses it
effectively, even if cumbersomely in bemoaning Gloucester's
death:

> And as the butcher takes away the calf,
> And binds the wretch, and beats it when it strays,
> Bearing it to the bloody slaughter-house,

[1] *Loeb* translation.

Even so remorseless have they borne him hence;
And as the dam runs lowing up and down,
Looking the way her harmless young one went,
And can do nought but wail her darling's loss;
Even so myself bewails good Gloucester's case, . . .

(2 Henry VI, iii.1.210)

It is to the *slaughter-house* that Cade returns in addressing his supporter Dick, the butcher of Ashford: 'They fell before thee like sheep and oxen, and thou behavedst thyself as if thou hadst been in thine own slaughter-house.' (2 *Henry VI* iv.3.3)

If one is to discover in 2 and 3 *Henry VI* the beginning of a *continuing* image, that is an image recurring to Shakespeare during the whole time his mind is engaged with the composition, then it may be found here in the *butcher* and the *slaughter-house*. The examples quoted are only two of the most effective but others occur. The degree to which he came to feel that England, bloody and distraught with civil war could be seen through this comparison appears in a passage given to Margaret in 3 *Henry VI*:

Henry, your sovereign,
Is prisoner to the foe, His state usurped,
His realm a *slaughter-house*, his subjects slain.

(v.4.76)

This use of *butcher* and *slaughter-house* is not only distinctive to these plays and to the other early histories, particularly, and very naturally, *Richard III* but it exhausts itself with these plays, except for rare later references. How frequent and powerful is the employment in the early histories example alone can show. The word *slaughter-house* itself is found nowhere outside the early histories. In *King John* Salisbury accuses Hubert of the death of Prince Arthur:

Away with me, all you whose souls abhor
Th' uncleanly savours of a *slaughter-house*
For I am stifled with this smell of sin.

(iv.3.111)

In *Richard III* Hastings on his way to his death exclaims:

Three times today my foot-cloth horse did stumble,
And started, when he looked upon the Tower,
And loth to bear me to the *slaughter-house*.

(iii.4.88)

Later Elizabeth addresses the Marquess of Dorset:

> go across the seas,
> And live with Richmond, from the reach of hell.
> Go hie thee, hie thee from this *slaughter-house*,
> Lest thou increase the number of the dead.
>
> (iv.1.44)

Even the more general words *slaughter*, *slaughtered* and *slaughterer* find their most frequent use in these plays. So it is with all the words *butcher*, *butchered*, *butcheries*, *butcherly* and *butchery*. A number of these are vivid as if the scene had been witnessed as a personal experience. So Warwick answers the Queen after the death of Gloucester:

> Who finds the heifer dead, and bleeding fresh,
> And sees fast by a butcher with an axe,
> But will suspect 'twas he that made the slaughter.
>
> (2 *Henry VI.* iii.11.18)

It is true that at any time this image of *slaughter-house*, *butcher* and *flies upon the carrion* can return to him, but the examples are rare. One of the most effective is in *Coriolanus*:

> Than boys pursuing summer butterflies
> Or butchers killing flies
>
> (iv.6.95)

It can, of course, in lighter mood be transfigured into a phantasy, and so Mercutio in *Romeo and Juliet*:

> The very butcher of a silk button, a duellist.
>
> (ii.4.24)

Or it can be used in a comic context as Falstaff does in *The Merry Wives of Windsor*: he asks Bardolf to fetch him a quart of sack and adds: 'Have I lived to be carried in a basket like a barrow of butcher's offal?' But in the main his mind had been impressed with some personal sight of a slaughter-house, hot and foul with carnage, on a summer's day with flies everywhere and blood, and the nauseous odour of slaughter. This affected him profoundly in the period of the composition of the history plays, and later returned intermittently as in the memorable lines in *Julius Caesar*:

> O pardon me thou bleeding piece of earth
> That I am meek and gentle with these butchers.
>
> (iii.1.255)

It may have been through this image of *butcher* and *slaughter-house* that Shakespeare came to feel that the untractable material of the *Henry VI* plays needed some simpler and more definite design for dramatic effectiveness.

From a less personal recollection, but natural to his theme are the comparisons of anarchy and rebellion to the savagery of wild animals. Furnivall long ago was impressed by the frequency of this usage.[1] Hall had some examples to offer the poet if he needed such guidance and the emblems of the nobles, the bear and the boar confirmed the appropriateness of the images. All this, however, lacks the force of the *slaughter-house* image.

With one exception he makes no attempt to vary the verse or the imagery from one character to another. Henry from the first is given biblical imagery and references as if to emphasise the contrast of his quiet and devout simplicity with the warring and corrupt forces around him. So in his early speech to Margaret:

> O Lord, that lends me life,
> Lend me a heart replete with thankfulness.
>
> (2 *Henry VI*, i.i.19)

Such references are frequent throughout the *Henry VI* plays.

Among outside influences in these earliest historical plays the strongest is that of Marlowe, particularly in 3 *Henry VI*. At first sight Shakespeare's language in this early period seems to fall short of the commanding power with which Marlowe's rhetoric searches the utmost corners of the earth and the farthest reaches of the firmament for comparisons. Yet the humbler and quieter range of Shakespeare's verse is a sign that their author is conscious of the problem of the function of poetry in drama. It was an early recognition that verse must be the servant of the dramatic intention. What Marlowe's verse lacked, both in *Tamburlaine* and in his other tragedies, was a texture varied enough to make it a suitable instrument for the diverse situations of drama. In the historical plays, even when it is less impressive poetically, Shakespeare's verse is from the first a more adaptable dramatic medium than Marlowe ever possessed. Very early Shakespeare must have realised that he could not develop his own resources by becoming an imitator of Marlowe, and by *Henry IV* the more extravagant gestures of Marlowe are diverted to parody.

[1] See Arden Shakespeare *II Henry VI*, introd. p. liv. edited Andrew S. Cairncross and the reference to Furnivall.

In these earlier plays the music of *Tamburlaine* is too much present in his mind to be crowded out altogether. For instance Richard in speaking to his father, the Duke of York, says:

> And, father, do but think
> How sweet a thing it is to wear a crown;
> Within whose circuit is Elysium
> And all that poets feign of bliss and joy.
>
> (3 *Henry VI*, i.2.28)

The comparison with *Tamburlaine* is too obvious to be ignored. This image of the crown remains in *Richard II*, and is now employed, not merely as a symbol of the inexhaustible pleasure of material bliss, but with a more subtle and imaginative reference:

> A thousand flatterers sit within thy crown,
> Whose compass is no bigger than thy head;
> And yet, incaged in so small a verge,
> The waste is no whit lesser than thy land.
>
> (ii.1.100)

Later, Richard, with a memory of the earlier lines, describes the dangers and uncertainty of kingship, and holds one side of the crown while making Bolingbroke hold the other:

> On this side my hand, and on that side yours.
> Now is this golden crown like a deep well
> That owes two buckets, filling one another;
> The emptier ever dancing in the air,
> The other down, unseen and full of water:
> That bucket down and full of tears am I,
> Drinking my griefs, whilst you mount up on high.
>
> (iv.1.183)

It is as if the idea had been transformed from Marlowe's exaltation of material power to Shakespeare's more philosophical and sensitive enquiry as to the nature and value of human experience.

The language of 2 and 3 *Henry VI* is more interesting than that of Part I. Here the flatness is relieved only in certain scenes, particularly those in which Talbot occurs. Here a single image is developed into the argument with an increasing power over the associations that unite to make poetic language. There is also, in some of these scenes, a sombre rhetoric, as in Talbot's speech when the body of his son is brought into his presence:

> Thou antic death, which laugh'st us here to scorn
>
> (iv.7.18)

The danger is that when emphasis is given to any passage the imaginative language falls out of control into rant, and a riot of words. So Sir William Lucy to La Pucelle:

> O, were mine eye-balls into bullets turn'd,
> That I in rage might shoot them at your faces!
>
> (iv.7.79)

In *Henry VI*, Parts II and III there are numerous passages of a stronger quality. With the lines just quoted may be compared the king's verbal assault on Suffolk in Part II:

> Thou baleful messenger, out of my sight!
> Upon thy eye-balls murderous tyranny
> Sits in grim majesty, to fright the world.
>
> (iii.2.48)

The same lapses into excess remain, as indeed they do throughout the history plays. Suffolk in *2 Henry VI* falls back upon the idiom of Marlowe to gain the extremes he requires for cursing his enemies:

> Gall, worse than gall, the daintiest that they taste!
> Their sweetest shade a grove of cypress trees.
>
> (iii.2.322)

and much of a similar quality is displayed in the lines of the speech that follows.

As a contribution to the development of Shakespeare's use of language in drama *2* and *3 Henry VI* are far more impressive than the text itself might suggest. The verse itself is often inadequate as compared with his later performance, but he has taken the measure of new problems even if he has not solved them. He broke his way through to the possession of new powers through his stern work in these history chronicles. He reviewed in his own mind the whole problem of imaginative writing for dramatic purposes. Among much else he discovered that the dramatic effect became stronger as the action became less diffuse and more clearly defined, and he turned not without some help from Marlowe in *Richard III* and *Richard II* to matter that could be more easily mastered within the pattern of a play.

CHAPTER IV

RICHARD III AND RICHARD II

How rapidly Shakespeare matured can be seen by a comparison of *Richard III* and *Richard II* with the Henry VI plays; and, further, by a comparison of *Richard III* and *Richard II*. In both plays he is still dependent on Holinshed's *Chronicle*, and for *Richard III* this means the narratives of Edward Hall and Sir Thomas More which Holinshed incorporated into his own work. Now after the stern apprenticeship in the Henry VI plays, but not without some help from Marlowe he could determine how much of the Chronicle's narrative could be digested in a play. The tyranny of unending incident has been subdued, and with the concentration on a single, central character he can expand the possibilities of each scene in the lucid framework of his plot. Some, though not all the tediousness of the verse has been expelled and the rhetoric though ample and violent is more purposeful. Above all, the dreary classical similes which so held up the action have been exorcised.

At times, he relaxes and allows the dull needs of explanatory material or the detail of historical narrative to take possession. Queen Elizabeth addressing Gloucester gives what is far from being an isolated example in *Richard III* of this pedestrian dullness:

> Brother of Gloucester, you mistake the matter.
> The king, of his own royal disposition,
> And not provoked by any suitor else;
> Aiming, belike, at your interior hatred,
> Which in your outward actions shows itself
> Against my children, brothers and myself
> Makes him to send;
>
> (i.3.62)

This does not touch the stubborn intractability of the following lines in *Richard II*:

> Then thus: I have from Port le Blanc, a bay
> In Brittany, received intelligence
> That Harry Duke of Hereford, Rainhold Lord Cobbam,
>
> .   .   .   .   .

That late broke from the Duke of Exeter,
His brother, Archbishop late of Canterbury,
Sir Thomas Erpingham, Sir John Ramston,
Sir John Norbery, Sir Robert Waterton, and Francis Quoint,
All these well furnish'd by the Duke of Bretagne
With eight tall ships, three thousand men of war,
Are making hither with all due expedience
And shortly mean to touch our northern shore.

(ii.1.277)

This passage is exceptional in *Richard II*, where with the theme under control the language has been sustained with an unprecedented liveliness.

Comparison between the two plays shows how far Shakespeare had advanced his whole conception of dramatic language in *Richard II* for it excels not only the Henry VI plays but also *Richard III*. Yet *Richard III* had for contemporary audiences a more appealing plot: there were six Quartos before the Folio of 1623, though *Richard II* follows closely in popularity with five Quartos in the same period. Much in *Richard III* is outrageous, both in theme and language, but all, or very nearly all, is theatrically effective, and obviously, most congenial to Elizabethan audiences. Samuel Johnson's comment still has much validity:

> This is one of the most celebrated of our author's performances; yet I know not whether it has happened to him as to others, to be praised when praise is not most deserved. That this play has scenes noble in themselves, and very well contrived to strike in the exhibition, cannot be denied. But some parts are trifling, others shocking, and some improbable.

Concentration is made on the central figure, Gloucester[1] himself, and upon him all the action of the play depends. Loyalty to the historical narrative necessitates the presence of the wailing royal ladies whose plangent rhetoric gives diffuseness to some passages. Mothers, widows, relations, they compete with each other in verbal stridency; Queen Elizabeth to Queen Margaret is an example:

> O! thou didst prophesy the time would come
> That I should wish for thee to help me curse
> That bottled spider, that foul bunchback'd toad.

(iv.4.79)

---

[1] I name him Gloucester while he is Duke and Richard when he is King.

Linguistically, the play is highly stylised with every device of rhetoric so employed that the total effect is not of tragedy but of irony, wit and melodrama. Not only is this effect attained, but it seems deliberate, as if Shakespeare were now employing language for a conscious dramatic purpose. Influences, of course, abound. Thus the language not less than the plot is under Marlowe's influence. Richard speaks to Queen Elizabeth:

> . . . the dignity and height of honour,
> *The high imperial type of this earth's glory.*

(iv.4.243)

Here is the very echo of Marlowe's line. Similarly, the devices of Senecan verse are employed, as in the *Stichomythia*, of the exchanges between Richard and Queen Elizabeth (iv.4.340) on his proposal that he shall marry her daughter:

Queen Elizabeth
> Under what title shall I woo for thee,
> That God, the law, my honour, and her love,
> Can make seem pleasing to her tender years?

King Richard
> Infer fair England's peace by this alliance.

Queen Elizabeth
> Which she shall purchase with still lasting war.

King Richard
> Say that the king, which may command, entreats.

Queen Elizabeth
> That at her hands which the king's King forbids.

So it continues for the long sequence of interchanges which follow. Despite these elements of style, obviously derived, and the way in which the text-books of rhetoric seem pillaged so that no example of their art should be missing, the total result is no cold collection of school-room devices in language, but of a play heightened by linguistic excess to the limit of its strange and violent theme. To such a general assertion there must obviously be exceptions. In two sentences of twenty lines with an opening reference to:

> The supreme seat, the throne majestical,
> The sceptred office of your ancestors.

(iii.7.118)

Buckingham contrives to pack all the figurative devices of the books of rhetoric.

All the subordinate characters declaim with loud-mouthed emphasis, either imaging the scenes of horror or distending the powers of speech in rhetorical vituperation. So Tyrrel, after the murder of the Princes in the Tower appears not in person but as the voice of a rhetorical chorus in clamant lines expressing all that can be felt about such a crime:

> The tyrannous and bloody deed is done,
> The most arch act of piteous massacre
> That ever this land was guilty of.
> Dighton and Forrest whom I did suborn
> To do this ruthless piece of butchery,
> Although they were flesh'd villains, bloody dogs,
> Melting with tenderness and kind compassion
> Wept like two children in their death's sad story.
>
> (iv.3.1)

With some of the characters this language falls back into cold and lifeless conceits. So Anne, as she mourns over the wounds in her husband's dead body:

> Lo, in these windows that let forth thy life,
> I pour the helpless balm of my poor eyes.
>
> (i.2.12)

In the next line Anne has thrown off these mild similitudes which seem as if they might have been borrowed from one of the lesser sonneteers, and is making her own contribution to the verbal violence of the much-abused royal ladies:

> Cursed be the hand that made them fatal holes!
> Cursed be the heart that had the heart to do it!
> Cursed the blood that let this blood from hence!
> More direful hap betide that hated wretch,
> That makes us wretched by the death of thee,
> Than I can wish to adders, spiders, toads,
> Or any creeping venom'd thing that lives!
>
> (i.2.13)

'Blood', as Sir Edmund Chambers wrote in a surprisingly[1] interesting passage on *Richard III* 'runs like a *leit-motif* through

---

[1] 'surprisingly' because this is the only detailed passage devoted to Shakespeare's language in the two volumes of *William Shakespeare*, 1930.

the play'. The verse seems sometimes like a nightmare where blood faces one in every direction, with hot and nauseating persistence: 'Thou bloodless remnant of that royal blood'; 'Curse the blood that let this blood from hence'; 'blood, From cold and empty veins, where no blood dwells'; 'thy murderous falchion smoking in his blood; a shadow like an angel, with bright hair, dabbled in blood'; 'That dog, that had his teeth before his eyes, To worry lambs and lap their gentle blood'; 'And make poor England weep in streams of blood.' Escape is impossible; wherever one turns the haunting image of 'blood' is ever present.

In contrast to the reckless violence of the action, where murder succeeds murder with calculated and remorseless cunning, and also in contrast to the rages of the tumultuous queens is Richard himself. Tyrrel's speech after the murder of the Princes has been quoted above: it is as if the voice of conscience were emerging everywhere even to the lowest and most evil elements in society. But a few lines later, Richard can speak of his proposed wooing of the young Elizabeth:

> To her I go, a jolly thriving wooer.
>
> (iv.3.43)

Here is the voice beyond conscience, beyond good and evil, the Machiavellian character, who because he is above compassion can move in a mood of wit amid the blood soaked horrors. So in a scene of Shakespeare's invention Gloucester woos Anne, widow of Prince Edward, as she is bearing the corpse of Henry VI to burial. Anne herself rises to a tempest fury rhetoric:

> O gentlemen, see, see! dead Henry's wounds
> Open their congeal'd mouths and bleed afresh!
> Blush, blush, thou lump of foul deformity.
>
> (i.2.55)

But Gloucester, cool and ironical, speaks as a lover with all the stylised art of one of the early comedies:

> It is a quarrel most unnatural,
> To be reveng'd on him that loveth thee.
>
> (i.2.134)

And Anne is brought into the same mood in her reply:

> It is a quarrel just and reasonable,
> To be reveng'd on him that kill'd my husband.

He woos her in the language of a minor Elizabethan sonneteer. To Anne, who has wished her eyes were 'basilisks, to strike him dead', he replies:

> I would they were, that I might die at once;
> For now they kill me with a living death.
> Those eyes of thine from mine have drawn salt tears,
> Sham'd their aspects with store of childish drops.
>
> (i.2.151)

So complete is Gloucester's awareness of his own verbal conceits that he asks Anne:

> To leave this keen encounter of our wits
> And fall something into a slower method, . . .
>
> (i.2.116)

Richard III succeeds because it is worked out in such distinct, brutal, and theatrically sustaining ways. It also succeeds because, except in a few scenes, it does not go beyond this blatant Machiavellian melodrama on which the action depends. Wherever it does depart from its own stylised formula the shallowness of the whole is revealed. Thus, for instance, the most imaginative lines in the play are given to Clarence. His dream, so brilliantly presented, has a humanity and pathos transcending all else:

> Methought I saw a thousand fearful wrecks;
> Ten thousand men that fishes gnaw'd upon;
> Wedges of gold, great anchors, heaps of pearl,
> Inestimable stones, unvalu'd jewels,
> All scatter'd in the bottom of the sea:
> Some lay in dead men's skulls; and in those holes
> Where eyes did once inhabit, there were crept,
> As 'twere in scorn of eyes, reflecting gems,
> Which woo'd the slimy bottom of the deep,
> And mock'd the dead bones that lay scatter'd by.
>
> (i.4.24)

In this, and the surrounding passages, moods are allowed to enter of compassion and human understanding which are excluded from the play as a whole.

In a different way the hard, limited, successful pattern of the play breaks down in Richard's soliloquy before Bosworth Field. Here is a mood of self-analysis where despair has penetrated the nonchalant self composure. But rhetoric will not serve this more subtle purpose and Shakespeare seems to have no effective linguistic instrument at hand. As a result, in one of the most crucial moments in the play the verse falters, and interest is maintained solely by the situation:

> Richard loves Richard; that is, I am I.
> Is there a murderer here? No. Yes, I am.
> Then fly. What from myself? Great reason why?
> Lest I revenge. What, myself upon myself?
> Alack I love myself. Wherefore? for any good
> That I myself have done unto myself?
> O, no! alas, I rather hate myself
> For hateful deeds committed by myself?
>
> (v.3.184)

The contrast is complete between these faltering lines and the compact strength of the soliloquy with which the play opens:

> But I, that am not shap'd for sportive tricks,
> Nor made to court an amorous looking-glass.
>
> (i.1.14)

'Conscience' is not a word with which one would have thought the play to have much concern. In the early scenes there are a few references, ironical with Richard, and declamatory with the royal ladies; then in the soliloquy scene Richard refers to 'conscience', with a solemn sense if not of repentance at least of fear:

> My conscience hath a thousand several tongues,
> And every tongue brings in a several tale,
> And every tale condemns me for a villain.
>
> (v.3.193)

Shakespeare in one of the few passages where irony moves towards comedy had already allowed the Second Murderer to make an anatomy of *conscience:*

> I'll not meddle with it: it makes a man a coward: a man cannot steal, but it accuseth him; a man cannot swear, but it checks him; he cannot lie with his neighbour's wife, but it detects him: 'tis a blushing shamefast spirit that mutinies in a man's bosom; it fills one full of obstacles: it made me once restore a purse of gold that I found; it beggars any man that keeps it; it is turned out of all towns and cities for a dangerous thing; and every man that means to live well endeavours to trust to himself and to live without it. (i.4.137)

This seems a prelude to Falstaff's analysis of 'Honour' in *Henry IV*, Part I.

Symbol occurred in *Henry VI*, Part III in the scene where the king saw a son bringing in the body of his father whom he had killed, and a little later a father bringing in the dead body of a son: in *Richard II*, symbol is impressively used. The hot, uncontemplative action of *Richard III* leaves no room for symbol though the direct and moving lines of the Scrivener make a close approach to such an effect. He enters with a paper in his hand:

> This is the indictment of the good Lord Hastings;
> Which in a set hand fairly is engross'd,
> That it may be this day read o'er in Pauls.
> And mark how well the sequel hangs together:
> Eleven hours I have spent to write it over,
> For yesternight by Catesby was it brought me;
> The precedent was full as long a-doing:
> And yet within these five hour's Hastings lived,
> Untainted, unexamined, free, at liberty.
> Here's a good world the while! Why who's so gross
> That seeth not this palpable device?
> Yet who's so bold, but says he sees it not?
> Bad is the world; and all will come to nought,
> When such ill dealing must be seen in thought.
>
> (iii.6.1)

Only for a moment is the mind allowed thus to contemplate the action in moral terms, and view the evil corruption of which Richard is the centre. Soon we are away again in the heady exaltation of his own Machiavellian ardour.

As in *Richard III*, Holinshed is Shakespeare's main source for *Richard II*. He is no longer overwhelmed by his material and the diversity of personages and incident. *Richard III*, and the influence of Marlowe had shown him how much of all the coagulated mass of chronicle could be digested in a play. As in *Richard III* all is related to the character of the king and in this way a pattern for dramatic action is discovered. But the supporting material is far more varied and lively than in *Richard III* and the violent excesses of rhetoric have been discarded. It is as if he had consciously learned a great deal in composing *Richard III*, and now with additional strength and confidence filled the whole play, or very nearly all of it, with a compelling language, dramatically effective, and also effective as verse. Again and again, he will take a phrase from Holinshed, or the mere hint of a phrase, and illuminate it with poetic strength. Holinshed, for instance, had a passage on how the bay trees withered:

> In this yeere in a manner throughout all the realme of England, old baie trees withered, and afterwards, contrarie to all men's thinking, grew greene againe, a strange sight, and supposed to import some unknowne event.

Shakespeare transfers the 'bay-trees' to Wales and gives them to the 'Welsh Captain' as the opening for a brilliant speech in which he explains why he cannot any longer wait for the king:

> Tis thought the king is dead: we will not stay.
> The bay-trees in our country are all wither'd,
> And meteors fright the fixed stars of heaven:
> The pale-faced moon looks bloody on the earth
> And lean-look'd prophets whisper fearful change:
> Rich men look sad, and ruffians dance and leap,
> The one in fear to lose what they enjoy,
> The other to enjoy by rage and war:
> These signs forerun the death or fall of kings.
>
> (*Richard II*, ii.4.7)

Even when the material is less tractable, he can take a few pedestrian phrases from Holinshed and give them that kinetic energy which his poetry came increasingly to possess. In Holinshed, a knight speaking on behalf of Bolingbroke accuses Mowbray in the following terms:

> Thomas Mowbraie duke of Norfolke hath received eight thousand nobles to pay the souldiers that keepe your towne of Calis, which he hath not doone as he ought.

Shakespeare eliminates the knight and makes Bolingbroke speak in his own person:

> Look, what I speak, my life shall prove it true;
> That Mowbray hath receiv'd eight thousand nobles
> In name of lendings for your Highness' soldiers,
> The which he hath detain'd for lewd employments,
> Like a false traitor and injurious villain.
>
> (i.1.87)

Apart from this liveliness in the language, maintained when

even the duller action of the play has to be pushed forward, he controls the verse as well as the action for the dramatic purposes which he has defined. There are passages where the verse falls back into the flat and heavy manner which had been so common in the Henry VI plays, and examples are most frequent in Act I and Act V. But this does not overcome the general impression of a maturing control and a well-defined purpose. A weak king rules with self-gratifying indulgence and his country falls into ruin. The verse on several occasions describes this sense of decay in passages which seem to have a symbolical significance. So the Duchess of Gloucester asks John of Gaunt, to ask his brother, the Duke of York, to meet her at Plashy:

> Alack, and what shall good old York there see
> But empty lodgings and unfurnish'd walls,
> Unpeopled offices, untrodden stones?
> And what hear there for welcome but my groans?
> Therefore commend me; let him not come there,
> To seek out sorrow that dwells everywhere.

(i.2.67)

John of Gaunt concludes his famous speech on England with a similar sense of decay:

> This land of such dear souls, this dear dear land,
> Dear for her reputation through the world,
> Is now leas'd out, I die pronouncing it,
> Like to a tenement or pelting farm.

(ii.1.57)

A *pelting* farm is a *paltry* farm.

While John of Gaunt's reference is prophetic Bolingbroke in accusing Richard's associate Bushy makes a more practical reference to the inventory of waste of Richard and his friends:

> You have fed upon my signories,
> Dispark'd my parks and fell'd my forest woods,
> From my own windows torn my household coat.

(iii.1.22)

In contrast to this emphasis on decay is Shakespeare's deliberate exaltation of England. To achieve this, he turns Gaunt from what Ure describes[1] as 'a turbulent and self-seeking magnate'

---

[1] Peter Ure, *Richard II*, 1955. p. 34. I am indebted to Peter Ure for other references in the analysis of the play

to 'a father and patriot of grandiose stature, a prophet whose dying speech on England attracted the attention of the anthologist for *England's Parnassus* as early as 1600':

> This royal throne of kings, this scepter'd isle,
> This earth of majesty, this seat of Mars,
> This other Eden, demi-paradise,
> This fortress built by Nature for herself
> Against infection and the hand of war,
> This happy breed of men, this little world,
> This precious stone set in the silver sea,
> Which serves it in the office of a wall
> Or as a moat defensive to a house,
> Against the envy of less happier lands,
> This blessed plot, this earth, this realm, this England.
>
> (ii.1.40)

Here the imagination happily accumulates the heap of images with which it would adorn the central idea. They are arranged without complexity, without the urgency present in more dramatic passages. This is a slow solemn rhetoric, magnificent for its own purpose, but not serviceable for much else.

Mowbray, discussing his exile in an otherwise rhetorical speech, refers to England with a frank and simple sincerity:

> The language I have learn'd these forty years,
> My native English, now I must forego.
>
> (i.3.159)

In a similar passage Bolingbroke discusses his exile, emphasising his consciousness of the loss of English sights and sounds, though a more personal element enters here. He is replying to a philosophical argument posed by his father:

> All places that the eye of heaven visits
> Are to a wise man ports and happy havens.
> Teach thy necessity to reason thus;
> There is no virtue like necessity.
>
> (i.3.275)

To this Bolingbroke answers:

> O, who can hold a fire in his hand,
> By thinking on the frosty Caucasus?
> Or cloy the hungry edge of appetite
> By bare imagination of a feast?

Or wallow naked in December snow
By thinking on fantastic summer's heat?
O, no! the apprehension of the good
Gives but the greater feeling to the worse:
Fell sorrow's tooth doth never rankle more
Than when he bites, but lanceth not the sore.

(i.3.294)

The most memorable of these speeches on England is given to
Richard himself where he describes the country which he is being
called to rule:

I weep for joy
To stand upon my kingdom once again.
Dear earth, I do salute thee with my hand.

(iii.2.4)

Bolingbroke, though he is an opponent of the king, speaks in very
similar terms:

And sigh'd my English breath in foreign clouds.

(iii.1.20)

These contrasting elements of decay and patriotism give the
mood in which the play exists. Confirmation of the pattern they
impose appears in the symbolism of the Garden Scene (iii.4.).
Shakespeare had numerous, possible sources of such imagery, and
already he had employed the imagery of gardens and weeds in
the Henry VI plays with a certainty of touch, which suggested that
in addition to any literary recollections his own rural memories
were still strong:

Now 'tis the spring, and weeds are shallow-rooted;
Suffer them now, and they'll o'ergrow the garden
And choke the herbs for want of husbandry.

(2 *Henry VI*, iii.1.31)

In *Richard II* with the strong organising power of a compelling
imagination Shakespeare summarises through a symbol the whole
meaning of the play. Why, the gardener's man suggests, should he
care for the garden while England itself decays from want of
loyalty and government. The gardener replies to his man that
Bolingbroke is now taking care of England, and he orders the man
to prune his plants as Richard should have attended to his kingdom. All this, overheard by the Queen and her ladies, makes a

most moving scene, concluding with the exchanges between the gardener and the Queen from which she learns, for the first time, that Richard has been taken by Bolingbroke.

The movement approaches symbol, a second time, in the Abdication Scene (iv.1.) where Richard dispossesses himself of the crown in an elaborately rhetorical speech:

> With mine own tears I wash away my balm,
> With mine own hands I give away my crown,
> With mine own tongue deny my sacred state,
> With mine own breath release all duty's rites.
>
> (iv.1.207)

At the conclusion of this speech he calls for a mirror to see if sorrow has not brought 'deeper wrinkles' to his face. Finding none, he condemns the mirror:

> O flattering glass
> Like to my followers in prosperity.
>
> (iv.1.279)

Then dashing the mirror to the ground, he asserts it to be as brittle as his own glory:

> For there it is, crack'd in an hundred shivers.
> Mark, silent king, the moral of this sport,
> How soon my sorrow hath destroy'd my face.
>
> (iv.1.289)

Richard II gains a distinguishing feature from the character of the king himself. Unlike all the other protagonists of the history plays he is a poet. Richard III was a Machiavellian villain, brilliantly portrayed, but the presentation exhausts the possibilities of the character. Richard II, introspective, self-conscious, theatrical, posturising, ever in the presence of an audience, if that audience is only himself, is a character capable in one or other of his aspects of almost indefinite development. In him, it would seem that Shakespeare had touched upon the range of human temperament that he would most wish to explore. From Richard the road winds with whatever turnings to Hamlet. Richard's verse is distinct not only from that of the other characters in the play but from all that has happened in the historical plays so far. Among his memorable speeches is his address to his followers on the coast of Wales, when he has learned that Bolingbroke has returned in arms against him. At first he uses the same violent

rhetoric against his own false friends as any royal character in
similar circumstances might use in the history plays:

> O villains, vipers, damn'd without redemption!
> Dogs, easily won to fawn on any man!
> Snakes, in my heart-blood warm'd, that sting my heart.
>
> (iii.2.128)

But later he turns to his own manner; reflective yet theatrical,
contemplative yet attitudinising, with his grief half-dissolved in
his own contemplation of it.

> Let's talk of graves, of worms and epitaphs;
> Make dust our paper, and with rainy eyes
> Write sorry on the bosom of the earth.
>
> (iii.2.145)

Yet employing the old conceits he uses them to a fresh purpose,
and the speech gathers strength and poignancy as it proceeds:

> For God's sake let us sit upon the ground
> And tell sad stories of the death of kings:
> How some have been deposed; some slain in war;
> Some haunted by the ghosts they have deposed;
> Some poison'd by their wives, some sleeping kill'd:
> All murder'd—for within the hollow crown
> That rounds the mortal temples of a king
> Keeps Death his court and there the antic sits,
> Scoffing his state and grinning at his pomp,
> Allowing him a breath, a little scene,
> To monarchize, be fear'd, and kill with looks.
>
> (iii.2.155)

In the abdication speech he combines again the same sombre
rhetoric with the self-contemplative mood. It is more than a device
that he should generalise from his fate, for the actor in him forces
him naturally to such a position. He is indulgent by temperament
and in grief he finds consolation in submerging himself deep in his
sorrow. So he addresses Aumerle when he knows that all is lost:

> A little, little grave, an obscure grave,
> Or I'll be buried in the king's highway.
>
> (iii.3.154)

This is only an introduction to the solemn movement of the
abdication speech itself:

> Now, mark me how I will undo myself.
> I give this heavy weight from off my head,
> And this unwieldy sceptre from my hand.
>
> (iv.1.203)

And so throughout the speech which follows.

With *Richard II* a stage in the language of the history plays had been reached, for *King John*, though strangely inconsistent breaks fresh and most interesting new ground. It was in these plays to *Richard II* that Shakespeare discovered the possibilities and problems of language, and, particularly, verse as a dramatic medium. That his mind was ever on the stage, seems confirmed by the images which he takes from the theatre. So, for instance, in *Richard III*, Buckingham is given the lines:

> Tut, I can counterfeit the deep tragedian,
> Speak and look back, and pry on every side,
> Tremble and start at wagging of a straw,
> Intending deep suspicion.
>
> (iii.5.5)

Again in *Richard II*, the Duke of York tells the Duchess of the downfall of Richard and the triumph of Bolingbroke through an image from the theatre:

> As in a theatre the eyes of men,
> After a well-grac'd actor leaves the stage
> Are idly bent on him that enters next
> Thinking his prattle to be tedious;
> Even so, or with much more contempt, men's eyes
> Did scowl on Richard.
>
> (v.2.23)

Considered as a whole, the language of the history plays presents no single or consistent picture. But a remarkable development can be seen from the flatness of the earliest scenes, and the stretches where verse is bogged down in incident. The louder and grosser ways of rhetoric are impressed all too frequently on the verse, but a resounding eloquence comes through, growing out of this rhetoric and often overcoming it. In imagery, personification, in the mastery of narrative and the adaptation of verse to plot and character, there are signs of a remarkable maturing of power. All may not be pleasing in the history plays but it was here that Shakespeare learned to mature his craft as a poet dramatist.

CHAPTER V

KING JOHN

IN the use of language for dramatic purposes *King John* is one of the most revealing of the plays. Much is new and enterprising, far beyond anything Shakespeare had yet achieved. He seems to have a conscious awareness in his employment of language, varying the style from one scene to another and between the separate characters. All this is combined with passages of the old-style declamatory blank verse, found at times in *King John* with almost unparalleled excess. It is almost as if after episodes of most brilliant and sensitive composition Shakespeare came to lose interest in the language as he had indeed in the play itself.

These exceptional features in the linguistic background of the play relate to the exceptional circumstances of its composition. For in *King John* Shakespeare was released from the task of discovering a plot or even ordering the sequence of scenes. He had before him a source, *The Troublesome Raigne of John King of England*, which contained all the necessary material. It is true that he used other subsidiary sources,[1] though these are not relevant to the present argument. What is important is that for the first time he had unloaded from himself the whole burdensome task of plot structure. Instead of the supremely exacting process of creation, he could employ his imagination in relation to his critical mind introducing such modification of incident and character as seemed to him desirable. His resources could also concentrate on other problems, particularly that of language, and it is this condition which makes the play exceptional among all others of this period. For while he borrowed the plot, the ordering of the scenes and sometimes the very development of the argument within a speech, he did not accept the language. Only two lines in *King John* follow exactly lines in *The Troublesome Raigne:* one is the line in v.4.42:

> For that my grandsire was an Englishman.

In the other King Philip is made to say:

[1] E. A. J. Honingmann, *King John*, 1954.

> Then I demand *Volquesson, Torain, Main*
> *Poitiers* and *Anjou*, these five provinces
>
> (i.4.158–9)

In *King John*, the King himself speaks:

> Then do I give Volquessen, Touraine, Maine,
> Poictiers and Anjou, these five provinces.
>
> (ii.1.527–8)

The maturity of the dramatic language is impressive not only when compared with *The Troublesome Raigne* but with much of Shakespeare's own early work. His language has become alert and self-conscious, not from any direct references to diction but from the presence of a number of vivid and at times conflicting styles, developed in an atmosphere of experiment. It was as if Shakespeare had seen new possibilities in dramatic language and was experimenting with them, though not always with complete confidence. This marks a stage in his development from the early histories to *Henry IV*, I and II and in some ways the language of *King John* looks far beyond any of the history plays to the great tragedies; but not without extraordinary lapses. The behaviour of genius when its resources are stretched is startlingly different from the orderly but duller processes of the pedestrian or even the merely talented mind.

The dominant manner in the historical plays has been that of a bold rhetoric often with a number of comparisons set out, one after the other, with an ever increasing emphasis. This rhetoric remains a formidable instrument in *King John*. For instance Faulconbridge, in the concluding lines, utters the famous passage which re-echoes the praise of England declared in John of Gaunt's speech in *Richard II*:

> This England never did, nor never shall,
> Lie at the proud foot of a conqueror,
> But when it first did help to wound itself.
> Now these her princes are come home again,
> Come the three corners of the world in arms,
> And we shall shock them. Nought shall make us rue,
> If England to itself do rest but true.
>
> (v.7.112)

Nor is this the only passage where a patriotic rhetoric is given an emphasis. This had been present, it is true, in *The Troublesome Raigne* but it is developed as a motive by Shakespeare. Even the

Archduke of Austria, with a little incongruity, is made to emphasise the island virtues:

> I will no more return,
> Till Angiers and the right thou hast in France,
> Together with that pale, that white-fac'd shore,
> Whose foot spurns back the ocean's roaring tides
> And coops from other lands her islanders,
> Even till that England, hedged in with the main,
> That water-walled bulwark, still secure
> And confident from foreign purposes,
> Even till that utmost corner of the west
> Salute thee for her king: . . .

(ii.1.21)

This declamatory rhetoric about England, whoever may speak it, is given, in *King John*, a distinctive quality of its own: it remains the poetic chorus of the play.

Some of the verse in *King John* belongs to that neutral language, inevitable in the history plays where a considerable body of matter has to be conveyed. Yet so varied is the verse that one is impelled to feel that Shakespeare is thinking consciously of the diversity of the characters and of the language which is appropriate to them. Nowhere is this clearer than in the speeches of Constance, mother of Arthur, who is permitted to exploit the dramatic effect of a massive and declamatory language to its utmost. Constance expresses her speeches of anger in a ranting language which knows no restraint, and it would require very little excess for them to topple over into a satire of their own intention. So when her son asks her to be content she replies:

> If thou, that bid'st me be content, wert grim,
> Ugly and slanderous to thy mother's womb,
> Full of unpleasing blots and sightless stains,
> Lame, foolish, crooked, swart, prodigious,
> Patch'd with foul moles and eye-offending marks,
> I would not care, I then would be content;
> For then I should not love thee, no, nor thou
> Become thy great birth nor deserve a crown.

(iii.1.43)

Nor is she permitted to vary from this language of excess. One cannot escape the conclusion that Shakespeare was, consciously, giving to her a language distinct from the other characters and removed from that general stream of blank verse into which all characters can dip.

Distinct from declamation is a language which is full of quibbling conceits, similar to the most conventional language of the sonnets. Hubert is given the following lines in referring to Lady Blanche and the young Dauphin:

> Such as she is, in beauty, virtue, birth,
> Is the young Dauphin every way complete:
> If not complete of, say he is not she;
> And she again wants nothing, to name want,
> If want it be not that she is not he:
> He is the half part of a blessed man,
> Left to be finished by such as she;
> And she a fair divided excellence,
> Whose fulness of perfection lies in him.
>
> (ii.1.432)

Some have been so offended by the lines that they feel Shakespeare cannot have composed them, and others have built up a charitable theory that 'Shakespeare used the nice balance of formal poetry to point to human formalities'.[1] But Johnson was closer to the truth in his general observation, already quoted: 'a quibble is to *Shakespeare* what luminous vapours are to the traveller! he follows it at all adventures . . . a quibble was to him the fatal Cleopatra for which he lost his soul and was content to lose it'.[2] Shakespeare wrote in this way because he was attracted by this style, overwhelmingly and possessively attracted. Nor was this unnatural for here was one of the manners, most admired at the time, the fashionable and elegant manner approved by the court.

All this belongs to that part of the language of the play which looks backward towards the earlier work. The only new element here is the greater degree with which declamation and 'conceit' are adjusted to character and scene. But apart from all these older features much in the rest of the play is full of linguistic prowess and experiment. In *King John* Shakespeare had, as has been already suggested, the leisure to amend and develop instead of creating and this gives his verse a dramatic effectiveness which he is far from gaining elsewhere in this period. The first line of the play is

[1] E. A. J. Honigmann, *King John*, 1954   [2] Page 4.

illustrative. Through all the tedious periphrasis of *The Trouble-some Raigne*'s introductory material Shakespeare defines in a single line the quarrel of France and England with which the play opens and the presence of Chatillon the Ambassador, who is to explore the issue:

> Now, say, Chatillon, what would France with us?

What Shakespeare can achieve in dramatic compression and linguistic concentration appears with brilliant clarity throughout the first scene where Faulconbridge's illegitimacy is disclosed. This is in marked contrast to the tediousness of the parallel scene in *The Troublesome Raigne*. Incidentally it is strange that while so much attention has been given to textual problems relating to the two plays so little has been written of their contrast in language and drama, yet linguistically the difference is most revealing. In *The Troublesome Raigne* much of the verse is just tedious; worse than anything Shakespeare does when he is using the dullest patterns of blank verse rhetorical writing, and when his mind is engaged elsewhere. Shakespeare had before him ample examples of this type of rhetoric at its most extravagant, ready for employment. So in *The Troublesome Raigne* Queen Eleanor addresses the Bastard:

> Ungracious youth, to rip thy mother's shame,
> The womb from whence thou didst thy being take.

Shakespeare does not reject this temptation to rhetoric altogether. Indeed, as has already been affirmed, it was not a new temptation: the desire towards all this verbal extravagance was a demon that continually haunted and occasionally illuminated his imagination. Yet he showed that he had the skill to avoid the indiscriminate use with which it was employed in *The Troublesome Raigne*. At his best he adapted it to character and scene and occasionally and more indolently used it in periods of creative lethargy. Fortunately in a play where his energies were so free he did much else. In many passages his powers were concentrated on passages possessing a most effective restraint.

A most egregious passage in *The Troublesome Raigne* is one in which the Bastard in a speech which has a visionary element announces that he has discovered his bastardy. This spurious combination of rhetoric and lyricism might well have been a temptation to Shakespeare:

> Birds in their flight make music with their wings,
> Filling the air with glory of my birth;
> Birds, bubbles, leaves and mountains, echo all
> Ring in mine ears that I am Richard's son.

Shakespeare cuts through all this by giving Queen Eleanor, the mother of Richard Cœur-de-Lion, the Bastard's father, a few trenchant and direct lines:

> He hath a trick of Cœur-de-Lion's face;
> The accent of his tongue affecteth him.
> Do you not read some tokens of my son
> In the large composition of this man?
>
> (i.1.85)

Again there is a little imagery, or rhetoric, but direct and most rewarding dramatic poetry.

While in all its main features one can trace Shakespeare controlling the diffuseness of *The Troublesome Raigne*, a new element enters with the Bastard's soliloquy, and this is wholly the poet's own invention. There were suggestions in *The Troublesome Raigne* that the Bastard had comic elements in his character but here is something newly invented, a verse which is sharp, witty, sardonic, compact and controlled. There is nothing like this in the plays so far: the nearest approach in the near future is to be some of Falstaff's prose. Such are the lines in which the Bastard imagines himself as a man of high honour, now that Richard Cœur-de-lion is recognised as his father:

> Well, now can I make any Joan a lady
> 'Good den, Sir Richard!'—'God-a-mercy, fellow!'
> And if his name be George, I'll call him Peter;
> For new-made honour doth forget men's names;
>
> (i.1.184)

There follows his imaginary discourse with a traveller, where again wit instructs the well-managed lines:

> Now your traveller,
> He and his toothpick at my worship's mess,
> And when my knightly stomach suffic'd
> Why then I suck my teeth and catechize
> My picked man of countries.
>
> (i.1.189)

Though Shakespeare introduces these new elements and seems fully to realise their opportunities for verse drama, he is not, as has already been suggested, prepared to exclude the rhetoric of the earlier histories and the temptation towards all the elaborate splendours of a 'conceited' diction are constantly present before him. The most remarkable example of a contrast of styles, present in a single scene, occurs in Act IV, Scene 1, in the famous encounter between Hubert and Arthur. The boy is given more than one speech in a simple, direct and realistic language:

> Have you the heart: When your head did but ache,
> I knit my handkercher about your brows,
> The best I had, a princess wrought it me,
> And I did never ask it you again;
> And with my hand at midnight held your head,
> And like the watchful minutes to the hour,
> Still and anon cheer'd up the heavy time,
> Saying 'What lack you?' and 'Where lies your grief?'
> Or 'What good love may I perform for you?'
>
> (iv.1.41)

It is one of the major problems of Shakespeare's language why when once he had captured this supreme simplicity in blank verse he did not use it more frequently as a dramatic medium. Much that is most effective in the plays was achieved by these simple means but the contemplation of a coloured and imaged language remained always for him a competitive fascination, and in Arthur's very next speech Shakespeare falls back from realism to a most complex and far-fetched conceit:

> Ah, none but in this iron age would do it!
> The iron of itself, though heat red-hot,
> Approaching near these eyes, would drink my tears
> And quench his fiery indignation
> Even in the matter of mine innocence;
> Nay, after that, consume away in rust,
> But for containing fire to harm mine eye.
> Are you more stubborn-hard than hammer'd iron?
>
> (iv.1.60)

W. P. Ker drew attention to the contrast in *Form and Style in English Poetry*:[1] 'Arthur at first goes riddling in conceits about his tears, innocence, and so on, "playing with counters". And then

[1] Pp. 248–9.

suddenly comes the thrilling change, where the poet drops these
fancies and with beautiful simplicity goes straight to poetic truth—
"universal" truth—for all feel, like Hubert, unable to resist the
passionate, despairing cry. The poet has discovered what would
happen in such a situation, given such persons. This truth is
"universal" in different senses of the word. It is "universal" in
the simple sense, appealing to common sympathy. But it is also
"universal" in a much deeper sense, taking hold of the real life
of the world, discovering one of the ways of the spirit of man. It is
the essence of innocence in distress, given by the poet, not in an
abstract allegorical manner, but dramatically.'

Yet the presence of these simpler passages, and there are a
number of them, shows that Shakespeare is exploring the possibilities of diction outside the range of the ranked cohorts of
rhetoric, and beyond the brilliance but temptation of conceit.
Further, though it might be wished that they were more frequent,
these simpler passages come to play an increasingly important part
in Shakespeare's dramatic diction.

The character of Faulconbridge permits the declamatory
language to be modified by a sardonic mood. For here is present
a character possessing elements of the introspection and analysis
of Falstaff, and ultimately of Hamlet. The most notable example
is to be found in his soliloquy on 'commodity', where syntactically
the speech is very similar to the resounding speeches of declamation to be found so frequently in the historical plays, but the thought
is analytical and based on a satirical mood:

> That smooth-faced gentleman, tickling Commodity,
> Commodity, the. bias of the world,
> The world, who of itself is peised well,
> Made to run even upon even ground,
> Till this advantage, this vile-drawing bias,
> This sway of motion, this Commodity,
> Makes it take head from all indifferency,
> From all direction, purpose, course, intent:
> And this same bias, this Commodity,
> This bawd, this broker, this all-changing word,
> Clapp'd on the outward eye of fickle France,
> Hath drawn him from his own determined aid,
> From a resolved and honourable war,
> To a most base and vile-concluded peace.

(ii.1.573)

One of the strange things in Shakespeare's language is that having mastered this skill and having penetrated through it in some speeches to a more elliptical and crowded diction he can still fall back into conventional and rhetorical blank verse.

As has been suggested much of the verse of *King John* belongs to that neutral language which is inevitable in the history plays where a considerable body of matter has to be conveyed to the audience. At the same time such is the variety that one feels at times that here Shakespeare is thinking consciously of the variety of characters and of the language which is appropriate to them. There is at least far greater differentiation of language in *King John*, in Faulconbridge, Constance, Hubert and Arthur, than there is in any of the earlier history plays. When one comes to examine much that is later most effective in his language one is led back to discover that it was in *King John* that the experiment first began. In the development of his own internal thought about language for drama it is among the most important of all the plays. This, of course, does not mean that the language itself parallels in interest the achievement of the mature plays.

In the development of language *Henry V* seems, at first, to have little to offer. Dramatically, it is not as impressive as either of the parts of *Henry IV*, but yet its linguistic virtues, however much concealed, are considerable.

The play is inadequate because it is a pageant, rounded off with a domestic scene, and a little bawdry. Shakespeare is often given to the use of 'seamy' language but the employment is almost always incidental. Here against his normal practice in Act III Scene 4, is a scene whose main climax is a little feeble and coy bawdry. I can find no explanation for it. The editors fail, modestly, to comment.

The foreign language emphasis of Act III Scene 4 is confirmed in the Fluellen scenes. While Act III, Scene 4 is unintelligible without a little knowledge of French, the Fluellen scenes depend for their humour on a knowledge of Welsh pronunciation. Such a humour, dependent on national linguistic curiosities, is unusual in Shakespeare. One is driven to conclude that the whole tempo of the prose comic scenes of Nym, Bardolph, Pistol and Fluellen is less effective than in the Henry IV plays. Shakespeare's problem is that Falstaff has been removed. It has been argued[1] that, as the

---

[1] *Henry V*, edited J. H. Walter, 1954.

play was originally planned, Falstaff accompanied Henry to France 'but for some reason or other it was decided to change this and to kill him off'. Following this assumption it is argued that many of the passages originally designed for Falstaff were given to Pistol. Whatever weight is given to these surmises the fact remains that the 'low' parts have lost much of their amusement and also of their depth and linguistic ingenuity because Falstaff is not present. The play attains a genuine pathos in the prose of the Hostess's famous lament over Falstaff: 'Nay, sure he's not in hell: he's in Arthur's bosom, if ever man went to Arthur's bosom.' This is the speech which contains Theobald's emendation, universally admired if not always accepted, of 'a babbled of green fields' for the Folio's 'and a Table of green fields'. The Hostess's speech has that maturity of prose which Shakespeare achieved here and in some of Falstaff's speeches and never excelled. Statement at its simplest, untouched by imagery and unadorned by rhetoric is given all the strength of deep emotion: 'So a'bade me lay more clothes on his feet: I put my hand into the bed and felt them and they were as cold as any stone; then I felt to his knees, and so upward and upward, and all was as cold as any stone.' (iii.3.23)

Falstaff, it has been suggested,[1] had to go because Oldcastle's descendants, the Brooke family, objected. But there were adequate artistic reasons why his presence in *Henry V* would be found troublesome. For the play depends on the heroic character of the king as revealed in action, and in his eloquent speeches, and the comic devices of the old ale-house companion would have been an unwelcome intrusion. The speech before Harfleur (iii.1) has become such a commonplace that its virtues are taken for granted. But here is eloquence in a blank verse closely compact in sense and fully fraught with an agile imagery: no longer the tediousness of rhetorical explanation but a rapid keenly caught image set with full appropriateness into the argument:

> I see you stand like greyhounds in the slips,
> Straining upon the start. The game's afoot:
> Follow your spirit, and upon this charge
> Cry, 'God for Harry, England and Saint George'.
>
> (iii.1.31)

The Choruses with which the acts are introduced are composed,

---

[1] J. H. Walter, *loc. cit.*

deliberately, in a more formal speech, with gestures of an antique style:

> Thus with imagined wing our swift scene flies
> In motion of no less celerity
> Than that of thought.

(iii.1.1)

In the same way in *Hamlet* Shakespeare ensures that the Player's speech shall be different from the verse of the tragedy itself.

The brilliance with which blank verse is manipulated is not confined to Henry's set speeches. The play has an admirable opening, plunging the listener directly into the action with the Archbishop of Canterbury's opening phrase, 'My Lord, I'll tell you.' This, one may compare with the slow tediousness of the narrative openings of any of the Henry VI plays. This sense of speed is maintained even in the explanatory scenes of the first Act. So the Archbishop of Canterbury refers to the reformed Henry:

> Turn him to any cause of policy,
> The Gordian knot of it he will unloose,
> Familiar as his garter.

(i.1.45)

One recalls, in contrast the narrative, classical similes, dreary and overplayed in the Henry VI plays.

The dullest speech is the Archbishop of Canterbury's rehearsal of Henry's claim to the French throne (i.2): this is unrelieved Holinshed, but essential to the action, and more interesting to Shakespeare's contemporaries than to a modern audience. It stands as an exception for elsewhere the images, with a quick irridescent brightness, illuminate the action.

In *Henry V* Shakespeare seems to control resources of language greater than the play needs, except in its more exalted moments. The quality of the language seems more mature than most of the play itself. The situation is so different from *King John* where the language seems struggling with purposes beyond its powers. *Henry V* seems a side-piece in Shakespeare's development: the real link with the later work lies in *Henry IV*.

CHAPTER VI

A MIDSUMMER-NIGHT'S DREAM

WITH *A Midsummer Night's Dream* Shakespeare returned to a play, boldly poetical, almost as if he enjoyed a sense of release from the ardours and difficulties of the historical plays. Though now, instead of going back to the wit and verbal excitability of *Love's Labour's Lost*, he takes the royal road to poetry by some magical transmutation of the English countryside into a fairy kingdom.

Theseus's famous speech at the opening of Act V, a passage thought by some to have been written during a period of revision, shows that Shakespeare had been contemplating the nature of poetic language. There are a number of passages in the plays in which he considers the nature of poetry and the imagination, but this is the earliest as it is one of the fullest until Hamlet's talk with the players. It would seem that after his work in the early comedies and histories he was reflecting on the nature of his medium, aware now of his own developing powers:

> I never may believe
> These antique fables, nor these fairy toys.
> Lovers and madmen have such seething brains,
> Such shaping fantasies, that apprehend
> More than cool reason ever comprehends.
> The lunatic, the lover and the poet
> Are of imagination all compact:
> One sees more devils than vast hell can hold,
> That is, the madman: the lover, all as frantic,
> Sees Helen's beauty in a brow of Egypt:
> The poet's eye, in a fine frenzy rolling,
> Doth glance from heaven to earth, from earth to heaven;
> And as imagination bodies forth
> The forms of things unknown, the poet's pen
> Turns them to shapes and gives to airy nothing
> A local habitation and a name.   (v.i.2)

No passage of criticism can compete with this in showing the origins and effects of poetic imagery. Particularly well does it show his own recognition of the widely varying resources of the associations from which he creates his imaginative comparisons. By the time he composed this passage he was aware in a conscious, even a critical way, of the powers he possessed, above all, his ability of bringing together in a single and inevitable phrase, objects and experiences previously remote, so that their union might illuminate some new aspect of truth.

In *The Two Gentlemen of Verona* one group of comparisons was used recurrently and related to the main theme of the play. There it was the image of the *vow* that he employed, and now, in a much stronger way, the *moon* passages have a strong associative relation with the atmosphere of the play as a whole. This is never mechanical enough to be allegorical, nor rigid enough to be a symbol, but it heightens the emotional content, and gives to the poetic language as a whole an effect over and above that to be discovered in any single passage.

The moonlight passages, whether descriptive, or derived from mythology, seem to evoke the inner meaning of the *Dream*. Hippolyta, in the opening speech, foreshadows the dominant mood:

> And then the moon, like to a silver bow
> New-bent in heaven, shall behold the night
> Of our solemnities.

(i.1.9)

and again in the same scene Lysander speaks:

> Tomorrow night, when Phoebe doth behold
> Her silver visage in the watery glass,
> Decking with liquid pearl the bladed grass,
> A time that lovers' flights doth still conceal,
> Through Athens' gates have we devised to steal.

(i.1.209)

The relation of a dominant motive in the language to the play as a whole has by some critics been over emphasised, particularly for the later plays. An effect only discoverable by the scholar in the study with the aid as it were of a microscope or a computing machine, is no effect which a dramatist should properly introduce into a play, whose operations must be intelligible to an audience in the theatre. Further, the obvious point, forgotten by some critics, is that there must be a simple and inevitable relation between the theme and the language of a play. Even the 'mechanicals' knew that the action was to be in moonlight. 'Doth the moon shine that night we play our play?' Snout asked. To which Bottom cried out, 'A calendar, a calendar! look in the almanac; find out moonshine, find out moonshine,' and Quince, who presumably has either a calendar or a good memory breaks in 'Yes, it doth shine that night' (iii.1.52). *The Two Gentlemen of Verona* did after all deal with a *vow* and it was inevitable that vows should be mentioned, as inevitable as that the poet should refer to the *moonlight* which is the setting of the *Dream*. Yet beyond this practical and necessary relationship there is a pursuit of a single associative group to give an emphasis which adds to the unity of poetic and dramatic intention, and this is a practice which grows stronger with Shakespeare.

The relation of language to plot has developed, markedly, since *Love's Labour's Lost*. Shakespeare learned in the histories, if not already in the early comedies, that the easy development of the action will be helped by passages of simple and direct speech. It was the beginning of the hard lesson that in drama verse could not be solely the instrument of wit or rhetoric but had to be controlled for the ends of the play. Simplicity, he had learned, had its own virtues, and those virtues were sometimes a dramatic necessity. As Theseus says of the play of Bottom and his fellows:

> I will hear that play;
> For never anything can be amiss,
> When simpleness and duty tender it.   (v.1.81)

Nothing could be more direct than Lysander's defence of himself in the first Act of the play:

> I am, my lord, as well derived as he,
> As well possess'd; my love is more than his;
> My fortunes every way as fairly rank'd,
> If not with vantage, as Demetrius';
> And, which is more than all these boasts can be,
> I am beloved of beauteous Hermia.   (i.1.99)

And so it is in many other passages. As indeed in Lysander's later speech:

> A good persuasion: therefore, hear me, Hermia.
> I have a widow aunt, a dowager
> Of great revenue, and she hath no child:
> From Athens is her house remote seven leagues;
> And she respects me as her only son.
> There, gentle Hermia, may I marry thee.   (i.1.156)

This comes immediately after the speech:

> Or, if there were a sympathy in choice
> War, death, or sickness did lay siege to it,
> Making it momentary as a sound,   (i.1.141)

where a comparison is played as far as ingenuity can pursue it.

No element in Shakespeare's language has been given so little emphasis as his power of using simple and direct language. The splendours of his imagery have drawn attention away from the effectiveness of these strong, dramatic effects made out of the most unpretentious elements. It is a power that increases with his maturity. In the *Dream* the direct passages are often thin and slow-moving compared with those in the great tragedies, nor are they given a large place. Further it may be recalled that in exploiting the resounding and elaborate elements in language he was answering the spirit of his age and the practice of his contemporaries, but the quiet language was a dramatic opportunity and necessity that he had to discover for himself, against the fashion of his time, and indeed in opposition to much that was dominant in his own temperament.

The mood in the *Dream* is lyrical and the scenes of the lovers invite a happy play of verbal conceits. In these scenes Shakespeare is not breaking new ground in language but is often doing something again, but with an added grace, because he has done it successfully before.

While using this serviceable if *flat* language in order to move the action, he reserves for the lovers an imagery similar to that which occupied his mind in the sonnets. So Theseus says to Hermia:

> Thrice-blessed they that master so their blood,
> To undergo such maiden pilgrimage;
> But earthlier happy is the rose distill'd,
> Than that which withering on the virgin thorn
> Grows, lives and dies in single blessedness.   (i.1.74)

This was the very comparison he had explored with singular beauty in the Fifth Sonnet:

> Then, were not summer's distillation left,
> A liquid prisoner pent in walls of glass,
> Beauty's effect with beauty were bereft,
> Nor it nor no remembrance what it was:
>   But flowers distill'd, though they with winter meet,
>   Leese but their show; their substance still lives sweet.

Much of the warm effusiveness of the language which Hermia and Lysander exchange belongs to the sonnet tradition, and the same is true of Helena and Demetrius. Hermia will swear 'by Cupid's strongest bow' (i.1.169), by 'the simplicity of Venus' doves' (i.1.171), and by a whole catalogue of such comparisons. Helena in speaking to Hermia uses the very idiom of the sonnet writers, with their play on words, the balance in the line, and the easy and ample imagery:

> Call you me fair? that fair again unsay.
> Demetrius loves your fair: O happy fair!
> Your eyes are lode-stars; and your tongue's sweet air
> More tuneable than lark to shepherd's ear,
> When wheat is green, when hawthorn buds appear.
>
> (i.1.181)

Hermia and Lysander play upon words, in the manner of the sonnets, until at length Hermia pleads that 'Lysander riddles very prettily' (ii.2.53).

As a contrast to the sonneteering moods of the lovers there come the happy interludes of rustic prose of Bottom and his friends. The aim here is usually direct and dramatic with a natural realism, and no involved trick in the language as in *Love's Labour's Lost*, though Quince, it is true, cannot avoid the rule of triplicity in giving their parts to his fellow actors: 'I am to *entreat* you, *request* you and *desire* you, to con them by tomorrow night' (i.2.101).

Apart from Theseus's speech on poetic imagination there is very little direct reference to language. In *Hamlet* the coming of the players is used for the most detailed and elaborate discussion of diction. The rehearsals of Bottom and his fellows give similar opportunities but they have not been taken up and the atmosphere is left uncritical and carefree in its comedy. The only exception is that Bottom is permitted to describe the ranting language which it would give him pleasure to employ: 'That will ask some tears in the true performing of it: if I do it, let the audience look to their eyes; I will move storms, I will condole in some measure. To the rest: yet my chief humour is for a tyrant: I could play Ercles rarely, or a part to tear a cat in, to make all split' (i.2.27). So Bottom would play Hercules Furens as Sir Philip Sidney had seen him played: 'leaning his hands upon his bill, and his chin upon his hands'.

The difference between all this and *Love's Labour's Lost* is that in the earlier play the employment of a witty and decorative language was the major occupation upon which plot and char- acters depended, while here, in one of the most original and balanced plays in all Shakespeare's work, plot, characters, atmos- phere, mood and language are brought into a single dramatic purpose. It may be that this very unity of creative intention makes the use of language far less self-conscious than in *Love's Labour's Lost*. Much of it is simple, as if no mental entanglement stood between Shakespeare and the presentation of the theme, as it did, much later, in the opening scenes of *The Winter's Tale*.

Despite its many affectations of language, *Love's Labour's Lost* did retain an interest in the English countryside and in rustic scenes, and the background of Athens in *A Midsummer-Night's Dream* is also this same England, where Bottom and his companion players can meet and where Puck is the 'merry wanderer of the night' (ii.1.43). But now, England is given a magic of faery, and that vision is in turn kept in touch with the rustic. Both are united in a lyrical, and mainly rhyming verse, while the moon imagery and atmosphere make the borderlands of faery and reality deliberately difficult to define. Thus, for instance, in the passages where Puck is questioned by the Fairy on his identity:

> are not you he
> That frights the maidens of the villagery;
> Skim milk, and sometimes labour in the quern
> And bootless make the breathless housewife churn;
> And sometime make the drink to bear no barm;
> Mislead night-wanderers, laughing at their harm?
> Those that Hobgoblin call you and sweet Puck,
> You do their work, and they shall have good luck:
> Are not you he? (ii.1.34)

It is in such descriptions that one is aware of the genuine rustic England out of which the more visionary elements have been con- structed. So Titania describes to Oberon the ways in which he has disturbed her 'sport' in a moving passage realistic in all its elements, though in the passage immediately preceding we have been on 'the farthest steppe of India' and 'through the glimmering night from Perigenia':

> Contagious fogs; which falling in the land
> Have every pelting river made so proud
> That they have overborne their continents:

> The ox hath therefore stretch'd his yoke in vain,
> The ploughman lost his sweat, and the green corn
> Hath rotted ere his youth attain'd a beard;
> The fold stands empty in the drowned field,
> And crows are fatted with the murrion flock;
> The nine men's morris is fill'd up with mud,
> And the quaint mazes in the wanton green
> For lack of tread are undistinguishable.
>
> (ii.1.90)

This passage, a part only of which is quoted, belongs to genuine observation of the rural scene. It is followed by the most deliberately magical passage in the play:

> That very time I saw, but thou couldst not,
> Flying between the cold moon and the earth,
> Cupid all arm'd: a certain aim he took
> At a fair vestal throned by the west,
> And loosed his love-shaft smartly from his bow,
> As it should pierce a hundred thousand hearts;
> But I might see young Cupid's fiery shaft
> Quench'd in the chaste beams of the watery moon,
> And the imperial votaress passed on,
> In maiden meditation, fancy-free.
>
> (ii.1.155)

There is no return to the language of *A Midsummer-Night's Dream.* Later Shakespeare's poetic speech becomes stronger and more complex, and shakes the imagination more profoundly, but here it is gathered up into the dominant mood of the *Dream,* where myth and romance and the gentle English scene are at one, and where all is easily intelligible, lyrical in mood and gentle. Sometimes in the lovers' exchanges, following the pattern of the sonnets, the language ranges over human experience for the comparisons. So Lysander says:

> For as a surfeit of the sweetest things
> The deepest loathing to the stomach brings,
> Or as the heresies that men do leave
> Are hated most of those they did deceive,
> So thou, my surfeit and my heresy,
> Of all be hated, but the most of me!
>
> (ii.2.137)

But normally the concentration is on the country scene, either with its real or its faery aspects, and it is in the sudden transfer from one to the other that the play gains some of its most brilliant effects.) So in a striking passage Puck describes the effect of the transformation of Bottom on his companions:

> When they him spy,
> As wild geese that the creeping fowler eye,
> Or russet-pated choughs, many in sort,
> Rising and cawing at the gun's report,
> Sever themselves and madly sweep the sky,
> So, at his sight, away his fellows fly.

(iii.2.19)

As often in the early plays, here is the memory of a rustic scene arising directly out of Shakespeare's personal experience. In other passages he recalls a memory of a nature scene, already half-idealised:

> I know a bank where the wild thyme blows,
> Where oxlips and the nodding violet grows,
> Quite over-canopied with luscious woodbine,
> With sweet musk-roses and with eglantine:
> There sleeps Titania sometime of the night,
> Lull'd in these flowers with dances and delight.

(ii.1.249)

The rural theme will, of course, be found later in the plays, for it is a memory which never dies out, but the primary emphasis on this motive disappears here in *A Midsummer-Night's Dream* after its dominance in the early comedies and the histories.) When it returns, actively, as in Falstaff's visit to Justice Shallow, the mood is that of the townsman, recalling half-regretfully something which he knows he has outlived. It is present in the last plays in a new and sophisticated way, yet intermingled with simpler passages, and all strangely moving, though some theorists have discovered too much in it. This I would record rather than attempt to explain. It would be easy to press the biographical motive and to say that in the plays that follow the town interests had replaced the native background. At times, certainly, as in *Romeo and Juliet* a conscious art gathers up the language so appropriately to the mood that there is no room for this rustic material. Whatever be the conclusion, *A Midsummer-Night's Dream* seems to mark the end of a period, the exhaustion of the first impulse, and the stretching out of genius towards fresh attainment.)

CHAPTER VII

ROMEO AND JULIET

IT is difficult to place the tragedy of *Romeo and Juliet* in the chronology of the plays but it is certain that Shakespeare had considerable experience in the exacting task of writing the history plays before he came to this, the first of the tragedies with a theme independent of English history. He had also written the early comedies, and possibly he had written *A Midsummer-Night's Dream*, though the usual view is that this follows *Romeo and Juliet*, and some would see a parody of the love theme of the tragedy in the Pyramus episode. Creative development does not follow necessarily on the order of chronological production, and whichever play came first, *A Midsummer-Night's Dream* is the logical conclusion of the early comedies, and *Romeo and Juliet*, despite many similarities with the comedies, marks a new beginning.

Linguistically one can feel a certain absence of pressure, as if the burden of incident and material, which weighs upon him continuously in the English history plays, had been removed. He seems rather to be looking back towards the language of the early comedies, and assessing its possibilities with a genially critical eye. He has reached some stage in his creative development that makes him as self-conscious in his employment, as he had been in *Love's Labour's Lost*, though less indulgent, and not in a troubled or fretful way. Throughout the history plays there are many conflicting purposes in the use of language, and ultimately, much uncertainty. Here, Shakespeare seems ever aware of the effects which his language is producing.

There is a release into new experiments, and into the attainment of a fresh beauty. The only place where the heavier tread of the language of the historical plays is to be heard is in the Prince's formal speech in the opening scene:

> Rebellious subjects, enemies to peace,
> Profaners of this neighbour-stained steel,—
> Will they not hear? What, ho! you men, you beasts,
> That quench the fire of your pernicious rage
> With purple fountains issuing from your veins,

> On pain of torture, from those bloody hands
> Throw your mistemper'd weapons to the ground,
> And hear the sentence of your moved prince.
>
> (i.1.88)

A deliberate weight and formality of movement separate this from the rest of the play.

In *Love's Labour's Lost* the interest in language was not only dominant but exclusive of all other considerations. In *Romeo and Juliet* the problem is to adjust the words to the action, and yet retain a lyrical mood, with all the liveliness and beauty of a romantic tragedy, and this Shakespeare achieves. Much of the mood belongs to that of the Elizabethan sonneteers, and Shakespeare, as often, approaches this romantic sentiment simultaneously parodying it, and presenting it with seriousness and genuine emotion. When Benvolio comments that Rosaline has 'sworn that she will still live chaste' it is in the very idiom of the sonneteers that Romeo replies:

> She hath, and in that sparing makes huge waste,
> For beauty starved with her severity
> Cuts beauty off from all posterity.
>
> (i.1.224)

Mercutio, the most intellectual character in the play, is allowed, on more than one occasion, to dissect the excesses of the imagery which Romeo and the sonneteers use: 'Now is he for the numbers that Petrarch flowed in: Laura to his lady was but a kitchen-wench; marry, she had a better love to be-rhyme her; Dido a dowdy; Cleopatra a gipsy; Helen and Hero hildings and harlots; this be a grey eye or so, but not to the purpose' (ii.4.40).

Yet in contrast, and marking Shakespeare's amphibious approach to the sonnet material is Lady Capulet's description of Count Paris, a somewhat formal, though serious, passage of description which is set out as a complete sonnet:

> Read o'er the volume of young Paris' face
> And find delight writ there with beauty's pen;
> Examine every married lineament
> And see how one another lends content,
> And what obscured in this fair volume lies
> Find written in the margent of his eyes.
> This precious book of love, this unbound lover,
> To beautify him, only lacks a cover:

> The fish lives in the sea, and 'tis much pride
> For fair without the fair within to hide:
> That book in many's eyes doth share the glory,
> That in gold clasps locks in the golden story;
> So shall you share all that he doth possess,
> By having him, making yourself no less.

(i.3.81)

The effect of this decorative passage is increased by the genuine realism of the Nurse earlier in the scene. The sonnet form, again, is used for the Chorus at the beginning of Act I and Act II.

In Romeo himself Shakespeare seems to have adjusted language to the character more precisely than has so far been his practice. This is a result of what I have described as the more self-conscious approach to language in *Romeo and Juliet*. By the time of *King Lear* the language is subtly distinguished as between the characters. Here, in the first scene, we meet Romeo before he has encountered Juliet, and when he is still in love with Rosaline. His language is made deliberately into a parody of the language of the sonneteers, and yet for that very reason it is appropriate to Romeo's unreal and forced sentiment in this pre-Juliet period. Such are the lines which he speaks on appearing after the street brawl:

> Here's much to do with hate, but more with love.
> Why, then, O brawling love! O loving hate!
> O any thing, of nothing first create!
> O heavy lightness! serious vanity!
> Mis-shapen chaos of well-seeming forms!
> Feather of lead, bright smoke, cold fire, sick health!

(i.1.181)

The whole of this passage is based upon that conceit of contrast which is so common in the Elizabethan sonneteers.

Romeo follows this passage with an attempt to express in verse the relationship between love and grief, and this he does in a plodding movement, such as Shakespeare is coming to assign increasingly to the dull characters or, as here, to a dull mood of a brighter intelligence:

> this love that thou hast shown
> Doth add more grief to too much of mine own.
> Love is a smoke raised with the fume of sighs;
> Being purged, a fire sparkling in lovers' eyes;

Being vex'd, a sea nourished with lovers' tears:
What is it else? a madness most discreet,
A choking gall and a preserving sweet.

(i.1.194)

The last phrase gives Romeo away, for he is expressing no genuine, spontaneous feeling, but sending 'the spaniel over the fields of memory' to use Dryden's phrase, in the hope that some comparison can be captured and so dragged into employment. This is the language of the sonneteering poetasters whom Sidney described so vividly in *Astrophel and Stella*:

You that do dictionary's method bring
Into your rhymes, running in rattling rows.

The only other character who uses a similar language is Capulet. When he sees Juliet weeping, allegedly for the death of Tybalt, he sets out on a linguistic experiment which proceeds at the pace of a slow and clumsy mechanism:

When the sun sets, the air doth drizzle dew;
But for the sunset of my brother's son
It rains downright.
How now! a conduit, girl? what, still in tears?
Evermore showering? In one little body
Thou counterfeit'st a bark, a sea, a wind;
For still thy eyes, which I may call the sea,
Do ebb and flow with tears; the bark thy body is,
Sailing in this salt flood; the winds, thy sighs;
Who, raging with thy tears, and they with them,
Without a sudden calm, will overset
Thy tempest-tossed body.

(iii.5.127)

Here is an early example of the adjustment of the language to the character. Capulet is old, garrulous, easy-going and stupid, and, in lurching through these dull comparisons, reveals a bleak and insensitive mind with an unrelenting persistence. Shakespeare is not writing lyrically but dramatically. He could have written far more magnificent lines, but they would not have been appropriate. At times, however, he needs a character, even a dull one, to give expression not to his own thoughts, but to all that can be felt of a poignant moment in the action. So at Juliet's death Shakespeare makes Capulet the spokesman of all that the most sensitive participant in the scene could feel:

> Death lies on her like an untimely frost
> Upon the sweetest flower of all the field.   (iv.5.28)

I believe that particular attention is to be attached to passages such as Capulet's dull speech. They have the appearance of being deliberate, as if Shakespeare were reviewing here the slack structure of much of his earlier writing. For what he now uses with a conscious critical intention is not unlike some of his earlier writing in the histories and the comedies which was the best he could do at the time, or was a result of those linguistic distempers, which though they became less frequent he was never able completely to throw off.

Romeo drops the imagery of the Rosaline period completely and abruptly with the introduction of Juliet. All that went before is shown for what it is. To use an unmatchable Chaucerian word it is 'disteyned' in the flaming audacity of his lines on first meeting with Juliet:

> O, she doth teach the torches to burn bright!
> It seems she hangs upon the cheek of night
> Like a rich jewel in an Ethiope's ear;
> Beauty too rich for use, for earth too dear!   (i.5.46)

If found in lyrical poetry this might be regarded as excessive, but here the aim of the image is dramatically to reveal the mind of the character. For a moment Romeo's romantic exaltation is allowed to flash out, and that is combined with the violent contrast of light and darkness which is present so frequently in the play. The image has not only excess, but glamour, the mystery of the East and a dazzling splendour.

In the scenes between Romeo and Juliet that follow the lovers are both given language which might have been found in a sonnet, but no longer is the mood unkindly. The situation is seen not with the critical eye of an outsider, but from the point of view of one who accepts the sentiment, and the poetry is consequently made much more effective. As has already been noticed, Shakespeare frequently uses the comparison of the vow of the pilgrim to the vow of the lover, and here Romeo and Juliet use this image again in a passage of dialogue which, taken as a whole, makes up a complete sonnet. It is as if he were here summarising a whole mood of sentiment proper to the early comedies and now reaching its consummation as far as his work is concerned:

ROMEO (*to* JULIET). If I profane with my unworthiest hand
    This holy shrine, the gentle fine is this:
My lips, two blushing pilgrims, ready stand
    To smooth that rough touch with a tender kiss.
JULIET. Good pilgrim, you do wrong your hand too much,
    Which mannerly devotion shows in this;
For saints have hands that pilgrims' hands do touch,
    And palm to palm is holy palmers' kiss.
ROMEO. Have not saints lips, and holy palmers too?
JULIET. Ay, pilgrims, lips that they must use in prayer.
ROMEO. O then, dear saint, let lips do what hands do;
    They pray, grant thou, lest faith turn to despair.
JULIET. Saints do not move, though grant for prayers' sake.
ROMEO. Then move not, while my prayer's effect I take.
    Thus from my lips, by yours, my sin is purged.

                                    (i.5.95)

    The development of Romeo's language does not end here, for
he is given in the concluding and tragic scenes a directness and
strength, not elsewhere present. One outstanding passage of such
a kind owes its origin, as Steevens commented, to some lines by
Samuel Daniel in *The Complaint of Rosamond* (1592):

    And nought respecting death (the last of paines)
    Plac'd his pale colours (th'ensign of his might)
    Upon his new-got spoil.

Out of this Shakespeare has found the following:

                O my love! my wife!
    Death, that hath suck'd the honey of thy breath,
    Hath had no power yet upon thy beauty:
    Thou art not conquer'd; beauty's ensign yet
    Is crimson in thy lips and in thy cheeks,
    And death's pale flag is not advanced there.

                                    (v.3.91)

    The contrast of the two passages shows the strange and varying
power that words have over the mind: while Daniel had gathered
together the material for the image but had left it as an amorphous
heap Shakespeare commanded already at the conclusion of this
play the power to unite all the associative elements of the comparison into one compelling experience.
    While Romeo's verse thus grows in strength, Mercutio is given
that witty and analytical approach to words which Hamlet was
later to employ. Part of this is only that love of jest and of punning

so frequently given to the Elizabethan gentleman and courtier. Further, Mercutio, like all the most intelligent of Shakespeare's characters, will not accept words at their face value. He wishes to examine them more closely, though the examination often leads only to playfulness. So when Tybalt charges Mercutio, 'thou consort'st with Romeo', he seizes upon the word 'consort', and in an arrogant and flaunting way plays with it: 'Consort! what, dost thou make us minstrels? an thou make minstrels of us, look to hear nothing but dischords: here's my fiddlestick; here's that shall make you dance. 'Zounds, consort!' (iii.1.48). Mercutio dies upon a pun and one can accept either that in such circumstances the Elizabethans would accept the pun as a linguistic instrument of serious emphasis or that Mercutio had the sort of temperament that would greet death with irony and humour.

Whatever may be said of the quibble with which he dies one has to face the problem that it was to this sardonic and questioning mind that Shakespeare chose for some reason to give the Queen Mab speech (i.4.53). A number of explanations may be advanced why this speech should go to Mercutio. He is a major character and falls early in the play, and it may well be that in the economy of the theatre it was necessary to enlarge the part of the actor who represented him. Yet part of Shakespeare's skill is that he can combine these practical necessities of the theatre with the exercise of his own dramatic and poetic art. For there is an appropriateness that one who finds life full of false sentiments should look to a world of faery for emotional satisfaction. Mercutio is conscious of what he is doing, for when Romeo rebukes him for his irrelevant fantasy—'Peace, peace, Mercutio, peace! Thou talk'st of nothing' —he is allowed to reply with a passage which analyses the nature of fantasy. This examination is not as closely argued as Theseus's speech in the fifth act of *A Midsummer-Night's Dream*, but it is looking in the same direction:

> True, I talk of dreams,
> Which are the children of an idle brain,
> Begot of nothing but vain fantasy,
> Which is as thin of substance as the air
> And more inconstant than the wind, who wooes
> Even now the frozen bosom of the north,
> And, being anger'd, puffs away from thence,
> Turning his face to the dew-dropping south.   (i.4.96)

Already in *The Two Gentlemen of Verona* and in *A Midsummer-Night's Dream* Shakespeare has allowed one associative figure to recur until it becomes an imaginative atmosphere or argument answerable to the mood of the play. So did the *vow* develop in *The Two Gentlemen* and the *moon* in *A Midsummer-Night's Dream*. Here the effect is at once stronger and more subtle. For, throughout, darkness and light are brought into contrast, until they dwell in the memory as a symbol of the tragic contrast of love and death which encircles the young lovers. Much of this is established outside the language, by the setting of the scenes themselves, with night, and the light of torches upon the night, the dawn, the bright sunlight, and straight keen shadows of the Italian day. The 'rich jewel in an Ethiope's ear' supplies the emotional image of the play, which the setting has confirmed.

If language has its power and achievement it also has its deceits and trivialities. With Sampson and Gregory in the opening scene there are the old puns and verbal trivialities, the 'colliers' and 'choler' (i.1.2), the 'heads of the maids' and 'maidenheads' (i.1.29). They probably delighted Shakespeare himself as much as they did his audience, and the theoretical evidence in their defence has already been analysed.[1] Yet it remains that this element in Shakespeare's language however appropriate to his contemporaries has not had the universality and endurance of so much else in his achievement.

Throughout the early comedies the imagery of nature and of rustic life had been generously employed as if from this source Shakespeare's imagination had been richly fed. Nothing confirms more strongly his rustic upbringing than the way that he falls back, even in the most unexpected places, on these rustic themes. In *Romeo and Juliet* this country background has disappeared, and nature even in its more formal aspects appears only rarely. We have Capulet's:

> When well-apparell'd April on the heel
> Of limping winter treads,

(i.2.27)

but little else.

One of the most original elements in the language where much is experimental is in the speeches of the Nurse. For here a conscious and successful attempt at realism enters. For the most

[1] p. 9.

part imagery and rhetoric have ousted plain speech out of the language of the play. But the Nurse, to the extent that blank verse will permit, speaks as the Nurse would have spoken in ordinary life:

> Even or odd, of all days in the year,
> Come Lammas-eve at night shall she be fourteen.
> Susan and she—God rest all Christian souls!—
> Were of an age: well, Susan is with God.

(1.3.16)

Shakespeare must have realised, as he did in Arthur's speeches in *King John*, that he had captured realism into verse. But it was not his intention to be restrained within its limits. The sombre tones of a massive and decorative speech, the far-reaching resources of associative language, all that a complex and intricate control of speech could yield, were to be worked into a texture far richer than realism alone would permit.

CHAPTER VIII

HENRY IV, Part I and Part II, and *HENRY V*

IN *Henry IV*, Parts I and II, Shakespeare matured his conception of the history play as a form distinct from tragedy and from the old chronicle play. At the same time he developed his use of language in a manner which separates these plays from the rest of his achievement. Verse occupies a larger and more important place in Part I, for in Part II Falstaff and the prose action is so important that in playing time on the stage it becomes the major action. In the verse passages the matter no longer dominates the style as in the *Henry VI* plays. Nor are we merely entertained with occasional passages of excellence as in *Richard II* and *Richard III*. At the same time the urgency of the matter will not permit a release of the style into any exercise of independent virtuosity. As so frequently there is a certain balance between the pressure of the theme and the ebullience of the medium through which it is expressed.

This sense of verbal power contained, though with difficulty, within a pattern of rhetoric, and expressed in a mounting and complicated imagery, where one motion is abandoned before it is fully developed as another comes crowding into the poet's mind, can be seen in the first speech by the King, opening with the lines:

> No more the thirsty entrance of this soil
> Shall daub her lips with her own children's blood;
> No more shall trenching war channel her fields,
> Nor bruise her flowerets with the armed hoofs
> Of hostile paces: those opposed eyes,
> Which, like the meteors of a troubled heaven,
> All of one nature, of one substance bred,
> Did lately meet in the intestine shock
> And furious close of civil butchery
> Shall now, in mutual well-beseeming ranks,
> March all one way and be no more opposed
> Against acquaintance, kindred and allies:
> The edge of war, like an ill-sheathed knife,
> No more shall cut his master.

(i.1.5)

Samuel Johnson rejected the image of the first two lines out-right: 'that these lines are absurd is soon discovered, but how this nonsense will be made sense is not so easily told.' He was seeking for a clear, visual image, embedded in a logical argument, where, in fact, all is mixed and excited. Yet the meaning of the whole play is illuminated by the passage; for Shakespeare pictures mother earth satiated with her children's blood, her soil, or entrance, normally thirsty now having no blood to daub on her lips.

Throughout, a greater strength and concentration in the verse gives a compact effect, so that a sense of pressure accompanies the creation. Only occasionally does Shakespeare relax into the more leisured and descriptive imagery which has been present in the earlier plays, and in this new atmosphere the effect seems inappropriate. Such a passage is found in the soliloquy in which the Prince first reveals himself to the audience:

> Yet herein will I imitate the sun,
> Who doth permit the base contagious clouds
> To smother up his beauty from the world,
> That, when he please again to be himself,
> Being wanted, he may be more wonder'd at,
> By breaking through the foul and ugly mists
> Of vapours that did seem to strangle him.
>
> (i.2.220)

It can be argued that here, as in some other scenes, a concluding and explanatory soliloquy is deliberately separated in style from the remainder of the action.

The directness and the very strength and concentration of style result in less variety than is present in the later tragedies. It is as if a picture had been painted in the strongest available colours so that everything should be very vivid and richly emblazoned. As in *Venus and Adonis*, Shakespeare seems to be stretching each description or each sentiment to hold all that it can possibly contain. Some of the results are most effective. As for instance Hotspur's description to the King of how after the battle of Holmedon, when he was 'breathless and faint' there came

> a certain lord, neat, and trimly dress'd,
> Fresh as a bridegroom; and his chin new reap'd
> Show'd like a stubble-land at harvest-home;
> He was perfumed like a milliner;

And 'twixt his finger and his thumb he held
A pouncet-box, which ever and anon
He gave his nose and took't away again;
Who therewith angry, when it next came there,
Took it in snuff; and still he smiled and talk'd,
And as the soldiers bore dead bodies by,
He call'd them untaught knaves, unmannerly,
To bring a slovenly unhandsome corse
Betwixt the wind and his nobility.
With many holiday and lady terms
He question'd me.   (i.3.33)

In a somewhat different way the same fullness of colour and emphasis is given to the speeches in which Glendower describes the magical quality of his birth and personality:

           that at my birth
The front of heaven was full of fiery shapes,
The goats ran from the mountains, and the herds
Were strangely clamorous to the frighted fields.
These signs have mark'd me extraordinary;
And all the courses of my life do show
I am not in the roll of common men.   (iii.1.37)

It may be that this strong and open effect of style leads to the absence of affectation in the language, or of any introspection about the possibilities of diction. It is as if the instrument of language were being used boldly and securely for well-defined purposes, and fed by an ample and unquestioning imagination.

The prose of the play is more self-conscious, and more experimental, than the verse. As often there is a contrast of effect between the verse and the prose and the creative elements, so far as they fore-shadow the future, seem to be announcing themselves in the prose.

Falstaff is given a passage which is a close and deliberate parody of Lyly's *Euphues*[1]: 'There is a thing, Harry, which thou hast often heard of and it is known to many in our land by the name of pitch: this pitch, as ancient writers do report, doth defile; so doth the company thou keepest: for, Harry, now I do not speak to thee in drink but in tears, not in pleasure but in passion, not in words only, but in woes also' (ii.4.452). In the same scene Falstaff

---

[1] *The First Part of King Henry the Fourth*, ed. R. P. Cowl and A. E. Morgan (1914), p. 94.

again parodies Lyly in the phrase: 'for though the camomile, the more it is trodden on the faster it grows, yet youth, the more it is wasted the sooner it wears' (ii.4.440). Further it is Falstaff, by far the most intellectual character in the play, who makes the only comments on language: 'for I must speak in passion, and I will do it in King Cambyses' vein' (ii.4.425). With the other characters words are an entry into action, but Falstaff, as Hamlet later, distrusts the instrument of words and is for ever examining it.

Not unnaturally, the word 'honour' dominates the action of *Henry IV*, Part I. For it is natural in a theme which so concerns 'honour' that the word should be found frequently. Yet one feels that at the back of his mind the word must have occurred as a recurrent motive, and that in writing one passage based on the theme the memory of others must have been still present. Each use of the word 'honour' is made closely illustrative of the temperament of the character who is speaking. Again the associations of the word in the prose passages are more subtle than in the verse.

Hotspur is the man of action to whom introspection and contemplation are unknown and in one of the more powerful and crowded groups of images he is allowed to describe his relationship to 'honour' in such terms:

> By heaven, methinks it were an easy leap,
> To pluck bright honour from the pale-faced moon,
> Or dive into the bottom of the deep,
> Where fathom-line could never touch the ground,
> And pluck up drowned honour by the locks.   (i.3.201)

It is not surprising that after this Worcester is made to say:

> He apprehends a world of figures here,
> But not the form of what he should attend.   (i.3.209)

Worcester is emphasising, as Shakespeare does so frequently, the contrast between the language of imagination and direct language, or the speech necessary for action.

The most dramatic contrast to Hotspur's lines is Falstaff's examination of the term 'honour'. For Falstaff is determined to explore cautiously the notion which Hotspur has so romantically embraced: 'Well, 'tis no matter; honour pricks me on. Yea, but how if honour prick me off when I come on? how then? Can honour set to a leg? no: or an arm? no: or take away the grief

of a wound? no. Honour hath no skill in surgery, then? no.
What is honour? a word. What is in that word honour? what is
that honour? air. A trim reckoning! Who hath it? he that died
o' Wednesday. Doth he feel it? no. Doth he hear it? no. 'Tis
insensible, then? Yea, to the dead. But will it not live with the
living? no. Why? detraction will not suffer it. Therefore I'll
none of it. Honour is a mere scutcheon: and so ends my cate-
chism' (v.1.130).

There is an ironic appropriateness in the final use of the word
in the play which occurs on the lips of Prince Hal in his last and
fatal encounter with Hotspur:

> I'll make it greater ere I part from thee;
> And all the budding honours on thy crest
> I'll crop, to make a garland for my head.   (v.4.71)

Such then is the bold and original verse of *Henry IV*, Part I,
relying on an emblazoned language which is now crowded with
imaginative suggestions, but not yet penetrating into the depths
of the more contemplative passages such as are to be found in the
later tragedies. In some ways the most typical passage, and indeed
the outstanding example of the verse and of the 'mounting'
imagery is in Vernon's description to Hotspur of the Prince of
Wales, of 'the nimble-footed madcap Prince of Wales' once he
has converted himself into a soldier:

> All furnish'd, all in arms;
> All plumed like estridges that with[1] the wind
> Baited like eagles having lately bathed;
> Glittering in golden coats, like images;
> As full of spirit as the month of May
> And gorgeous as the sun at midsummer;
> Wanton as youthful goats, wild as young bulls.
> I saw young Harry, with his beaver on,
> His cuisses on his thighs, gallantly arm'd,
> Rise from the ground like feather'd Mercury,
> And vaulted with such ease into his seat,
> As if an angel dropp'd down from the clouds,
> To turn and wind a fiery Pegasus
> And witch the world with noble horsemanship.

(iv.1.97)

[1] Possibly, as Johnson suggested, this should read *wing*: 'They were not
only plumed like estridges, but their plumes fluttered like those of an estridge
on the wing, mounting against the wind.'

It was Walter Pater[1] who noted that after this description of
'the grandiose aspects of war, and its magnificent trappings'
Shakespeare recoils, almost immediately, in the following speech
of Hotspur:

> They come like sacrifices in their trim,
> And to the fire-eyed maid of smoky war
> All hot and bleeding will we offer them.

(iv.1.113)

The language of 2 *Henry IV* differs notably from that of
1 *Henry IV*, and a study of the contrast leads one to the realisation
of the divergence in the whole dramatic pattern of these two plays.
Fortunately, within living memory we have had a chance of seeing
2 *Henry IV* on the stage with Sir Ralph Richardson's brilliant
interpretation of the part of Falstaff. We are in a position therefore in this generation to re-estimate much of the nineteenth-
century and early twentieth-century disparagement of these plays.
This is not the only occasion when one has to go back to Johnson
to find a just comment of the two Parts of the play:

> None of *Shakespeare's* plays are more read than the First and
> Second Parts of *Henry IV*. Perhaps no author has ever in two
> plays afforded so much delight. The great events are interesting, for
> the fate of kingdoms depends upon them; the slighter occurrences
> are diverting, and, except one or two, sufficiently probable; the inci-
> dents are multiplied with wonderful fertility of invention, and the
> characters diversified with the utmost nicety of discernment, and
> the profoundest skill in the nature of man.

The opening of *Henry IV*, Part II, deals with the historical side
and is told with a language that is stiff and laboured. Shakespeare
seems enervated by the fact that the historical plot is one of
rebellion, and therefore a repetition of *Henry IV*, Part I, while he
now lacks the characters to give the historical side a lively movement
and the rebellion itself ends not in battle but in an underhand
struggle.

The real life of the play rests with Falstaff, and with the comic
scenes which are contemporary with Shakespeare's own time.
As has already been suggested they occupy even quantitatively a
very different place from the scenes in *Henry IV*, Part I, for now
they are a major part even by a counting of lines, and, when one
adds dramatic business, they occupy, by far, the larger part of the

[1] *Appreciations*.

action. The language of these scenes is in prose, but it has a bold, realistic quality far exceeding in originality anything in the historical sections. The contrast is most noticeable in the early part of the play for it is here that the historical writing is at its dullest. A typical passage of these early historical scenes can be found in Morton's pleading with Northumberland:

> The lives of all your loving complices
> Lean on your health; the which, if you give o'er
> To stormy passion, must perforce decay.
> You cast the event of war, my noble lord,
> And summ'd the account of chance, before you said
> 'Let us make head.' It was your presurmise,
> That, in the dole of blows, your son might drop:
> You knew he walk'd o'er perils, on an edge,
> More likely to fall in than to get o'er;
> You were advised his flesh was capable
> Of wounds and scars and that his forward spirit
> Would lift him where most trade of danger ranged.
>
> (i.1.163)

With this one may contrast the brilliant, if Hogarthian, entry of Falstaff with his dwarf page in the next scene: 'I am not only witty in myself, but the cause that wit is in other men. I do here walk before thee like a sow that hath overwhelmed all her litter but one' (i.2.11).

One seems aware of a conscious effort by Shakespeare to warm up the language of the historical scenes as if his imagination was being denied that easy service upon which he was so often able to call. So in the speech of the Archbishop rhetoric, which is effective but somewhat forced, has a spirit which much of these early scenes do not possess:

> Let us on,
> And publish the occasion of our arms.
> The commonwealth is sick of their own choice;
> Their over-greedy love hath surfeited:
> An habitation giddy and unsure
> Hath he that buildeth on the vulgar heart.
> O thou fond many, with what loud applause
> Didst thou beat heaven with blessing Bolingbroke,
> Before he was what thou wouldst have him be!
> And being now trimm'd in thine own desires,
> Thou, beastly feeder, art so full of him,

> That thou provokest thyself to cast him up.
> So, so, thou common dog, didst thou disgorge
> Thy glutton bosom of the royal Richard;
> And now thou wouldst eat thy dead vomit up,
> And howl'st to find it.

(i.3.85)

At the same time there developed in the historical plays, to be matured later in *Troilus and Cressida* and the tragedies, a group of ideas on *order* and *chaos*. To Shakespeare's mind the ultimate danger of rebellion was the breakdown of order and the development of chaos. These ideas always fire his imagination with alert and effective language, gaining their final expression in the great speech of Ulysses in *Troilus and Cressida*. But the nucleus of the conception is already here in Northumberland's speech:

> Let heaven kiss earth! now let not Nature's hand
> Keep the wild flood confined! let order die!
> And let this world no longer be a stage
> To feed contention in a lingering act;
> But let one spirit of the first-born Cain
> Reign in all bosoms, that, each heart being set
> On bloody courses, the rude scene may end,
> And darkness be the burier of the dead!

(i.1.153)

In these early historical scenes one passage of narrative imagery stands altogether apart. Lord Bardolph is discussing the prospects of the rebellion, and he enters into a comparison based on the building of a house. It is the longest narrative comparison in Shakespeare:

>   a cause on foot
> Lives so in hope as in an early spring
> We see the appearing buds; which to prove fruit,
> Hope gives not so much warrant as despair
> That frosts will bite them. When we mean to build,
> We first survey the plot, then draw the model;
> And when we see the figure of the house,
> Then must we rate the cost of the erection;
> Which if we find outweighs ability,
> What do we then but draw anew the model
> In fewer offices, or at last desist
> To build at all? Much more, in this great work,
> Which is almost to pluck a kingdom down

And set another up, should we survey
The plot of situation and the model,
Consent upon a sure foundation,
Question surveyors, know our own estate,
How able such a work to undergo,
To weigh against his opposite; or else
We fortify in paper and in figures,
Using the names of men instead of men:
Like one that draws the model of a house
Beyond his power to build it; who, half through,
Gives o'er and leaves his part-created cost
A naked subject to the weeping clouds
And waste for churlish winter's tyranny.   (i.3.37)

Shakespeare sometimes becomes involved in a narrative simile
because having entered into the theme he seems unable to work
his way out. At other times he deliberately gives the space to a
comparison because he wishes to illustrate the workings of a dull
mind, but here the detail, although excessive for the occasion, is
interesting. It is difficult to resist surmising that it must be based
upon a personal experience. It is as if amid these laboured scenes
of the early part of the play Shakespeare's mind had gone back to
some memory of the building of a house and once his imagination
had been so attracted he was unable to dislodge it. Professor
Spurgeon associated the passage, more precisely, with Shakespeare's building of New Place in 1597.

There is, however, as often with Shakespeare, another, and more
literary motive. For his lines parallel very closely Luke xiv, 28-30:
'For which of you, intending to build a tower, sitteth not down
before, and counteth the cost, whether he have sufficient to perform it? Lest that after he hath laid the foundation, and is not
able to perform it, all that behold it, begin to mock him, saying,
This man began to build, and was not able to make an end.'[1]
Nor is it difficult to see how Shakespeare had come to remember
this passage. He had given to Lord Bardolph a passage in which
he described the rashness of Hotspur:

                    who lined himself with hope,
        Eating the air on promise of supply,
        Flattering himself in project of a power
        Much smaller than the smallest of his thoughts:

---

[1] The verses are quoted from the Genevan version, but the spelling is
modernised.

> And so, with great imagination
> Proper to madmen, led his powers to death
> And winking leap'd into destruction.

(i.3.27)

This corresponds closely to the thought in Luke xiv, 31: 'Or what king, going to make war against another king, sitteth not down first and taketh counsel whether he be able with ten thousand to meet him that cometh against him with twenty thousand.' The building passage is immediately preceding. This does not, of course, preclude the possibility that there is also a direct auto-biographical memory as Professor Spurgeon suggests.

To the subtle realistic language of the Falstaff scenes justice has seldom been done. This is one of the instances where Professor Spurgeon's theory of imagery and her scholar's dislike for this play, whose real life belongs to the theatre, lead her to disprize the skill and the development of his art which Shakespeare has shewn in the prose scenes. Professor Spurgeon writes: 'I do not think it is mere chance that Falstaff's images in the second part of the play shew less trace of genuine feeling, cultivation and reading, and partake more of grotesque and ribaldry than in the first part. Witty they always are, for else Falstaff would no longer be Falstaff, but I believe that, in the course of the two plays, Shakespeare definitely pictured a certain deterioration of spirit in the fat knight, which is subtly reflected in his images.

'One may compare, for instance, the charm of tone of his gesting references to romance and the moon: "Marry, then, sweet wag, when thou art king, let not us that are squires of the night's body be called thieves of the day's beauty: let us be Diana's foresters, gentlemen of the shade, minions of the moon; and let men say we be men of good government, being governed, as the sea is, by our noble and chaste mistress the moon, under whose countenance we steal" (1 *Henry IV*, 1.2.25) with the roughness of his same satirical threat later to Prince John, that if his valour be not recognised he will have a ballad made to commemorate his deeds: "with mine own picture on the top on't, Coleville kissing my foot: to the which course if I be enforced, if you do not all show like gilt two-pences to me, and I in the clear sky of fame o'ershine you as much as the full moon doth the cinders of the element, which show like pins' heads to her, believe not the word of the noble:" (2 *Henry IV*, iv.3.53).'

But this is to deal with the evidence in an arbitrary manner, and certainly to abandon that statistical principle on which Professor Spurgeon normally attempts to rely. Falstaff had already thought of ballads in 1 *Henry IV* and indeed Shakespeare repeats phrases and ideas much more frequently than is realised:

> Go hang thyself in thine own heir-apparent garters! If I be ta'en, I'll peach for this. An I have not ballads made on you all and sung to filthy tunes, let a cup of sack be my poison (1 *Henry IV*, ii.2.47).

The prose of *Henry IV*, Part II, is the culmination of that prose which had been developing in strength and variety in the comedies.

Much of the invention and originality of the prose lies not in imagery but in the capturing of moods, sometimes comic but often poignant, made from the simplest elements of colloquial speech. Such, for instance, is the speech made by the hostess after a rowdy scene when she succumbs to Falstaff's request for money:

> Well, you shall have it, though I pawn my gown. I hope you'll come to supper. You'll pay me all together? (2 *Henry IV*, ii.1.171).

Her speech is one of those indications that whatever Falstaff might be losing at Court he was able to lord it at Eastcheap with a personality that endeared itself to companions who knew that he was utterly unreliable.

The most impressive scene in the whole play is Act II, Scene 4, the major scene at the Boar's Head Tavern in Eastcheap. Some of the prose in this scene differs not only from what has preceded it but from all else in Shakespeare's work. As is often true when he is using language for a new purpose he inserts some passage which shews that he is thinking consciously about language. In this scene he permits Pistol to speak in a ranting tone with a parody on Marlowe's *Tamburlaine*:

> These be good humours, indeed! Shall pack-horses
> And hollow pamper'd jades of Asia,
> Which cannot go but thirty mile a-day,
> Compare with Caesars, and with Cannibals,
> And Trojan Greeks? nay, rather damn them with
> King Cerberus; and let the welkin roar.
> Shall we fall foul for toys?
>
> (2 *Henry IV*, ii.4.177)

Pistol's parody is Shakespeare's announcement that he is secure now from the dangers which Marlowe's influence once had. It marks the beginning of a dissatisfaction with rhetorical language and the recognition of a difference between the crude forms of rhetoric and the simple and dramatic effects which blank verse can produce.

There are many passages among Pistol's speeches which seem almost like a parody of Shakespeare's own style in the more ranting passages in the early historical plays:

> What! shall we have incision? shall we imbrue?
> Then death rock me asleep, abridge my doleful days!
> Why, then, let grievous, ghastly, gaping wounds
> Untwine the Sisters Three! Come, Atropos, I say!
>
> (2 *Henry IV*, ii.4.210)

In contrast the prose of this scene has not only comedy but a poignant human sentiment, and is expressed in a diction which is colloquial, often monosyllabic, and completely direct:

> FALSTAFF. What stuff wilt have a kirtle of? I shall receive money o' Thursday: shalt have a cap to-morrow. A merry song, come: it grows late; we'll to bed. Thou'lt forget me when I am gone.
>
> DOLL. By my troth, thou'lt set me a-weeping, an thou sayest so: prove that ever I dress myself handsome till thy return: well, hearken at the end.
>
> (2 *Henry IV*, ii.4.297)

This new-found power of direct and simple prose is used in its most effective way in the conclusion of this great scene. I will not comment on it, for each member of the audience must draw from it as much as his experience or his intelligence will permit:

> BARDOLPH. You must away to court, sir, presently; a dozen captains stay at door for you.
>
> FALSTAFF (*to the Page*). Pay the musicians, sirrah. Farewell, hostess; farewell, Doll. You see, my good wenches, how men of merit are sought after: the undeserver may sleep, when the man of action is called on. Farewell, good wenches: if I be not sent away post, I will see you again ere I go.
>
> DOLL. I cannot speak; if my heart be not ready to burst—well, sweet Jack, have a care of thyself.
>
> FALSTAFF. Farewell, farewell. (*Exeunt Falstaff and Bardolph*).
>
> HOSTESS. Well, fare thee well: I have known thee these twenty-nine years, come peascod-time; but an honester and truer-hearted man, —well, fare thee well.
>
> BARDOLPH. (*Within*) Mistress Tearsheet!

HOSTESS. What's the matter?
BARDOLPH. (*Within*) Bid Mistress Tearsheet come to my master.
HOSTESS. O, run, Doll, run; run, good Doll: come. (*She comes blubbered*). Yea, will you come, Doll?

(2 *Henry IV*, ii.4.401)

The prose of this great scene at Eastcheap is paralleled by the rural scene with the simple talk of Silence and Shallow, which suggests, as did the long narrative simile on the building of a house, that Shakespeare's mind during the composition of this play was in Stratford and his own associations and projects there. These scenes have the intelligent and sardonic imagination which Falstaff's alert even if corrupt intelligence can always reach. So in his description of Shallow he uses an imagery far more lively than has as yet been found in the historical parts of the play:

I do remember him at Clement's Inn like a man made after supper of a cheese-paring: when a' was naked, he was, for all the world, like a forked radish, with a head fantastically carved upon it with a knife: a' was so forlorn, that his dimensions to any thick sight were invincible: a' was the very genius of famine; yet lecherous as a monkey, and the whores called him mandrake: a' came ever in the rearward of the fashion, and sung those tunes to the overscutched huswives that he heard the carmen whistle, and sware they were his fancies or his good-nights (iii.2.331).

As a background to all this Shakespeare has somehow contrived to give the poignancy of the coming of old age in a man of high intelligence even if he be a man whose conduct from a moral point of view deserves no sympathy:

We have heard the chimes at midnight, Master Shallow.

(iii.2.229)

It is merely statement but it is statement which has more emotion than many passages of metaphor and imagery can supply.

Professor Spurgeon's depreciation of Falstaff's language in this second part of the play continues to trouble me. She must have come to it with a mind too squeamish for some of its major delights for apart from the speech on 'Honour' in Part I there is little in the whole of Shakespeare's language to compare with his praise of sherris-sack:

A good sherris-sack hath a two-fold operation in it. It ascends me into the brain; dries me there all the foolish and dull and crudy vapours which environ it; makes it apprehensive, quick, forgetive, full of nimble fiery and delectable shapes; which, delivered o'er to the voice, the tongue, which is the birth, becomes excellent wit. The second property of your excellent sherris is, the warming of the blood; which, before cold and settled, left the liver white and pale, which is the badge of pusillanimity and cowardice; but the sherris warms it and makes it course from the inwards to the parts extreme: it illumineth the face, which as a beacon gives warning to all the rest of this little kingdom, man, to arm; and then the vital commoners and inland petty spirits muster me all to their captain, the heart, who, great and puffed up with this retinue, doth any deed of courage; and this valour comes of sherris. So that skill in the weapon is nothing without sack, for that sets it a-work; and learning a mere hoard of gold kept by a devil, till sack commences it and sets it in act and use. Hereof comes it that Prince Harry is valiant; for the cold blood he did naturally inherit of his father, he hath, like lean, sterile and bare land, manured, husbanded and tilled with excellent endeavour of drinking good and good store of fertile sherris, that he is become very hot and valiant. If I had a thousand sons, the first humane principle I would teach them should be, to forswear thin potations and to addict themselves to sack (iv.3.103).

It is only through an appreciation of Falstaff's language in this Second Part that one can realise how far Shakespeare had moved in his control of language both direct and imaged. The lesson which he had taught himself would appear again in the great tragedies, in *Othello* and *King Lear* particularly. The discovery of a speech closer to realism was not to deny the expanding power of the more poetic side of his diction. The cohorts of splendid words were always there ready to be used, and tempting his attention away from what he had achieved. But there is in some of the Falstaff scenes a quality of moving realism very rare in the plays. He had discovered something which he was never fully to exploit. In the development of Shakespeare's language *Henry V* has little to add except in the prose passages. The tradition of a bold rhetorical language is continued and there are set speeches which have been justly famous. But the real link between the early histories and Shakespeare's later work lies in *Henry IV*.

CHAPTER IX

THE MIDDLE COMEDIES:

The Merry Wives of Windsor; *The Merchant of Venice*;
Much Ado About Nothing; *As You Like It*; *Twelfth Night*

AMONG the most happily conceived and popular of Shakespeare's plays, these comedies, with the exception of *The Merchant of Venice*, show very little development in his verse, though there is much new in the prose of the comic episodes. Two of them, *Much Ado About Nothing* and *As You Like It*, have many evidences of hasty composition. *Twelfth Night* is brilliantly executed and is one of his outstanding achievements in comedy, yet linguistically there is little to mark a development from what had been achieved in *A Midsummer-Night's Dream*. This conclusion must not be identified with any assumption that much in these comedies is not new, for indeed all is most fresh and attractive. In *Much Ado About Nothing* the plot has a dexterity worthy of a better theme, and Benedick and Beatrice are more mature than any previous characters in the comedies: *As You Like It* has a careless audacity in technique and a measureless charm. The whole however is constructed without the genius of the writer being fully stretched, with a gracious and seemingly unlabouring ease. At last, almost as if he realised that the end had come of this particular way of writing he gathered up the dominant motives into *Twelfth Night* and gave them their final and most perfect expression. Achievement, then, there is in plenty though it is not in the main a linguistic development.

The Merry Wives of Windsor is an occasional piece, and lies outside our main argument. With the exception of a few speeches it is in prose, and confirms the evidence of a number of the comedies that Shakespeare gained an ease and flexibility in his prose which later he applied to his verse. *The Merry Wives* comes in the period when, as it were, the prose is ahead of the verse.

The language of *The Merchant of Venice* is somewhat different from the other comedies of the period, though here verse plays a very full part. But it is verse used easily, not exploring new purposes, confidently controlled and well-defined in all that is

attempted and accomplished. Verse prescribes the mood in which
we accept the play, gathering up the fairy-story of the caskets,
the shabbiness of Bassanio's motives and the elements of incipient
tragedy of the Shylock and Antonio theme, and holding them
united in a charmed and magical world. Shakespeare might be
asking that the motives for action should not be examined by the
dull and calculating arguments of realism, but that all should be
accepted in the rainbow hues of romance which the poetry has
provided. Accept the music of the verse, Shakespeare would seem
to say with Lorenzo, and all else will become acceptable:

> therefore the poet
> Did feign that Orpheus drew trees, stones and floods;
> Since nought so stockish, hard and full of rage,
> But music for the time doth change his nature.
> The man that hath no music in himself,
> Nor is not moved with concord of sweet sounds,
> Is fit for treasons, stratagems and spoils.   (v.1.79)

As a result the language has great riches, and wide ranges of
experience are claimed by Shakespeare as the resources of his
imagery. The language is almost uniformly beautiful. Shylock,
it is true, is allowed to explore more closely the harsher elements
in life, and Gratiano has the licence of a wit. But in the main, the
images of disease, war, strife, all the emphasis on the darker
motives for human action are excluded. Deliberately Shakespeare
seems to bathe the play in music, to wash it over with a richly
emblazoned verse. So it is on the theme of music again that Portia
reflects as she awaits Bassanio to make his choice of the caskets:

> Let music sound while he doth make his choice;
> Then, if he lose, he makes a swan-like end,
> Fading in music: that the comparison
> May stand more proper, my eye shall be the stream
> And watery death-bed for him. He may win;
> And what is music then? Then music is
> Even as the flourish when true subjects bow
> To a new-crowned monarch: such it is
> As are those dulcet sounds in break of day
> That creep into the dreaming bridegroom's ear
> And summon him to marriage.   (iii.2.43)

This summoning of the resources of romance gains its greatest
emphasis in the fifth act where Lorenzo and Jessica rehearse the

legends of the classical characters who knew nights similar to the
one they were then enjoying:

> The moon shines bright: in such a night as this,
> When the sweet wind did gently kiss the trees
> And they did make no noise, in such a night
> Troilus methinks mounted the Troyan walls
> And sigh'd his soul toward the Grecian tents,
> Where Cressid lay that night.   (v.1.1)

Lorenzo, in this scene, gives the ultimate effect of poetry in
this play, disengaging life from all tarnishing influences, all the
incidents and motives which ordinarily encourage dismay and
despair. Through its music, poetry opens out, as it were, into a
world romantic but spiritual, a life that is void of all that is con-
taminating and sordid:

> Look how the floor of heaven
> Is thick inlaid with patines of bright gold:
> There's not the smallest orb which thou behold'st
> But in his motion like an angel sings,
> Still quiring to the young-eyed cherubins;
> Such harmony is in immortal souls;
> But whilst this muddy vesture of decay
> Doth grossly close it in, we cannot hear it.   (v.1.58)

This is not ordinary existence Shakespeare seems to emphasise,
but a moment of brightness created for pleasure. It is as if Portia's
lines on her final return to her house were a symbol for the play
as a whole:

> That light we see is burning in my hall.
> How far that little candle throws his beams!
> So shines a good deed in a naughty world.   (v.1.89)

With such an atmosphere we cannot expect complex, or introspective passages. Not thought, but pleasure, is the mood, and
Bassanio, addressing Portia, in one of the most interesting
passages in the whole play, reflects how words can have an effect
of pleasure on the senses while the reason is numbed into temporary acquiescence:

> Madam, you have bereft me of all words,
> Only my blood speaks to you in my veins;
> And there is such confusion in my powers,
> As, after some oration fairly spoke
> By a beloved prince, there doth appear

> Among the buzzing pleased multitude;
> Where every something, being blent together,
> Turns to a wild of nothing, save of joy,
> Express'd and not express'd.   (iii.2.177)

This is one of the few comments on language in the play.
The other references, as so often in Shakespeare, deal with the
difference between plain statement and the compromising influence of elaborate or decorative speech. It was as if conscious of
his own power over words he was continually reflecting upon the
ways it could be employed. So (iii.1.12):

> SALANIO. But it is true, without any slips of prolixity or crossing
> the plain highway of talk, that the good Antonio, the honest
> Antonio,—O that I had a title good enough to keep his name
> company!—
> SALARINO. Come, the full stop.
> SALANIO. Ha! what sayest thou? Why, the end is, he hath lost a ship.

'Prolixity or crossing the plain highway of talk'—these were
the very temptations that had affected Shakespeare himself in
Love's Labour's Lost where the play of linguistic extravagance had
so possessed him. Now all is so fully in command that the very
temptation to err seems absent. Launcelot, alone, as the fool, is
allowed his quibbles and puns and wit-snappings, so that Lorenzo
is led to comment:

> O dear discretion, how his words are suited!
> The fool hath planted in his memory
> An army of good words; and I do know
> A many fools, that stand in better place,
> Garnish'd like him, that for a tricksy word
> Defy the matter.   (iii.5.70)

While the romantic background is so admirably maintained by
the verse, there is variety as the action moves from one scene to
another. Shylock himself is given a language of realism, often
simple, direct and forceful. Shakespeare has learned the power
of statement, unadorned with imagery, strong in its own content
and movement:

> Pray you, tell me this;
> If he should break his day, what should I gain
> By the exaction of the forfeiture?
> A pound of man's flesh taken from a man
> Is not so estimable, profitable neither,
> As flesh of muttons, beefs, or goats.   (i.3.163)

Further in his distress for the loss of Jessica and the theft of his treasure Shylock is given the abrupt and broken phrases that he might have used in actual life: 'Out upon her! Thou torturest me, Tubal: it was my turquoise; I had it of Leah when I was a bachelor: I would not have given it for a wilderness of monkeys' (iii.1.125).

The control of language is emphasised by the number of speeches which have the formal arrangement of an oration. The outstanding example is Portia's 'Mercy' speech. Each phrase has its counterpart, and each sentence is balanced, and so the argument, with its sentiments, is constructed until the whole has a formal and classical strength. Incidentally there are so many competing claimants as the original of this speech that one is driven back upon the hypothesis that perhaps the sentiments are so commonplace that invention was unnecessary, though poetically they are supremely expressed:

> it is twice blest;
> It blesseth him that gives and him that takes:
> 'Tis mightiest in the mightiest: it becomes
> The throned monarch better than his crown.

(iv.1.186)

While Portia's address is the most obvious example, a number of the speeches follow a formal pattern. Thus Shylock's great defence of the Hebrew people gains its strength not through imagery or through an imaginative language, but through simple and direct statements so arranged and repeated that they obtain an effect of profound emotional power: 'Hath not a Jew eyes? hath not a Jew hands, organs, dimensions, senses, affections, passions? fed with the same food, hurt with the same weapons, subject to the same diseases, healed by the same means, warmed and cooled by the same winter and summer, as a Christian is?' (iii.1.61).

While these are the two main examples there are a number of speeches which display a formal pattern, used for emphasis and merely for the delight with which the ear receives them. So Portia, even in her talk with Bassanio can set her speech into the rule of triplicity:

> *Happy* in this, she is not yet so old
> But she may learn; *happier* than this,
> She is not bred so dull but she can learn;

> *Happiest* of all is that her gentle spirit
> Commits itself to yours to be directed,
> As from her *lord*, her *governor*, her *king*.   (iii.2.162)

This formal structure used seriously throughout the play is employed in the last act, light-heartedly, to restore the mood of
comedy after the solemnities of the trial scene.

> BASSANIO.   Sweet Portia,
> If you did know to whom I gave the ring,
> If you did know for whom I gave the ring
> And would conceive for what I gave the ring
> And how unwillingly I left the ring,
> When nought would be accepted but the ring,
> You would abate the strength of your displeasure.
>
> (v.1.192)

To which Portia replies in a sentence of a similar pattern.

All this emphasises the impression that the language is easily in
control and looks back towards Shakespeare's earlier achievement.
It is adjusted to the needs both of the scene and the characters.
An example occurs in the early scenes. Antonio is given lines
which are slow in their movement, quiet in contemplation, without
the brightness of an image:

> In sooth, I know not why I am so sad:
> It wearies me; you say it wearies you.   (i.1.1)

In contrast Gratiano speaks with the astringency of wit:

> Why should a man, whose blood is warm within,
> Sit like his grandsire cut in alabaster?   (i.1.83)

Against both of these is the quiet but sinister development by
Shylock of his biblical image of Jacob's ewes, as he tries to convince Antonio and Bassanio that usury is just and that his own
aims are innocent.

One of the happiest effects comes from the language connected
with the sea, above all of the traffic at sea of ships which merchant
adventurers in Venice send from port to port. Much of the
action depends on the losses at sea which Antonio, the rich merchant, was believed to have suffered. Antonio's losses cannot find
a place in the action itself, and yet they must be present in the
minds of the audience. So, from the first scene imagery is employed for this purpose of *definition*: 'Your mind', says Salarino
to Antonio, 'is tossing on the ocean';

> There, where your argosies with portly sail,
> Like signiors and rich burghers on the flood,
> Or, as it were, the pageants of the sea,
> Do overpeer the petty traffickers,
> That curtsy to them do them reverence,
> As they fly by them with their woven wings.
>
> (i.1.8)

This passage which so aptly compares the ships to the signiors and rich burghers of Venice seems to give the whole scene of the city. So Salarino again:

> When I thought
> What harm a wind too great at sea might do.
> I should not see the sandy hour-glass run,
> But I should think of shallows and of flats,
> And see my wealthy Andrew dock'd in sand,
> Vailing her high-top lower than her ribs
> To kiss her burial. Should I go to church
> And see the holy edifice of stone,
> And not bethink me straight of dangerous rocks,
> Which touching but my gentle vessel's side,
> Would scatter all her spices on the stream,
> Enrobe the roaring waters with my silks,
> And, in a word, but even now worth this,
> And now worth nothing?
>
> (i.1.23)

Once again in the very middle of the scene of Jessica's escape the mind of Gratiano is allowed to go back to the peril and uncertainty of sea traffickings, and so to recall and redefine the danger that awaits Antonio:

> How like a younker or a prodigal
> The scarfed bark puts from her native bay,
> Hugg'd and embraced by the strumpet wind!
> How like the prodigal doth she return,
> With over-weather'd ribs and ragged sails,
> Lean, rent and beggar'd by the strumpet wind!
>
> (ii.6.14)

So the sea, merchandise, the wealth of merchants, and the loss of wealth are re-emphasised in some of the play's most luxurious images.

It is all very satisfactory, as if Shakespeare had come to a period when he knew more about language than it was necessary for him immediately to employ. He had forces in reserve. All this would change when he came to the dark comedies and the tragedies.

In *Much Ado About Nothing* a great deal of the play is in prose, not only the comic scenes, but the exchanges of wit and sentiment that would elsewhere have been graced by blank verse. The only comment on language is made by Benedick, where he speaks of the change in Claudio, once he is in love: 'He was wont to speak plain and to the purpose, like an honest man and a soldier; and now is he turned orthography; his words are a very fantastical banquet, just so many strange dishes' (ii.3.17). It is the distinction between honest, plain speaking and an elaborate diction, already made by Mercutio, and one which appears in the early histories, while the concept of words as 'a very fantastical banquet' seems to go back to the 'taffeta phrases' of *Love's Labour's Lost*.

There is a subtlety in the comic language which is not to be found in the passages of sentiment and romance. Indeed Shakespeare's developing linguistic power lies rather in his treatment of Dogberry than of Hero or Claudio. He had from the first allowed his clowns to play on errors in language, either of sound or meaning, but Dogberry does this with greater ingenuity: 'This is your charge: you shall comprehend all vagrom men' (iii.3.25), and 'I would have some confidence with you that decerns you nearly' (iii.5.3); 'comparisons are odorous' (iii.5.19); 'our watch, sir, have indeed comprehended two auspicious persons' (iii.5.49); 'only get the learned writer to set down our excommunication and meet me at the gaol' (iii.5.68). It is almost as if James Joyce and Dogberry would have had some common understanding of linguistic invention. As Hardin Craig has commented, Dogberry has 'a form of humour which seems to be peculiarly Shakespearian. Clowns, of course, always misused their words: it is impossible to think of a clown who does not do so. But in this case there is a touch of pedantry. There is a certain amount of ridicule of pedantry in Lyly, but no humour derived from a misunderstanding or misuse of learned terms.'[1]

Claudio is one of the most unsatisfactory characters in the comedies, and his language has in it nothing remarkable. When in blank verse, it resembles the language young lovers have already used in the romantic comedies:

[1] Hardin Craig and the examples noted are quoted by Sister Joseph in *Shakespeare's Use of the Arts of Language* (1943).

How sweetly you do minister to love,
That know love's grief by his complexion!
But lest my liking might too sudden seem,
I would have salved it with a longer treatise.

(i.1.314)

Much of this is gently diffuse and unexacting, recalling the easy movement of passages in the early plays and showing no confirmation of that increasing concentration, which marks the development of Shakespeare's language. Don Pedro gives a typical example in the scene at Hero's tomb:

and look, the gentle day,
Before the wheels of Phoebus, round about
Dapples the drowsy east with spots of grey.

(v.3.25)

This leisurely and decorative gesture is found frequently in the verse, as when, for instance, Hero in telling Margaret to call Beatrice to hide in the garden, develops her instruction in the slow-moving charm of this conceit:

And bid her steal into the pleached bower,
Where honeysuckles, ripen'd by the sun,
Forbid the sun to enter, like favourites,
Made proud by princes, that advance their pride
Against that power that bred it.

(iii.1.7)

Nature and rustic life, which appeared so strikingly in the early comedies, occur intermittently in *Much Ado About Nothing*. Beatrice runs 'like a lapwing' 'Close by the ground' (iii.1.24). Benedick is said by Don Pedro to have 'a February face, so full of frost, of storm and cloudiness' (v.4.41). Ursula uses the gentle and slow idiom of the verse in her image of the 'angling of Beatrice':

The pleasant'st angling is to see the fish
Cut with her golden oars the silver stream,
And greedily devour the treacherous bait:
So angle we for Beatrice.

(iii.1.26)

It is typical of the linguistic indifference shown in this play that Claudio had used the same comparison, though less poetically, in the prose of the previous scene:

Bait the hook well; this fish will bite   (ii.3.113)

Shakespeare's mind explores in a genial laziness images which are
later modified in an urgent and compressed way in the tragedies.
So Leonato speaking of Hero says:

> O, she is fallen
> Into a pit of ink, that the wide sea
> Hath drops too few to wash her clean again
> And salt too little which may season give
> To her foul-tainted flesh!

(iv.1.141)

This may, of course, be dismissed as merely a witty passage, but
the situation is a serious one, and must be treated as such if the
play is to proceed. The quality of the texture comes out when the
lines are contrasted with Lady Macbeth's: 'all the perfumes of
Arabia will not sweeten this little hand' (*Macbeth*, v.1.57).

In the first scene Benedick jests with the sign of the 'blind
Cupid' which was the door sign of a brothel: 'pick out mine eyes
with a ballad-maker's pen and hang me up at the door of a brothel-
house for the sign of blind Cupid' (i.1.254). It is moving to recall
that in one of the most terrible passages in *King Lear*, when the
blindness is the real blindness of Gloucester and not a jest the
'blind Cupid' image is employed to express the cruel savagery of
Lear's distracted mood: 'Dost thou squiny at me? No, do thy worst
blind Cupid; I'll not love' (iv.6.140).

While *Much Ado* has thus no new approach to language, in the
verse, nor any of that continuity of intention in the imagery, discovered already in *The Two Gentlemen of Verona* and in *A Midsummer-Night's Dream*, it has its own verbal liveliness. Apart
from Dogberry's malapropisms, on which comment has already
been made, there are numerous topical allusions to be caught by
the audience to whom they were first addressed. Such is Bora-
chio's tantalizing passage in which he defines the effect of fashion
on 'the hot bloods between fourteen and five-and-thirty? sometimes fashioning them like Pharaoh's soldiers in the reechy
painting, sometimes like god Bel's priests in the old church-
window, sometime like the shaven Hercules in the smirched
worm-eaten tapestry, where his codpiece seems as massy as his
club?' (iii.3.141). There are further the happy but unexpected
comparisons, unexpected in themselves and in the characters who
use them. So is Don Pedro's simile when he warns Claudio that
he must not leave with him for Arragon immediately after his

wedding: 'Nay, that would be as great a soil in the new gloss of your marriage as to show a child his new coat and forbid him to wear it' (iii.2.5).

Despite the slow movement of much of the blank verse, and the slow pace of the images and associative reference, it is in liveliness and quickness that much that is most attractive in the language of the play is to be found. Such is Benedick's talk and that of Beatrice, as for instance, her comparison of 'wooing, wedding, and repenting' to 'a Scotch jig, a measure, and a cinque pace' (ii.1.76), or in Benedick's 'She told me, not thinking I had been myself, that I was the prince's jester, that I was duller than a great thaw' (ii.1.249). These two characters both habitually indulged in wit, yet achieved their most effective moment and their most memorable phrases in moods of seriousness. 'You were born in a merry hour', says Don Pedro to Beatrice, and she replies in some of the most beautiful lines in the play: 'No, sure, my lord, my mother cried; but then there was a star danced, and under that was I born' (ii.1.347). Benedick is as effective, though in a different way, when in the Church scene he breaks out with the simple sincerity of 'This looks not like a nuptial' (iv.1.69).

As You Like It has a claim to be the most popular of all the comedies and yet, as far as its verse is concerned, apart from the lyrics and a few isolated passages there is little of fresh interest. The lyrics are well-known, especially—'Blow, blow thou winter wind', and 'It was a lover and his lass', while Jaques's speech 'All the world's a stage' is perhaps the most often quoted from Shakespeare. But most of the play is in prose and its charm lies in situation and incident, and in the happy exchange of wit rather than in an original approach to vocabulary. Much of the action is conducted in straight-forward prose, a willing servant of the action. So in the first scene Charles to Oliver: 'I came to acquaint you with a matter. I am given, sir, secretly to understand that your younger brother Orlando hath a disposition to come in disguised against me to try a fall' (i.1.128). Similarly in the second scene Celia says to Rosaline: 'You know my father hath no child but I, nor none is like to have: and, truly, when he dies, thou shalt be his heir, for what he hath taken away from thy father perforce, I will render thee again in affection' (i.2.18).

There is a charm in much of the prose which escapes easy definition. Rosaline speaks with a lightness and ease unparalleled

by any of the earlier characters in Shakespeare's comedy. It is as
if here he has his reward for all the experiment in dramatic prose
which he had pursued in the earlier comedies. Her speech is less
formal than in the earlier comedies, and there is less to comment
on, but it is there that its brilliance lies. Its touch is as light as a
feather, witty, and romantic. Though, of course, and especially
with Touchstone, she is given her share of the quibbles.

The quality of direct and unadorned speech is found also in
much of the verse. So Le Beau answers Orlando's question as to
which of the two ladies at the wrestling was the daughter of the
Duke:

> Neither his daughter, if we judge by manners;
> But yet indeed the lesser is his daughter:
> The other is daughter to the banish'd duke,
> And here detain'd by her usurping uncle,
> To keep his daughter company.
>
> (i.2.283)

While Touchstone and the other characters in the comic scenes
have lively exchanges and a play on words, the action itself is
made to proceed in direct, even subdued statement. I am not
prepared to assign with confidence the motives for this change
but this period of restraint has its influence, in mediating between
the self-assertive brilliance of the early comedies and the original
but disciplined language of the mature plays. Shakespeare was
still thinking about the relation of language to meaning and,
strangely enough, in a brilliant and profound passage Touchstone
and Audrey are the spokesmen of his conclusions:

> TOUCHSTONE. When a man's verses cannot be understood, nor a
> man's good wit seconded with the forward child Understanding,
> it strikes a man more dead than a great reckoning in a little room.
> Truly, I would the gods had made thee poetical.
> AUDREY. I do not know what 'poetical' is: is it honest in deed and
> word? is it a true thing?
> TOUCHSTONE. No, truly; for the truest poetry is the most feigning.
>
> (iii.3.12)

Twelfth Night gathers into itself all that is most fragrant in the
romantic comedies, and the fullness of its perfection can only be
discovered by examining the whole action, its characters, and the
neat arrangement of its situations. Its language is more distinguished than that of *As You Like It*, for while the matter and

methods of the comic scenes remain much the same, and though
prose retains an important place, there is now a more prominent
and pleasing use of verse. While little may be original yet the
total effect of the language is different from that in any of the
preceding plays. Much of the expression of sentiment looks back
to the idiom of the sonnets, already exploited in the earlier comedies and in *Romeo and Juliet*. So Viola describes the beauty of
Olivia:

> Lady, you are the cruell'st she alive,
> If you will lead these graces to the grave
> And leave the world no copy.
>
> (i.5.259)

Similarly the Duke addresses Viola:

> I have unclasp'd
> To thee the book even of my secret soul.
>
> (i.4.13)

This conventional sonnet image is picked up in the next scene by
Olivia in her talk with Viola:

> OLIVIA. Where lies your text?
> VIOLA. In Orsino's bosom.
> OLIVIA. In his bosom! In what chapter of his bosom?
>
> (i.5.24c)

As in *As You Like It* the rural element remains, but only intermittently. Malvolia describes Viola: 'Not yet old enough for a
man, nor young enough for a boy; as a squash is before 'tis a
peascod, or a codling when 'tis almost an apple' (i.5.165). Sir
Toby describes Sir Andrew's hair: 'it hangs like flax on a distaff;
and I hope to see a housewife take thee between her legs and spin
it off' (i.3.108). The Duke plays, more romantically, with a similar
theme:

> The spinsters and the knitters in the sun
> And the free maids that weave their thread with bones
> Do use to chant it: it is silly sooth,
> And dallies with the innocence of love,
> Like the old age.
>
> (ii.4.45)

It is not in the imagery itself, but in the mastery and control
of the blank verse as a dramatic instrument that the strength lies.
In part this is found in the way that argument and imagery are

employed in close and easy relationship as in the opening lines
which so happily define the mood of the comedy:

> If music be the food of love, play on;
> Give me excess of it, that, surfeiting,
> The appetite may sicken, and so die.
> That strain again! it had a dying fall:
> O, it came o'er my ear like the sweet sound,
> That breathes upon a bank of violets,
> Stealing and giving odour!

(i.1.1)

There is a similar sense of command in Olivia's image to Viola,
where she derives the comparison from bear-baiting:

> Have you not set mine honour at the stake
> And baited it with all the unmuzzled thoughts
> That tyrannous heart can think?

(iii.1.129)

Further, much of the language is direct, relying on its appropriateness for strength rather than on decorative and fantastic elements.
Even some of the lyrics are composed of simple statements:

> What is love? 'tis not hereafter;
> Present mirth hath present laughter;
>   What's to come is still unsure:
> In delay there lies no plenty;
> Then come kiss me, sweet and twenty,
>   Youth's a stuff will not endure.

(ii.3.48)

Similarly a number of the speeches are equally direct. So Sebas-
tian in his puzzled soliloquy:

> This is the air; that is the glorious sun;
> This pearl she gave me, I do feel't and see't;
> And though 'tis wonder that enwraps me thus,
> Yet 'tis not madness. Where's Antonio, then?
> I could not find him at the Elephant:
> Yet there he was; and there I found this credit,
> That he did range the town to seek me out.

(iv.3.1)

The whole of this passage, and much of the speech that follows,
with the exception of the phrase, 'and though 'tis wonder that
enwraps me thus', is statement without any colouring of associative language. One has the sense of a greater power without that

power being for the present fully used. There is an increase of concentration, and a feeling that resources are being held in reserve. All this appears in such happy and compressed comparisons as the Duke's single line:

> Methought she purged the air of pestilence!   (i.1.20)

One feels that the approach to the language is easy, effortless, almost a lazy consciousness of strength. Many of the old counters are played, and the same idea, or more than one aspect of an idea, will be used more than once.

Though *Twelfth Night* has its own distinctive atmosphere, Shakespeare makes no use of any recurrent group of associations for the imagery as in *A Midsummer-Night's Dream*. As is appropriate in a play where rescue from a wreck is one of the main themes, the language dwells often on the sea, as in the Duke's first speech, which is one of the more complex passages in a linguistically easy play:

> O spirit of love! how quick and fresh art thou,
> That, notwithstanding thy capacity
> Receiveth as the sea, nought enters there,
> Of what validity and pitch soe'er,
> But falls into abatement and low price,
> Even in a minute.   (i.1.9)

But the sea is not so emphasised that the symbol hunters need erect any mysterious motive for its employment. Rather the language is a pleasant medley: nature, and legend; 'Arion on the dolphin's back' (i.2.15); Thyamis 'the Egyptian thief' (v.1.121); and, as if to note that the theme already interested him, 'Lord Pandarus of Phrygia, sir, to bring a Cressida to this. Troilus' (iii.1.58); topical and tantalizingly untraceable references such as Fabian's 'you will hang like an icicle on a Dutchman's beard' (iii.2.28); and happy phrases, so smooth that they seem proverbial, though now newly-minted:

> she pined in thought,
> And with a green and yellow melancholy
> She sat like patience on a monument,
> Smiling at grief.   (ii.4.115)

Shakespeare defined in *Twelfth Night* supremely what he could achieve in romantic comedy, but it is not a play where language progressed into new patterns.

CHAPTER X

HAMLET

No tragedy has endured such a weight of commentary as *Hamlet*, or such a variety of interpretation on the stage. Every actor aspires to play the part, and every critic feels a compulsion to add his piece to the endless discussion of texts, origins and character. The play, meanwhile, remains indestructibly alive. Some modern critics have emphasised the alleged 'imperfections' of this the earliest of the great tragedies, yet no work of dramatic genius has had a comparable appeal, even in translation, and in continents where the values of the original can only be dimly appreciated. Somehow Shakespeare created a tragedy acceptable at different levels of aesthetic enjoyment and Hamlet himself, the renaissance prince, in all the complexity of his moods, his learning and his motives for action, has provided for ordinary men everywhere some image of their own personality, and of the universal capacity for self-pity.

The language of the tragedy has never had the attention it deserves. For despite the crowded action, Shakespeare has had time to develop a self-conscious interest in words, and in the problems of language. This separates *Hamlet* from all the other great tragedies, for this, along with all its other qualities, is a tragedy of wit, where the turn of phrase and the quality of the vocabulary are treasured for their own sake. Hamlet, the renaissance prince, is a philologist, as is Polonius, and they alone of the characters in the tragedies could have witnessed a performance of *Love's Labour's Lost* and known what the comedy was about. Indeed nowhere in Shakespeare's work since *Love's Labour's Lost* had words gained such an *independent* importance. Though now, despite all their independence, words are subdued into the service of the action. In *Hamlet* the cunning is, that while words are explored for their own sake, by some creative ingenuity the interest in language is brought to the service of the action and of the characterisation so as to render it a natural and integral part of the conception.

While much in the language is fresh and original there are

parallels in some places with other plays. The close identity of
phrase and idea with *Measure for Measure* will be noted later.[1]
One other remarkable recollection occurs in the speech made by
Claudius while he is praying:

> What if this cursed hand
> Were thicker than itself with brother's blood,
> Is there not rain enough in the sweet heavens
> To wash it white as snow? Whereto serves mercy
> But to confront the visage of offence?
> And what's in prayer but this two-fold force,
> To be forestalled ere we come to fall,
> Or pardon'd being down?

(iii.3.43)

This is the very thought and idiom of Portia's speech on *mercy*
in *The Merchant of Venice*. This conception of language associated
with the same group of words must have been strong with Shakespeare for Isabella speaks a similar way in *Measure for Measure*.[2]

The exceptional importance in *Hamlet* of the linguistic interest
may be illustrated by Osric, who can claim the position of one of
the most 'minor' characters in the tragedy. He occurs only in the
fifth act, unless the ingenuity of a producer invents a place for
him in the earlier scenes. His function is confined, first to presenting to Hamlet the King's message about the duel, and secondly
to handing the swords to Hamlet and Laertes ('Give them the
foils, young Osric' (v.2.270)). In some recent productions Osric
appeared prominently in the early scenes, and his position at
Court was thus plausibly established prior to his appearance as
the King's chosen messenger to Hamlet in the matter of the duel.
In the theatre this is dramatically effective and also emphasises
Osric's complicity in the King's plot; he is, as Dr. Dover Wilson
has pointed out, in a position to guide Laertes's selection of the
unpoisoned foil. Whether all this expansion of Osric's role was
Shakespeare's actual intention remains debatable, and whatever
ingenuity can achieve for him he still remains a very minor
character.

Small as is his place in the action, Osric, the gilded, affected,
wealthy young courtier, with his peacock clothes and his elaborate

---

[1] See pp. 133–136. It must be recalled that the general view is that *Measure
for Measure* precedes *Hamlet*. Yet the comedy is the final phase of what has
gone before in Shakespeare's work while *Hamlet* looks to the future.

[2] See p. 133.

decoration of vocabulary wins a permanent place among English
dramatic characters. Apart from the clothes, it is Osric's language
and Hamlet's satiric imitation of it that gives interest to the part:

> OSRIC. Sir, here is newly come to court Laertes; believe me, an absolute
> gentleman, full of most excellent differences, of very soft society
> and great showing: indeed, to speak feelingly of him, he is the
> card or calendar of gentry, for you shall find in him the continent
> of what part a gentleman would see.
>
> HAMLET. Sir, his definement suffers no perdition in you.
>
> (v.2.110)

In one sense here is a linguistic satire, independent of the action,
for the play could go on if all this talk with Osric did not exist.
Yet the lively interest in an affected mode of speech, apart from
Hamlet's topical comment after Osric's departure on the fopperies
of speech and manner, is made to contribute to the emotional
content of the action. For the shallow affectation of Osric serves
to emphasise the loneliness of Hamlet, and the verbal dalliance of
their encounter brings out the contrasting strength of Hamlet's
sincere language which follows immediately afterwards: 'We defy
augury: there's a special providence in the fall of a sparrow. If it
be now, 'tis not to come; if it be not to come, it will be now; if it
be not now, yet it will come: the readiness is all' (v.2.230).

The constant interest in language in *Hamlet* reveals itself not
only in these specific references to language but also in the subtlety
with which language is employed throughout for dramatic purpose.
If verse is used with a gay self-consciousness in *Love's Labour's
Lost*, before the problems of its use as a dramatic medium have
been explored, in *Hamlet* there is a return to the language of wit
with a full knowledge that now the relation of speech and action
can be fully controlled.

One indication of this maturity can be found in Shakespeare's
skill in maintaining an argument in blank verse. The tragedy contains what is, to my mind, the most sustained period in blank
verse to be found anywhere in the plays, and it is remarkable that
no element of lucidity is destroyed by the most complex structure
of the syntax. The passage occurs when Hamlet and his companions, waiting for the appearance of the Ghost, hear 'a flourish
of trumpets, and ordnance, shot off, within' (i.4.6). Questioned
by Horatio on the meaning of these noises, Hamlet describes the
drinking in which the King indulges. Horatio asks if it is a custom,

to which Hamlet answers that it is 'a custom more honour'd in
the breach than the observance' (i.4.15) and it is to the second
sentence of this reply that I am now referring:

> This heavy-headed revel east and west
> Makes us traduced and tax'd of other nations:
> They clepe us drunkards, and with swinish phrase
> Soil our addition; and indeed it takes
> From our achievements, though perform'd at height,
> The pith and marrow of our attribute.
> So, oft it chances in particular men,
> That for some vicious mole of nature in them,
> As, in their birth—wherein they are not guilty,
> Since nature cannot choose his origin—
> By the o'ergrowth of some complexion,
> Oft breaking down the pales and forts of reason,
> Or by some habit that too much o'er-leavens
> The form of plausive manners, that these men,
> Carrying, I say, the stamp of one defect,
> Being nature's livery, or fortune's star,—
> Their virtues else—be they as pure as grace,
> As infinite as man may undergo—
> Shall in the general censure take corruption
> From that particular fault.

                                        (i.4.17)

The ease with which the argument is maintained, through all
elaborations and qualifying clauses and phrases, within the pattern
of a blank verse of complete lucidity, is as masterly as the thought
itself is subtle. Indeed it could be urged that in this sentence
Shakespeare defines the conception of character which is illustrated through the protagonists of his tragedies.

In *Hamlet* Shakespeare differentiated the language of each of
his major characters, though this was not carried through with
such precision, as later in *Othello* and *Macbeth*. There remained
a common 'pool' of blank verse for argument, reflection, images,
and lyricism on which any character could draw. In such passages
the character is speaking not for himself but with the voice of
Everyman: Horatio's romantic description of the dawn in the
opening scene—

> But, look, the morn, in russet mantle clad,
> Walks o'er the dew of yon high eastward hill.

                                        (i.1.166)

—belongs less to his own serious and thoughtful mind as to a lyrical mood which emphasises for the spectator the movement of time in the scene.

Similarly Polonius is given speeches which are in keeping with his character of a councillor garrulous, pedantic, and ageing, yet not without wisdom or knowledge of the world, who delighted in a conceit or a verbal pattern, even when the matter was serious. He creates a dramatic suspense by his delays in the speech where he tells the King and Queen of his belief that Hamlet is in love with Ophelia. He uses, appropriately to his character, a foppery in speech, and then recognises it for the 'toy' that it is:

> That he is mad, 'tis true: 'tis true 'tis pity;
> And pity 'tis 'tis true: a foolish figure.   (ii.2.97)

When Polonius is giving advice to Laertes he is drawing from that great neutral store of blank verse which can be employed from time to time by any character:

> Those friends thou hast, and their adoption tried,
> Grapple them to thy soul with hoops of steel;
> But do not dull thy palm with entertainment
> Of each new-hatched, unfledged comrade.   (i.3.62)

The outstanding example of this detachment of the speech from the character is the Queen's long and romantic description of the death of Ophelia:

> There is a willow grows aslant a brook,
> That shows his hoar leaves in the glassy stream;
> There with fantastic garlands did she come
> Of crow-flowers, nettles, daisies, and long purples
> That liberal shepherds give a grosser name,
> But our cold maids do dead men's fingers call them:
> There, on the pendent boughs her coronet weeds
> Clambering to hang, an envious sliver broke;
> When down her weedy trophies and herself
> Fell in the weeping brook. Her clothes spread wide;
> And, mermaid-like, awhile they bore her up:
> Which time she chanted snatches of old tunes;
> As one incapable of her own distress,
> Or like a creature native and indued
> Unto that element: but long it could not be
> Till that her garments, heavy with their drink,
> Pull'd the poor wretch from her melodious lay
> To muddy death.   (iv.7.167)

This is not the voice of the Queen in her own person but a necessary epitaph, that defines the emotional place of Ophelia in the tragedy. Despite its beauty, the speech, as many an actress must know, fits awkwardly into the dramatic action, for Laertes preludes the Queen's remarks with 'Drown'd! O, where?' and on the conclusion of the Queen's lines adds, somewhat oddly, 'Alas, then, she is drown'd?'

The exploitation of language for its own sake would not have been possible had not Hamlet himself possessed a profound linguistic interest, and this is shared by some of the other characters. It remains an unacknowledged bond of intellectual sympathy between Polonius and Hamlet, despite the strong cleavage that separates them on all major issues. When Hamlet, feigning madness, tries to give Polonius quibbling answers, the old courtier has the philological alertness to follow the Prince's equivocations: 'how pregnant sometimes his replies are! a happiness that often madness hits on, which reason and sanity could not so prosperously be delivered of' (ii.2.212). Polonius shows a critical interest in language in the scene with the players. When Hamlet declaims a speech of 'the rugged Pyrrhus' it is Polonius who comments, ''Fore God, my lord, well spoken, with good accent and good discretion' (ii.2.488); and later, when the player takes up the speech, he comments that it is too long, and again seizes on the phrase 'the mobled queen': 'That's good; "mobled queen" is good' (ii.2.526). Polonius has concentrated his attention sufficiently on the actor to see that he has worked himself into tears: 'Look, whether he has not turned his colour and has tears in's eyes' (ii.2.542).

Some of Polonius' literary interest belongs to the world of arid categorizing: it is this that leads him to 'the best actors in the world, either for tragedy, comedy, history, pastoral, pastoral-comical, historical-pastoral' and so on interminably (ii.2.415). But Polonius is also given some of the most penetrating phrases of dramatic comment: 'scene individable, or poem unlimited: Seneca cannot be too heavy, nor Plautus too light. For the law of writ and the liberty, these are the only men' (ii.2.418). Few phrases are as pregnant with dramatic criticism as 'the law of writ and the liberty' (ii.2.420) for they define the whole contrast of classical and romantic drama. Incidentally they shew how familiar Shakespeare was with the critical disputes current in his own day. Yet such material could not have been relevantly employed here had he not been portraying a renaissance councillor who is as versed in literary theory as he is in court intrigue.

Polonius's more specific expression of an interest in language occurs in the most entertaining scene, where he conveys to the King and Queen his conviction that Hamlet is in love with Ophelia. It is one of the many scenes where a comedy of wit is allowed a place in this tragedy. Polonius holds up his reading of the crucial evidence, namely Hamlet's poem to Ophelia, when he comes to the word 'beautified' in order to show his stylistic disapproval:

> 'To the celestial and my soul's idol, the most
> beautified Ophelia,'—
> That's an ill phrase, a vile phrase; 'beautified' is a vile
> phrase: but you shall hear.
>
> (ii.2.110)

This suspension of his narrative for the sake of style follows the self-conscious precision and elaboration of style of his opening speech in this scene where linguistic considerations occupy him far more than the direct conveyance of urgent matter. The Queen is led to enter a protest: 'More matter, with less art' (ii.2.95). All this is contrived to portray the character of Polonius, the aged courtier with a long-winded interest in the niceties of style. It adds also one of those many moods of comedy which give this tragedy such a varied interest. Dramatically it is arresting, for Polonius's amusing tediousness is a period of suspense to the King and the Queen.

I would note here, incidentally, that one of the linguistic problems of the play is why Hamlet, who is a fastidious master of language, should have addressed to Ophelia lines such as:

> *Doubt thou the stars are fire;*
> *Doubt that the sun doth move;*
> *Doubt truth to be a liar;*
> *But never doubt I love.*
>
> *O dear Ophelia, I am ill at these numbers; I have not art to reckon*
> *my groans: but that I love thee best, O most best, believe it.*
>
> (ii.2.116)

I would only hazard as an explanation that in the theatre the passage raises no problems. It is appropriate that the verse of Hamlet's letter should be different from the verse of the play

itself, just as the verse of the Play within the Play is different
from that of the rest of the tragedy. There is deliberately a broader
and cruder brush-work in such passages, and it is dangerous to
examine too minutely in the study effects which have been designed for the conditions of the stage. If the passage is right in
the theatre, then its employment is justified whatever the closet
critics may say.

To Claudius's language Shakespeare seems to have paid particular attention, and it shows him as a man of quick and lively
intelligence, despite his capacity for evil. The King is first shown
presiding over his Court, and making an official and insincere
expression of grief for the death of Hamlet's father. For this
Shakespeare employs the opaque rhetoric which is his customary
medium on such occasions.

> Therefore our sometime sister, now our queen,
> The imperial jointress to this warlike state,
> Have we, as 'twere with a defeated joy,—
> With an auspicious and a dropping eye,
> With mirth in funeral and with dirge in marriage,
> In equal scale weighing delight and dole,—
> Taken to wife.   (i.2.8)

Everything here from the ceremonial 'imperial jointress', the
elaborate 'an auspicious and a dropping eye', the balance of 'mirth
in funeral and with dirge in marriage', and the alliteration of
'delight and dole', all combine to represent an official oration
where the required sentiments are enunciated, without much
reference to what is going on in the speaker's mind.

When the official business of the Court is over the King changes
to a happy informality in addressing Laertes, whose business is
of a private nature:

> And now, Laertes, what's the news with you?
> You told us of some suit; what is't, Laertes?
> You cannot speak of reason to the Dane,
> And lose your voice.   (i.2.42)

It is with a similar note of domestic kindliness that he attempts
to ingratiate himself with Hamlet: 'But now, my cousin Hamlet,
and my son' (i.2.64). Once this has failed he returns to his stately
manner in the formal plea which he addresses to Hamlet that he
should cease to mourn his father's death:

> to persever
> In obstinate condolement is a course
> Of impious stubbornness.
>
> (i.2.92)

The later scenes shew how quickly and with what determination his mind acts. When he and Polonius have spied on Hamlet and discovered that his distemper does not rise from a love of Ophelia he summarises the situation immediately:

> Love! his affections do not that way tend,   (iii.1.170)

and with equal rapidity he concludes how to act:

> I have in quick determination
> Thus set it down: he shall with speed to England,
> For the demand of our neglected tribute.
>
> (iii.1.176)

His speech, when he tells Hamlet that he must go to England, is similarly typical of his character. Opening with a rotund phrase where he hides his mind, he changes into keen and abrupt terms of instruction and command:

> Hamlet, this deed, for thine especial safety,—
> Which we do tender, as we dearly grieve
> For that which thou hast done,—must send thee hence
> With fiery quickness: therefore prepare thyself;
> The bark is ready, and the wind at help,
> The associates tend, and every thing is bent
> For England.
>
> (iv.3.42)

Nowhere is this same gift for the quick order of command and the forthright decision seen more clearly than when, on Laertes' return (iv.5.97), he fears that the castle is surrounded. He contrives to crowd his whole meaning into a single line:

> Where are my Switzers? Let them guard the door.

Hamlet's own language stands apart from all else in the plays, for Hamlet alone carries with him into a great tragic action the mind of a scholar, a satirist, a critic of drama and language, almost the mind of a metaphysical poet whose melancholic but witty anatomizing plays round any situation in which he finds himself. Macbeth is given more highly poetical language, charged with a rare and urgent metaphorical quality, but it is the instrument of a mind exploring action and motive, not of a philosopher who

watches as a fastidious critic the manner and quality of his own
expression and experience. Ophelia is given the lines which
describe Hamlet as Shakespeare saw him:

> The courtier's, soldier's, scholar's, eye, tongue, sword;
> The expectancy and rose of the fair state,
> The glass of fashion and the mould of form,
> The observed of all observers.

(iii.1.159)

The first moment of crisis in Hamlet's emotional life, inside
the play, comes on hearing the recital by his father's ghost, of the
way he was murdered. What is Hamlet's response? 'My tables,
meet it is I set it down' (i.5.107), or otherwise 'Where is my
memorandum book? I must make a note of it'. When he swears
to the ghost that he will clear his mind of all except revenge it is
the memory of books that first comes to his mind:

> I'll wipe away all trivial fond records,
> All saws of books, all forms, all pressures past,

(1.5.99)

and it is as a book that he speaks of his mind: 'the book and volume
of my brain' (i.5.103).

To Hamlet, the renaissance scholar, Shakespeare gives a more
ample classical imagery than to any of his other tragic characters:
'So excellent a king; that was, to this, Hyperion to a satyr' (i.2.139);
'she follow'd my poor father's body, Like Niobe, all tears' (i.2.148);
'My father's brother, but no more like my father Than I to Hercules' (i.2.152); 'And my imaginations are as foul As Vulcan's
stithy' (iii.2.88). To these must be added his magnificent description of his father in his address to his mother after the Play Scene:

> See, what a grace was seated on this brow;
> Hyperion's curls; the front of Jove himself;
> An eye like Mars, to threaten and command;
> A station like the herald Mercury
> New-lighted on a heaven-kissing hill.

(iii.4.55)

This is not a return to the school-room classicism of the early
plays, for it is worked into the imaginative language of the play
as a whole.

Hamlet is conscious of the 'fopperies' and conceits of language.
I have already referred to his encounter with the Players and with
Osric. It was Osric who led him to the comment, 'he—and many

more of the same breed that I know the drossy age dotes on—
only got the tune of the time and outward habit of encounter'
(v.2.196). In his encounters with Rosencrantz and Guildenstern
he plays with language very much as a young sonneteer. So he
tries to make Guildenstern play on a pipe and then pursues his
inability in a long comparison which hints at every aspect of their
relationship: 'You would play upon me; you would seem to
know my stops' (iii.2.380). Later, when the grave-digger (v.1)
shows that he, too, can play with words, Hamlet is led to a comment that again shows the observant student of language: 'We
must speak by the card, or equivocation will undo us. By the
Lord, Horatio, these three years I have taken note of it; the age
is grown so picked that the toe of the peasant comes so near the
heel of the courtier, he galls his kibe' (v.1.148).

This scholarly, analytic approach is illustrated many times, but
never more emphatically than in the scene in which Laertes and
Hamlet throw themselves into the grave of Ophelia. It could be
urged that Hamlet's action is based largely on philological motives.
He cannot tolerate the anaemic ranting of Laertes, and so he comes
forward to show in his own cascade of rhetoric how the thing should
be done, if indeed one wants to do it at all. 'What is he', Hamlet
says,

>   whose grief
> Bears such an emphasis? whose phrase of sorrow
> Conjures the wandering stars, and makes them stand
> Like wonder-wounded hearers?
>
>   (v.1.277)

Then Hamlet, in a speech of torrential rhetoric, so outdoes
Laertes' phrases that they seem in comparison the puny products
of an underfed imagination. Further, it is clear that whatever
may be his emotions, Hamlet is conscious of the verbal battle
with Laertes in which he is so easily a victor:

>   Dost thou come here to whine?
> To outface me with leaping in her grave?
> Be buried quick with her, and so will I:
> And, if thou *prate* of mountains, let them throw
> Millions of acres on us, till our ground,
> Singeing his pate against the burning zone,
> Make Ossa like a wart! *Nay, an thou'lt mouth,*
> *I'll rant as well as thou.*   (v.1.300)

I am not suggesting that Hamlet is devoid of feeling for Ophelia at this moment, but his sentiments are accompanied by an *independent* interest in the language in which they are expressed. It is this which separates him so completely from the other great figures in the tragedies.

This linguistic interest, while not deserting Hamlet in these supreme moments, is even more apparent in the few incidents in which he is portrayed in a more leisured mood. As compared with the other great tragedies, *Hamlet* has this distinguishing quality, that it depends on a period of hesitation and delay between the exposition of the action and the final crisis. Shakespeare fills this interval with a number of ingenious devices, the majority of which are related somehow to a linguistic interest. Thus the coming of the players is made an opportunity for him to express through Hamlet some of his own thoughts on acting, dramatic composition, audiences, and on the speaking of verse. Again these comments can be enjoyed independently, and indeed they constitute some of the most notable, practical criticism of the drama in the language, yet they are relevant and appropriate, because the protagonist is this renaissance prince, with a profound knowledge and interest in the arts. With an interval to fill, and with a character who could be reasonably represented as sharing such an interest, Shakespeare spoke not of words only, but of the speaking of words: 'Be not too tame neither, but let your own discretion be your tutor: suit the action to the word, the word to the action; with this special observance, that you o'erstep not the modesty of nature' (iii.2.19).

Hamlet's first line in the tragedy had been marked by a play in words:

A little more than kin, and less than kind, (i.2.65)

and it is with changing emphasis on a single word that he first shows his mother his contempt with her conduct:

Seems, madam! nay, it is; I know not 'seems' (i.2.76)

It is with a play of words that Hamlet hides his real mind from Polonius, and from Rosencrantz and Guildenstern. When necessary he can master a direct and concentrated language. There are few passages in Shakespeare more compressed than Hamlet's letter to Horatio telling of his escape on the pirate ship: 'Ere we were two days old at sea, a pirate of very warlike appointment gave us chase. Finding ourselves too slow of sail, we put on a compelled valour, and in the grapple I boarded them: on the instant they got clear of our ship; so I alone became their prisoner'. (iv.6.14). At the other extreme, Hamlet, when he is hiding his mind, can use the opaque speech, the elaborate and over-weighted words which Shakespeare so frequently employs in such circumstances. So, in his first speech to his mother, he hides his mind in a verbal elaboration by telling her that he cannot be truly revealed by his 'inky cloak':

> Nor customary suits of solemn black,
> Nor windy suspiration of forced breath,
> No, nor the fruitful river in the eye,
> Nor the dejected 'haviour of the visage.

(i.2.78)

All these features of the language which I have selected for comment still leave much that is most memorable in the play without definition. No counting of images will give the impression of what Shakespeare has achieved. In no play are Professor Spurgeon's statistical methods less illuminating, and she, with her usual honesty, realised this. She has noted the image of corruption, present in the tragedy, and figuring out the main theme:

> diseases desperate grown
> By desperate appliance are relieved,
> Or not at all.

(iv.3.9)

Again in Hamlet's address to his mother after the Play Scene the same association returns:

> Mother, for love of grace,
> Lay not that flattering unction to your soul,
> That not your trespass, but my madness speaks:
> It will but skin and film the ulcerous place,
> Whiles rank corruption, mining all within,
> Infects unseen.

(iii.4.144)

Yet Professor Spurgeon is aware of the compelling quality of beauty in *Hamlet* which counteracted the dominant image of disease, infection and ulceration: 'the whole lighted up by flashes of sheer beauty in the imagery; beauty of picture, of sound and association, more particularly in the classical group and in the personifications. Thus, the tragic, murky atmosphere of Hamlet's interview with his mother, with its ever-repeated insistence on physical sickness and revolting disease, is illuminated by the glow of his description of his father's portrait, the associations of beauty called up by Hyperion, Jove, and Mars, or the exquisite picture evoked by the contemplation of the grace of his father's poise:

> like the herald Mercury
> New-lighted on a heaven-kissing hill.'[1]

(iii.4.58)

In *Othello* the imagery of disease and infection is so persistent, and without any counteracting element, that it stays in the memory as a dominant memory. In *Hamlet*, though Shakespeare gives due emphasis to the theme of corruption, the language of wit and speculation has such entertainment and material for contemplation that the mind is sustained by a great variety of experience, and, above all, the associations of the imagery are so universal that the whole of human experience is stored within it for the refreshment of the imagination. In no play has Shakespeare so transfigured commonplace and proverbial phrases that they seem profound and original poetical statements. No play tempts one more to the conclusion that Shakespeare's power lay rather not in revealing new experience but in bringing to the expression of the common wisdom of humanity a strength and magnificence of style, so that what is most ordinary seems something new and uniquely experienced.

It is rather in contrast, therefore, than in any single element that the language of the tragedy gains its distinguishing quality. Nowhere else in Shakespeare is there a character such as Hamlet who can so suddenly and deliberately descend from the sublime to ironic analysis. An example occurs in his talk with Rosencrantz and Guildenstern after the play scene. In a mood, over-curious and metaphysical, and with an undertone of the comic he dissects the earth as 'this brave o'erhanging firmament, this majestical roof fretted with golden fire, why, it appears no other thing to me than foul and pestilent congregation of vapours' (ii.2.312). Immediately there follows the magnificent praise of humanity, which seems in its bold rhetoric to incorporate all that renaissance man, in his most ambitious moments, believed of himself and his capabilities: 'What a piece of work is man! how noble in reason! how infinite in faculty! in form and moving how express and admirable!

[1] *Shakespeare's Imagery.*

in action how like an angel! in apprehension how like a god! the beauty of the world! the paragon of animals!' (ii.2.316). Yet a moment later he has turned back into his own morbid introspection: 'And yet, to me, what is this quintessence of dust? man delights not me: no, nor woman neither, though by your smiling you seem to say so' (ii.2.321).

We have in Hamlet a mind that strikes out to undiscovered beauties, and then, by some complex anatomizing of experience, destroys the beauty he has created. 'Why', he asked Horatio, 'may not imagination trace the noble dust of Alexander, till he find it stopping a bung-hole?' Horatio answered with a comment that might apply to a number of Hamlet's speculations: ''Twere to consider too curiously, to consider so' (v.1.224). Hamlet can employ this analytical quality with bitter effectiveness, as he does in his conversations with Polonius and Ophelia, but, at times, and particularly in some passages of soliloquy, or in his talks with Horatio, he can use a language of power, or of unadulterated beauty. So he describes to Horatio his reaction to the death of Rosencrantz and Guildenstern:

> They are not near my conscience; their defeat
> Does by their own insinuation grow:
> 'Tis dangerous when the baser nature comes
> Between the pass and fell incensed points
> Of mighty opposites.
>
> (v.2.58)

It is to Horatio that he addressed the lines whose sentiment is all the more moving because they are spoken by one who could fret his way through the distempers of speech:

> If thou didst ever hold me in thy heart,
> Absent thee from felicity awhile,
> And in this harsh world draw thy breath in pain,
> To tell my story.
>
> (v.2.357)

Hamlet has that increased concentration of language which marks the tragedies in contrast to the earlier plays. A claim could be made that one of the phrases used by the Ghost is among the most concentrated in the whole of Shakespeare's work. After a brief description of the life after death Hamlet's father breaks off to say, 'But this *eternal blazon* must not be' (i.5.21). Those two

words 'eternal blazon' have a great imaginative compression, for
'to blazon' means to paint, in all the heraldic detail of arms and
distinctions according to the rules of chivalry, and so here, as the
Ghost applies the term to the whole picture of eternity, an endless
experience is brought within the compass of two words.

I would quote only one other example of this concentration,
which occurs in one of Hamlet's last speeches:

> You that look pale and tremble at this chance,
> That are but mutes or audience to this act,
> Had I but time—as this fell sergeant, death,
> Is strict in his arrest—O, I could tell you—
> But let it be. Horatio, I am dead;
> Thou livest; report me and my cause aright
> To the unsatisfied.
>
> (v.2.345)

Amid the urgency of the simple phrases has been set a picture
complete in a few words—*as this fell sergeant, death, Is strict in his
arrest*—and as so often in Shakespeare the abstract idea is set
bravely and dramatically in a moving and concrete form.

Shakespeare gave Polonius the term 'poem unlimited' to use in
describing one type of drama, and that conception of the *illimitable*
could be applied to the language of *Hamlet*. At times it is made
out of the simplest elements, yet used most movingly; on occasion
it indulges in the most elaborate and decorative figures of rhetorical
speech; and while it gathers into itself a language which dwells
among contaminated things, it has also a soaring quality. So
much of the whole mood is gathered into Horatio's words over
Hamlet:

> Now cracks a noble heart. Good night, sweet prince;
> And flights of angels sing thee to thy rest!
>
> (v.2.370)

Even here all is not as simple as it seems for Horatio's 'sweet
prince' re-echoes the last words that he had heard Ophelia speak:
'Good night, sweet ladies; good night, good night' (iv.5.73). But
the line which follows gives that sense of radiance which the play
possesses, whatever may be the tragic circumstance which it
embodies.

CHAPTER XI

MEASURE FOR MEASURE; ALL'S WELL THAT ENDS WELL; TROILUS AND CRESSIDA

To turn from the language of the romantic comedies to that of these plays is to move into a new world.

The problem of their relative chronology is difficult. The order suggested by Sir E. K. Chambers is *Troilus and Cressida* (1601-2); *All's Well That Ends Well* (1602-3) and *Measure for Measure* (1604-5). It may well be that this is true, though it is agreed that a strong element of conjecture has to enter in. I depart from the chronological order, treating *Measure for Measure* first because its language seems to me to have the strongest links with the preceding plays. I leave *Troilus and Cressida* until last because it stands so much in an almost aggressive isolation linguistically. Ultimately it must be remembered, as I have ventured several times to emphasise, that order of production is not necessarily the order of composition, nor is the order of composition of necessity the order of conception.

The contrast is most complete if *The Merchant of Venice*, with all its emblazoned beauty, is compared with even the least harsh of them, which is *Measure for Measure*. Some of the contrasts are obvious enough; for now, only occasionally, is the phrase or image pleasing in itself. Claudio's lines,

> If I must die,
> I will encounter darkness as a bride,
> And hug it in mine arms

(iii.1.83)

stand in vivid contrast to the general mood which is more typically and cruelly expressed by:

> Our natures do pursue,
> Like rats that ravin down their proper bane,
> A thirsty evil; and when we drink we die.

(i.2.132)

This change of associative background is accompanied by other developments, less easy to define. There is a compression of the

sense, a closely packed argument, replacing the gentle, unhurried
movement found, so frequently, in the earlier plays. Verse is
now more closely, or possibly even more aridly conditioned to an
argument from which gracious similitudes and an easy flow of
language are eliminated. So from the very opening lines the play
breaks into a proposition, precisely dissected:

> Of government the properties to unfold,
> Would seem in me to affect speech and discourse.
>
> (i.1.3)

This change to argument and analysis from a balanced rhetoric
is so complete that the rare passages where the earlier movement
occurs seem like some inappropriate survival, or some memory of
an earlier manner. The most notable interlude, with this now
abandoned style is in Isabella's speech to Angelo (ii.2.58-63 and
75-79):

> Well, believe this,
> No ceremony that to great ones 'longs,
> Not the king's crown, nor the deputed sword,
> The marshal's truncheon, nor the judge's robe,
> Become them with one half so good a grace
> As mercy does. . . .
> How would you be,
> If He, which is the top of judgment, should
> But judge you as you are? O, think on that;
> And mercy then will breathe within your lips,
> Like man new made.

Here in a speech which seems to have memories of *The Merchant
of Venice*, and possibly of *Hamlet*; the commonplace is adorned,
but with no subtlety of approach to the argument. Such a manner
is now to be replaced by a way of thought more subtle and introspective and with an answering style.

This change in the language, while marked with many brilliant
passages, is accompanied by some uncertainty and hesitation.
This can be discovered in the repetition of the same words and
phrases, not deliberately for emphasis, but as if the argument led
to a diminished attention to the associative resources of the
imagery. So the Duke questioning the quality of Angelo to
Escalus says:

> What *figure* of us think you he will bear?   (i.1.17)

and in the same scene Angelo says to the Duke:

> Now, good my lord,
> Let there be some more test made of my metal,
> Before so noble and so great a figure
> Be stamp'd upon it.   (i.1.48)

This repetition is of a different order from the emotional emphasis gained by the *continuing* image in a number of the plays.

In *Measure for Measure*, and in *All's Well That Ends Well* Shakespeare found himself engaged with themes and problems that were too strong for the stories that tried to contain them. Properly the themes he would discuss were tragic, though the plots which try to hold them were the plots of comedy. Thus he exchanged, and the order of exchange depends upon one's theory of chronology in order of composition, a number of images between *Measure for Measure* and *Hamlet* and the closeness of the repetition is rare in any other period of his work. So the Duke reflects in the first scene:

> Spirits are not finely touch'd
> But to fine issues, nor Nature never lends
> The smallest scruple of her excellence
> But, like a thrifty goddess, she determines
> Herself the glory of a creditor,
> Both thanks and use.   (i.1.36)

and later Lucio says:

> Our doubts are traitors
> And make us lose the good we oft might win
> By fearing to attempt.   (i.4.77)

So Hamlet reflects after he has seen the army of Fortinbras:

> Sure, he that made us with such large discourse,
> Looking before and after, gave us not
> That capability and god-like reason
> To fust in us unused. Now, whether it be
> Bestial oblivion, or some craven scruple
> Of thinking too precisely on the event,
> A thought which, quarter'd, hath but one part wisdom
> And ever three parts coward, I do not know
> Why yet I live to say 'This thing's to do;'
> Sith I have cause and will and strength and means
> To do't.   (iv.4.36)

This passage is not an isolated example. Sometimes the parallels exist not very precisely in individual words and phrases and in the structure of the sentence, but when Claudio contemplates death the identity is apparent both in the movement of thought and its expression:

> Ay, but to die, and go we know not where;
> To lie in cold obstruction and to rot;
> This sensible warm motion to become
> A kneaded clod; and the delighted spirit
> To bathe in fiery floods, or to reside
> In thrilling region of thick-ribbed ice;
> To be imprisoned in the viewless winds,
> And blown with restless violence round about
> The pendent world.
>
> (iii.1.118)

This could serve almost as an addition or a gloss on passages in Hamlet's *To be or not to be* speech:

> To die; to sleep;
> To sleep: perchance to dream: ay, there's the rub;
> For in that sleep of death what dreams may come
> When we have shuffled off this mortal coil,
> Must give us pause.
>
> (iii.1.64)

And again, later in his speech:

> the dread of something after death,
> The undiscover'd country from whose bourn
> No traveller returns.
>
> (iii.1.78)

Among the parallels with *Measure for Measure* more difficult to define is one which belongs to that anatomizing experience, that questing, metaphysical turn of mind, so strong in *Hamlet*. An example is the prince's speculation, for which Horatio rebukes him (' 'Twere to consider too curiously, to consider so') when he speculates; 'Why may not imagination trace the noble dust of Alexander, till he find it stopping a bung-hole?' (v.1.224). No one has this degree of inquisitive refinement in *Measure for Measure* but there are tendencies in this direction. So Isabella:

> And the poor beetle, that we tread upon,
> In corporal sufferance finds a pang as great
> As when a giant dies.   (iii.1.79)

So, too, the Duke addresses Claudio when he tells him to contemplate death easily:

> Friend hast thou none;
> For thine own bowels, which do call thee sire,
> The mere effusion of thy proper loins,
> Do curse the gout, serpigo, and the rheum,
> For ending thee no sooner.   (iii.1.28)

It was part of some new vision, enquiring, distrustful, and anti-
romantic which rose increasingly into authority, and led to that
emphasis on thought and argument, apparent so strongly throughout *Measure for Measure*. As will be seen in *Hamlet* these elements
were combined with much that was radiant and beautiful, which
enlarged the vision in a way which is not permitted in *Measure
for Measure*.

Further there move in the background certain images, connected
with the argument, as if Shakespeare were pursuing a problem
which perplexed him. So he imagines the ruler as one who
mounts a horse, and can either check, or curb it severely, or
give it free rein, that is to say, as one who can be severe, or
lenient, in his punishments. The image is not present for the
pleasure its detail can give, but for its usefulness in the argument,
and its repetition is not to erect a mounting emphasis, but symbolical of Shakespeare's re-working of a problem to which there
is no clear solution:

> Or whether that the body public be
> A horse whereon the governor doth ride,
> Who, newly in the seat, that it may know
> He can command, lets it straight feel the spur.   (i.2.163)

To another aspect of the same image, the Duke returns, still con-
sidering the same problem:

> We have strict statutes and most biting laws,
> The needful bits and curbs to headstrong steeds.[1]
>
>   (i.3.19)

To the same group of associations Angelo again returns when he
is tempted to seduce Isabella:

> I have begun,
> And now I give my sensual race[2] the rein.   (ii.4.159)

[1] F. reads *weeds*: I accept Theobald's reading of *steeds*.
[2] *race is* 'nature'.

More remarkable and more persistent, for it recurs frequently
in the earlier acts, is an image which, in one way or another,
contrasts the real object and its reflexion in a glass, the shadow
and the thing. Again the insistence on one group of associations
seems to lie with a mind struggling to define an idea, and less
interested in the play of the imagery than in the idea which is
being studied. Shakespeare seems at once fascinated and disturbed
by men's conduct and their real motives, by the parade of moral
conformity and the actuality of sensual desire. The image of the
impression of a face on a coin and the face itself, to which reference
has already been made, is only another attempt to discover the
imagery that will answer the idea. But it is the mirror or glass
that mainly serves as an illustration. One of the clearest statements
is by Isabella:

> proud man,
> Drest in a little brief authority,
> Most ignorant of what he's most assured,
> His glassy essence, like an angry ape,
> Plays such fantastic tricks before high heaven
> As make the angels weep.

(ii.2.117)

She returns later to the deception of the glass in addressing
Angelo:

ANGELO. Nay, women are frail too.
ISABELLA. Ay, as the glasses where they view themselves;
   Which are as easy broke as they make forms.

(ii.4.124)

Throughout, the comparison is between the real thing and the
unreal imitation, and Shakespeare seeks out one association after
another to confirm it. As Angelo says:

> Their saucy sweetness that do coin heaven's image
> In stamps that are forbid.

(ii.4.45)

and later in the same scene, to Isabella:

> as these black masks
> Proclaim an enshield beauty ten times louder
> Than beauty could, display'd.

(ii.4.79)

Still with the same contrast in mind Angelo had commented at the opening of the act:

> We must not make a scarecrow of the law,
> Setting it up to fear the birds of prey,
> And let it keep one shape, till custom make it
> Their perch and not their terror.
>
> (ii.1.1)

Claudio, the only character who is allowed a romantic language, had explored the same idea in the lines:

> but this new governor
> Awakes me all the enrolled penalties
> Which have like unscour'd armour, hung by the wall
> So long that nineteen zodiacs have gone round
> And none of them been worn.
>
> (i.2.169)

Angelo, who explores the idea, or some aspect of it, in so many different ways, makes his most profound exploration through an image, akin to the others, of the glass of divination through which the shadows of the future may be seen:

> The law hath not been dead, though it hath slept:
> Those many had not dared to do that evil,
> If the first that did the edict infringe
> Had answer'd for his deed: now 'tis awake,
> Takes note of what is done; and, like a prophet,
> Looks in a glass, that shows what future evils,
> Either new, or by remissness new-conceived,
> And so in progress to be hatch'd and born,
> Are now to have no successive degrees,
> But, ere they live, to end.
>
> (ii.2.90)

Measure for Measure, thus, with the other dark comedies, marks a profound stage in the development of Shakespeare's language. Delight in the patterns of speech for their own sake has gone, and so have the more decorative of rhetorical flourishes. Instead there is argument, analysis, compression, a curious, or as Horatio might indicate, an over-curious searching. No longer an acceptance of experience with an employment, sometimes almost breathless in its crowded variety, of a mounting imagery, but a questioning, with a sterner use of words to explore the enigma.

There are, of course, other elements. The low language is here, with a vivid imagery of its own. Shakespeare's attention to the sexual side of life was more concentrated than before. Mercutio could speak 'greasily' but now the references to sex are physical and harsh, almost as if they were a revenge on the earlier romanticism. Pompey gives an example, in referring to Claudio's offence as 'groping for trouts in a peculiar river' (i.2.91). Claudio alone, and then only occasionally, is given a romantic language.

Some similar problems are aroused by *All's Well* though the language falls far short of that in *Measure for Measure*. Editors have brought evidence that the play was revised and that it shows the mixture of an earlier and a later vision. Certainly a number of passages belong to earlier moods, to the romantic comedies, and the sonnets, with others of the later, more enquiring spirit, including that of *Measure for Measure*. There remains some ill-balance between the two moods, for the earlier is now inappropriate and the latter appears not fully considered, as if the vision had not fully conceived the new way which the creative power was leading it.

Examples of the earlier manner are copious. So the Countess uses the old, gentle, slow comparison in describing Helena: ''Tis the best brine a maiden can season her praise in. The remembrance of her father never approaches her heart but the tyranny of her sorrows takes all livelihood from her cheek' (i.1.55). At times the language drops into the movement and imagery of the sonnets, such as Shakespeare had affected in the early comedies. So in a speech given to the Countess:

> Even so it was with me when I was young:
>   If ever we are nature's, these are ours; this thorn
> Doth to our rose of youth rightly belong;
>   Our blood to us, this to our blood is born;
> It is the show and seal of nature's truth,
> Where love's strong passion is impress'd in youth:
> By our remembrances of days foregone,
> Such were our faults, or then we thought them none.

> (i.3.134)

Some of the passages in couplets capture the very mood and manner of *A Midsummer-Night's Dream* with some gestures even of the vocabulary:

> Ere twice the horses of the sun shall bring
> Their fiery torcher his diurnal ring,

> Ere twice in murk and occidental damp
> Moist Hesperus hath quench'd his sleepy lamp,
> Or four and twenty times the pilot's glass
> Hath told the thievish minutes how they pass,
> What is infirm from your sound parts shall fly,
> Health shall live free and sickness freely die.
>
> (ii.1.164)

Further, though the theme is now serious, Bertram and Diana in discussing the exchange of rings use the same play and balance in the sentence as did Bassanio and Portia:

> BERTRAM. It is an honour 'longing to our house,
> Bequeathed down from many ancestors;
> Which were the greatest obloquy i' the world
> In me to lose.

to which Diana replies:

> Mine honour's such a ring:
> My chastity's the jewel of our house,
> Bequeathed down from many ancestors;
> Which were the greatest obloquy i' the world
> In me to lose.
>
> (iv.2.42)

While the memories of the earlier style stream into the play they seem no longer to carry conviction, for the atmosphere as a whole no longer supports them. There are some verbal similarities with the tragedies, though not so many as in *Measure for Measure*. Helena in one of the most striking passages re-echoes, or anticipates Hamlet:

> Our remedies oft in ourselves do lie,
> Which we ascribe to heaven: the fated sky
> Gives us free scope, only doth backward pull
> Our slow designs when we ourselves are dull.
>
> (i.1.231)

Yet there is not here any persistent recollection of any one of the tragedies for this sentiment is a general one, and occurs also in *Julius Caesar*.

The strength of *Measure for Measure* lies in the argument and in the fresh mobilisation of language for that end. In *All's Well* the argument fails to develop, so that we are left with some incidentals of the newer style without its fundamental purpose. Had

the argument been expanded it would have been a variation on
the same theme, the strange deception that there is in life, above
all in the life of emotion or passion:

> But, O strange men!
> That can such sweet use make of what they hate,
> When saucy trusting of the cozen'd thoughts
> Defiles the pitchy night.

(iv.4.21)

As in *Measure for Measure*, though less emphatically, there
appears a mind that is over curious, determined so to analyse life
that experience loses its quality. So the king to Bertram:

> Strange is it that our bloods,
> Of colour, weight, and heat, pour'd all together,
> Would quite confound distinction, yet stand off
> In differences so mighty.

(ii.3.125)

What clearly asserts itself is the anti-romantic element of which
Parolles is the main spokesman. All this is different from the
comic bawdiness of the earlier plays, which even when it had been
obscure was light-hearted. There is now something more savage,
at times almost cruel. The undesirable self-restraint of virginity
had once been the theme of the sonnets. Now, in a different
accent, Parolles anatomizes: 'Virginity breeds mites, much like a
cheese; consumes itself to the very paring, and so dies with feeding
his own stomach' (i.1.153). It is a long road from this back to the
gentle, romantic quality of the sonnets:

> Unthrifty loveliness, why dost thou spend
> Upon thyself thy beauty's legacy?
> Nature's bequest gives nothing but doth lend,
> And being frank she lends to those are free.
> Then, beauteous niggard, why dost thou abuse
> The bounteous largess given thee to give?

(*Sonnet* iv)

Measure for Measure and *All's Well That Ends Well* have their
problems of language but they are elementary compared with
those of *Troilus and Cressida*. The one element of similarity is
that there remain passages which seem so firmly attached to an
earlier manner that they would support the theory that the play
was originally conceived at one period and then revised much

later when a more complex vision was predominant. This early manner with all its fluency, its wealth of reference, and its ease of understanding is found in one of Troilus's earliest speeches:

> But I am weaker than a woman's tear,
> Tamer than sleep, fonder than ignorance,
> Less valiant than the virgin in the night
> And skilless as unpractised infancy.

> (i.1.9)

All this could go into *Two Gentlemen of Verona* without any verbal incongruity, while a little later, in the same scene, Troilus, in describing Cressida, speaks with the authentic accent of *Romeo and Juliet*:

> Her bed is India; there she lies, a pearl:
> Between our Ilium and where she resides,
> Let it be call'd the wild and wandering flood,
> Ourself the merchant, and this sailing Pandar
> Our doubtful hope, our convoy and our bark.

> (i.1.103)

It was in this same imagery of the sea, slowly and ploddingly developed, and showing so clearly the mediocrity of his intelligence, that Capulet had described Juliet's tears:

> For still thy eyes, which I may call the sea,
> Do ebb and flow with tears; the bark thy body is,
> Sailing in this salt flood.

> (iii.5.133)

Cressida herself in describing Troilus falls into couplets parallel with the simplest, least individual form of verse that Shakespeare wrote even in the earliest plays:

> But more in Troilus thousand fold I see
> Than in the glass of Pandar's praise may be;
> Yet hold I off. Women are angels, wooing:
> Things won are done; joy's soul lies in the doing.

> (i.2.310)

All these passages lie far removed from what is new and individual in the language of the play.

It is true that it could be urged that Shakespeare was using these naive lines for contrast to keep this meditation in soliloquy distinct from all that surrounds it. But the degree of simplicity is remarkable in a play where so much is complex. In the main language of *Troilus and Cressida* there is indeed some mystery for so much seems to stand utterly apart from all else in his creation. 'The Prologue armed' with which the play opens, seems to confirm that he realised that here was something remote from his audience, unseasonable, and strangely wrought:

> but not in confidence
> Of author's pen or actor's voice.   (*Prologue*, 23)

The language seems like some great desert, bare, strangely lit, but with massive shapes of words found here and there in the darkness, words never employed before, and never to be employed again. For here is the most arresting feature, the words often abstract in meaning that rise up in this play: *conflux, tortive, errant, protractive, persistive, mastic, insisture, scaffoldage, propugnation, appertainments, assubjugate, plantage, soilure, embrasures, maculation,* and so many others. They deny all the qualities that the earlier language possessed, the easy reference to human experience, the warm and rich associative background with scenes and emotions that all men could identify as their own. These new words deny visual reference for they seem strange and shapeless, fashioned for argument rather than delight. To quote Agamemnon's phrase they are 'that unbodied figure of the thought' (i.3.16). They seem endowed with a deliberate harshness to which the frequent ending of *ive* as in *persistive* and *ure* as in *soilure* give emphasis. What was already apparent in *Measure for Measure* has here an increased emphasis for the problem or the argument is supreme over the story and indeed the story fails to respond to it,[1] and in this lies the restlessness of the whole action. In *Measure for Measure* with much that was new, some of the earlier and romantic elements were retained, even when argument was dominant, but in *Troilus and Cressida* this is not so. A new landscape appears, where there is no recall to rural scene, or the homely ways of life. 'I stalk about her door', says Troilus,

> Like a strange soul upon the Stygian banks
> Staying for waftage.   (iii.2.9)

As so often when Shakespeare seems to be re-assessing the powers of language there are passages in which he analyses the effect of verse and imagery. So Troilus asserts that his own fidelity

---

[1] This sentence must be revised if *Troilus and Cressida* is to be placed before *Measure for Measure*.

will be used by poets in their comparisons as superlative to all other similitudes:

> True swains in love shall in the world to come
> Approve their truths by Troilus: when their rhymes,
> Full of protest, of oath and big compare,
> Want similes, truth tired with iteration,
> As true as steel, as plantage to the moon,
> As sun to day, as turtle to her mate,
> As iron to adamant, as earth to the centre,
> Yet, after all comparisons of truth,
> As truth's authentic author to be cited,
> 'As true as Troilus' shall crown up the verse,
> And sanctify the numbers.   (iii.2.180)

It is the desert country which must be traversed, dangerous, without any defined route, and often bare, but with its own compelling quality, holding the mind. There is, indeed, an African reference which gives some confirmation to the desert imagery which I have employed. 'Were his brain as barren As banks of Libya' (i.3.327) says Nestor of Achilles; and, later, Ulysses, also speaking to Achilles, comments:

> And we were better parch in Afric sun
> Than in the pride and salt scorn of his eyes,
> Should he 'scape Hector fair.   (i.3.370)

This union of the abstract word with an intense insistence on argument breaks, at times, into moments of rare beauty, and of most concentrated expression. The most impressive example is in the opening of one of Ulysses's speeches to Achilles:

> Time hath, my lord, a wallet at his back,
> Wherein he puts alms for oblivion.   (iii.3.145)

Much of the power of Shakespearian language lies in the union of the concrete and the abstract but never more forcefully, though sometimes perplexingly, than in this play. An example occurs in the discussion between Nestor and Ulysses as to whether Hector's challenge shall be met by Achilles or Ajax. Nestor is arguing that though the contest is a personal one its effect will be general over the two armies. He first makes a direct statement, capable of a simple interpretation:

> Though't be a sportful combat,
> Yet in the trial much opinion dwells.   (i.3.335)

This he begins to elaborate and to render more abstract, without adding to the meaning:

> Our imputation shall be oddly poised
> In this wild action; for the success,
> Although particular, shall give a scantling[1]
> Of good or bad unto the general.

(i.3.339)

But this is not enough.

The passage is immediately elaborated, and now the metaphor is introduced, whose use is rare in Shakespeare, of an index which, in Elizabethan manner prefixes a volume, and this image enlarges out to a striking and complex figure, abstractly expressed, and indeed barely intelligible if the idea had not already been twice explored in the preceding lines:

> And in such indexes, although small pricks
> To their subsequent volumes, there is seen
> The baby figure of the giant mass
> Of things to come at large.

(i.3.343)

This philosophical interest in *Troilus and Cressida* gains its main emphasis in Ulysses's great speech on 'degree':

> Degree being vizarded,
> The unworthiest shows as fairly in the mask.
> The heavens themselves, the planets and this centre
> Observe degree, priority and place,
> Insisture, course, proportion, season, form,
> Office and custom, in all line of order.

(i.3.83)

Here, instead of imagery for the purpose of pleasure, there is a concentration on the argument, while the nouns are heaped up, one after the other as different aspects of the problem are brought under consideration. Only a bold and practised hand could sustain such matter within the blank verse pattern, and an artist who had abandoned all the earlier fopperies of verse, and now had hardened into a firm and uncompromising control for the sake of argument.

There is an outspoken and revealing passage on the language of *Troilus and Cressida* in the posthumous volume of that penetrating and individual critic A. A. Jack: '*Troilus* is often treated as one of

---

[1] pattern.

the patch-work Plays, but I have never found myself reading it from this point of view. I am as uninterested as Shakespeare was in his *Troilus and Cressida* story, and I think for the same reason, his new and delighted interest in the new management of poetical rhetoric. Shakespeare, here, indulges himself in the style "orgulous". He wished by the invention of a *particular* kind of swelling and swollen language to make the political commonplaces of statecraft—"Time hath, my lord, a wallet at his back"—"Peaceful commerce from individual shores"—as impressive in their way as the outcries of passion—"Farewell the plumed troop and the big wars"—and it has seemed always to me that the huge success he has made of this has never been fittingly acknowledged.'[1]

This mature control of the medium shows itself in a number of ways. Shakespeare has mastered and can use at will a realistic speech, that rejects all ornament, and whose only device is to appear as if there were no device at all. It comes through in a speech such as Pandarus makes to Cressida in describing how Helen spied a white hair 'on Troilus' chin': ' "Two and fifty hairs", quoth he, "and one white: that white hair is my father, and all the rest are his sons." "Jupiter!" quoth she, "which of these hairs is Paris my husband?" "The forked one", quoth he, "pluck't out, and give it him." But there was such laughing! and Helen so blushed, and Paris so chafed, and all the rest so laughed, that it passed' (i.2.175). More individual and more difficult to contrive was the mastery of argument in the verse, with quick, concentrated images, illuminating each stage of the discussion without disturbing its development. So Troilus to Hector:

> I take today a wife, and my election
> Is led on in the conduct of my will;
> My will enkindled by mine eyes and ears,
> Two traded pilots 'twixt the dangerous shores
> Of will and judgement: how may I avoid,
> Although my will distaste what it elected,
> The wife I chose? there can be no evasion
> To blench from this and to stand firm by honour:
> We turn not back the silks upon the merchant,
> When we have soil'd them, nor the remainder viands
> We do not throw in unrespective sieve,
> Because we now are full.

                                             (ii.2.61)

---

[1] *Young Hamlet* (1950).

Though much of the imagery is of a special quality, opaque rather than clearly visual, the language is highly metaphorical. The narrative image has now been on the whole discarded, though a few are retained. Nestor is allowed to develop an image of a storm, and it is noticeable that the sea and the wind occupy a large part in the imaginative language:

> In the reproof of chance
> Lies the true proof of men: the sea being smooth,
> How many shallow bauble boats dare sail
> Upon her patient breast, making their way
> With those of nobler bulk!
> But let the ruffian Boreas once enrage
> The gentle Thetis, and anon behold
> The strong-ribb'd bark through liquid mountains cut,
> Bounding between the two moist elements,
> Like Perseus' horse: where's then the saucy boat
> Whose weak untimber'd sides but even now
> Co-rivall'd greatness? Either to harbour fled,
> Or made a toast for Neptune. Even so
> Doth valour's show and valour's worth divide
> In storms of fortune.

(i.3.33)

Troilus and Cressida thus marks an important stage in Shakespeare's linguistic development though the language is so often remote, particularly where it is most original, from his practice elsewhere.

CHAPTER XII

OTHELLO AND *MACBETH*

I STUDY these two plays together, for they present such contrasting themes at a time when Shakespeare's poetic powers were at their height, and, as a consequence, they illustrate the varied ways in which he brought verse supremely to the service of his drama. *Othello* is the nearest approach to a domestic theme in the tragic period, and the main protagonist stands apart from the others, simple in mind, brave in action, untutored in any subtlety of intellect, and superstitious in his background. Macbeth is a character of a different order, introspective, poetical, self-torturing, ever pre-figuring the evil that he is about to commit, ever assessing his own sin, yet powerless to check his corruption. Intrigue in Iago overcomes the guileless and simple goodness of Othello but the action, though intense and unremitting is a *private* one. In *Macbeth* the evil let loose is given a cosmic significance, so that the whole of our human destiny seems involved in the fact that such malignity can exist, and that reason is such a feeble prisoner of passion. The verse not only answers all the needs of these two contrasting actions, defining the main protagonists and those with whom they are involved, but by imagery and associative suggestion it gathers the whole of the language by some super-added emotional relevancy into a single symbol defining its wider import.

In neither play is Shakespeare indebted to his source for any significant part of his language. Cinthio supplied Shakespeare only with the story of *Othello*, and even there he departed widely from his original. In *Macbeth* Shakespeare followed Holinshed but here again it was the narrative and not the language that in the main he derived. There are however some passages which recall Holinshed. So Macbeth's striking image:

> this even-handed justice
> Commends the ingredients of our poison'd chalice
> To our own lips.

> (i.7.10)

has its parallel in Holinshed: 'For the pricke of conscience (as it

chanceth ever in tyrants and such as atteine to anie estate by un-
righteous means) caused him ever to feare, least he should be
served of the same cup, as he had ministered to his predecessor.'

In the scene in England where Macduff meets Malcolm, Shakespeare follows Holinshed closely. The verse here is in a deliberate
contrast to the more original and highly poetical style of the rest
of the play. As elsewhere it is difficult to discover any dominant
influence out of his reading for the language or the associative
background of the comparisons. Rather it would seem that whatever he read and saw and heard, he used, knowing instinctively
what to employ and what to reject, and so, adding one thing or
another and changing all with the quick and creative stimulus of
his own mind, he produced a highly original language whose
source cannot be discovered in travelling down any single track.
Alfred Hart, in a memorable study,[1] has shown how Shakespeare
derived certain ideas from the Tudor Homilies. 'Shakespeare', he
writes, 'borrowed the doctrines of the divine right of kings, passive
obedience and the sin of rebellion from the homilies.' But Hart
at the same time emphasises that Shakespeare was 'no pick purse
of another's wit', and did not indulge in petty pilferings as did
the tribe of sonneteers. Occasionally he made glorious booty of
Plutarch's purple patches; his description of the meeting of
Cleopatra and Antony, Volumnia's appeal to her son, the speech
of Coriolanus to Aufidius, transmute North's admirable prose
into even more admirable poetry. But neither in *Antony and
Cleopatra* nor in *Coriolanus* nor in any other play, do we find
phrases, lines or passages, 'lifted' or 'conveyed' from the work of
any other writer than the author used as a source for the play.
In *Othello* and in *Lear* I find to some degree an exception to the
general proposition which Mr. Hart is stating. For in these
tragedies there seems a wash of memories from his reading of
Philemon Holland's translations, especially of Pliny's *Natural
History*. Pliny had the Cannibals, the Anthropophagi, and the
men 'whose heads Do grow beneath their shoulders' to whom
Othello referred in his speech (i.3.144) before the Duke. It was
Pliny again who gave the material for Othello's magnificent out-
burst when Iago tells him that his mind may change:

> Never, Iago. Like to the Pontic sea,
> Whose icy current and compulsive course

[1] *Shakespeare and the Homilies* (1934).

6

Ne'er feels retiring ebb, but keeps due on
To the Propontic and the Hellespont,
Even so my bloody thoughts, with violent pace,
Shall ne'er look back, ne'er ebb to humble love,
Till that a capable and wide revenge
Swallow them up.

(iii.3.453)

One of the continuing images in *Othello* lies in the contrast
of the *bookish* and the *unbookish*. Iago refers contemptuously to
Othello's distemper as an 'unbookish jealousy'. Earlier he has
spoken with equal contempt of Cassio as one:

That never set a squadron in the field,
Nor the division of a battle knows
More than a spinster; unless the bookish theoric,
Wherein the toged consuls can propose
As masterly as he: mere prattle, without practice,
Is all his soldiership.

(i.1.22)

Philemon Holland in the Preface to his translation of Livy had
written: 'who would say, the souldier were to have recourse unto
the universitie for militarie skill and knowledge; or the scholler
to put on armes and pitch a campe'. All this could be pursued too
hard. I am convinced that he read often in Philemon Holland
during these years when the tragedies were composed, but once
one leaves the outstanding memories which have left mark in a
few striking images, one follows a doubtful path of conjecture, in
pursuing words and phrases that may have come as easily from
another source as from Philemon Holland. The main body of the
language has still no single identifiable source, but in each of the
two plays is highly individual.

In theme, and in the conceptions which lie behind the language,
though not in the language itself, *Othello* has the closest parallel
with the 'dark' comedies. Very little that is beautiful is allowed
to enter, and such lines as there are have mostly been given to
Othello himself or to Desdemona. Instead of beauty there is a
continuous and emphatic imagery which renders gross and contemptible the sexual act on whose contemplation the action of the
play depends. He has 'boarded a land carack' says Iago to Cassio
of Othello's suit to Desdemona (i.2.50). Later, in telling Roderigo
of love, he says that 'it is merely a lust of the blood and a per-

mission of the will' (i.3.339), where 'will', as Professor F. P. Wilson has reminded us, means 'sensual desire'; and ''twixt my sheets He has done my office' (i.3.393) is his method of phrasing the accusation that Othello has seduced Emilia. To Brabantio he calls out:

> Even now, now, very now, an old black ram
> Is tupping your white ewe,
>
> (i.1.88)

and later he employs the same repulsive image when he is asking Othello what further proof he needs of the supposed love of Desdemona and Cassio:

> how satisfied, my lord?
> Would you, the supervisor, grossly gape on—
> Behold her topp'd?
>
> (iii.3.394)

This emphasis, maintained with an almost intolerable insistence, is supported by a continuing reference to the mind and its emotions in the terms of disease, or infection, or plagues of toads and flies, and 'the slime That sticks on filthy deeds' (v.2.148). Where love is a heat of the blood, a lechery, contemptible, and foul, the whole of life from which it springs is like some shambles on a feverish day, blackened with swarms of summer flies. Iago referring again to his belief that Othello has seduced Emilia says:

> the thought whereof
> Doth, like a poisonous mineral, gnaw my inwards;
> And nothing can or shall content my soul
> Till I am even'd with him, wife for wife.
>
> (ii.1.305)

Othello in one of his heart-rending speeches to Desdemona says how he could have borne 'All kinds of sores and shames on my bare head' (iv.2.49) if only he could have been protected from the final degradation of losing his peace of mind, 'there where I have garner'd up my heart,

> Where either I must live, or bear no life;
> The fountain from the which my current runs,
> Or else dries up; to be discarded thence!
> Or keep it as a cistern for foul toads
> To knot and gender in!
>
> (iv.2.57)

Iago in one of his ugly passages describes to Roderigo what will be Desdemona's course of love with Othello: 'her delicate tenderness will find itself abused, begin to heave the gorge, disrelish and abhor the Moor' (ii.1.235). The examples could be multiplied. They are most numerous in the speeches and soliloquies of Iago, but they spread out like an infecting plague into the language of Othello as he falls, increasingly, under Iago's influence. The statistical methods here fail us, for while it may be proved that images of disease are strongly represented in *Hamlet*, they are, in fact, triumphantly answered by associations of other and happier kinds, but here the mind is not allowed to escape the concept of corruption.

Disease, corruption, man as an animal, infected and lecherous, such conceptions the language of the tragedy forces upon us with the hard consistency of an argument. In *Measure for Measure* this development of the action as an illustration for an argument is also present, and it marks the more mature parts of *Troilus and Cressida*. Here the speeches of Iago to Othello along with his soliloquies have an almost painful insistence.

With this language which answers the general values of the play Shakespeare has defined the function and character of each of the major figures in the tragedy by the language they employ, and never more clearly. Othello's own early speeches explore his proud, manly, and simple character. He is direct in speech, without any of the subtleties of the 'curled darlings' of Venice. So in his defence before the Duke, he uses simple words without imagery, or rhetoric, or argument:

> Her father loved me; oft invited me;
> Still question'd me the story of my life,
> From year to year, the battles, sieges, fortunes,
> That I have pass'd.

> (i.3.128)

His references to the Cannibals and 'The Anthropophagi and men whose heads Do grow beneath their shoulders' (i.3.144) give a touch of the primitive to his transparent and guileless nature, with a background of the superstitious.

Once this essential character has been defined Shakespeare permits us to see the public figure, the great soldier, who with an ample gesture of formal dignity accepts the invitation to be a leader in war:

The tyrant custom, most grave senators,
Hath made the flinty and steel couch of war
My thrice-driven bed of down.

(i.3.230)

Away from this diction of the public occasion he greets Desdemona on their reunion in Cyprus with a moving and direct simplicity, which re-asserts all that is fundamental in his character:

If it were now to die,
'Twere now to be most happy; for, I fear,
My soul hath her content so absolute
That not another comfort like to this
Succeeds in unknown fate.

(ii.1.191)

It is true that his opening speech in this scene had an image to
describe the storm which had its elements of formality:

And let the labouring bark climb hills of seas
Olympus-high and duck again as low
As hell's from heaven!

(ii.1.189)

Professor Spurgeon noted that there is an ample use of the sea in
the tragedy, both in the language of Iago and Othello, and this
she assigns to the sea-faring atmosphere of Venice. Certainly the
sea is in the play, and Othello in his final tragic speech uses the
sea for one of his most poignant phrases:

here is my butt,
And very sea-mark of my utmost sail.

(v.2.267)

In the present scene the sea image stands alone, in contrast to the
easy and unadorned movement of Othello's other speeches:

Honey, you shall be well desired in Cyprus;
I have found great love amongst them. O my sweet,
I prattle out of fashion, and I dote
In mine own comforts.

(ii.1.206)

Othello next appears after the brawl which has followed Cassio's
drunkenness. He is given the language of the general in action;
bold, effective, with no word wasted, straight statements of an
assured mind, with none of the qualifications that arise from a
lack of self-confidence:

>He that stirs next to carve for his own rage
>Holds his soul light; he dies upon his motion.
>Silence that dreadful bell: it frights the isle
>From her propriety.

(ii.3.173)

This is the last scene in which we see Othello as a normal character. From now onwards Iago's harrowing arguments are first to affect, and, ultimately, to undermine him. A larger movement of emotion comes into his language, but only gradually. To Iago's earlier suggestions he responds as one determined to cling to the life of reason:

>Think'st thou I'd make a life of jealousy,
>To follow still the changes of the moon
>With fresh suspicions?

(iii.3.177)

As the mood grows, and as the 'green-eyed god' works its will upon him, he is given a wider range of imaginative language to announce his distress. For the first time, his language identifies itself with that imagery of corruption out of which the central values of the tragedy develop:

>I had rather be a toad,
>And live upon the vapour of a dungeon,
>Than keep a corner in the thing I love
>For others' uses.

(iii.3.270)

In the earlier stages these changes in Othello express themselves in rhetorical speeches, which are formal in pattern and reach their crescendo in the passage:

>I had been happy, if the general camp,
>Pioneers and all, had tasted her sweet body,
>So I had nothing known. O, now, for ever
>Farewell the tranquil mind! farewell content!
>Farewell the plumed troop, and the big wars,
>That make ambition virtue! O, farewell!
>Farewell the neighing steed, and the shrill trump,
>The spirit-stirring drum, the ear-piercing fife,
>The royal banner, and all quality,
>Pride, pomp and circumstance of glorious war!
>And, O you mortal engines, whose rude throats
>The immortal Jove's dread clamours counterfeit,
>Farewell!

(iii.3.345)

This speech seems to mark consciously the contrast between the normal Othello of the earlier acts, and the tragically infected and distraught Othello of the later scenes. The language changes as Othello's mood modifies and nowhere is the control of style illustrated more brilliantly than in this interpretation of Othello afflicted by the disease of jealousy. Pathos marks his despairing attempt to cling to a life of reason, before abandoning himself to the horrors that await him:

> By the world,
> I think my wife be honest and think she is not;
> I think that thou art just and think thou art not.
> *I'll have some proof.*
>
> (iii.3.383)

At first the sway of his rising emotion is expressed, as often before in Shakespeare, rhetorically, and it is here that the magnificent image of the Pontic and Propontic Sea is called into service, but later, his distraught mind is shown realistically. The large phrases are abandoned, verse is discarded, even grammar is thrown away, and there remains the heap of broken phrases of a mind out of control: 'Lie with her! lie on her! We say lie on her, when they belie her. Lie with her! that's fulsome. Handkerchief—confessions—handkerchief! . . . It is not words that shake me thus. Pish! Noses, ears, and lips. Is't possible?—Confess—handkerchief!—O devil!' (iv.1.35).

Apart from a few brief and moving words with Iago ('O, the world hath not a sweeter creature: she might lie by an emperor's side and command him tasks' (iv.1.194), his next appearance is with Desdemona in one of the scenes of greatest cruelty in Shakespeare. Here Othello returns in one gesture to the larger and more formal rhetoric of the earlier scenes, and uses an image among the most impressive but mysterious in the play:

> but, alas, to make me
> A fixed figure for the time of scorn
> To point his slow unmoving finger at!
>
> (iv.2.53)

It is here, where Othello charges Desdemona with being a whore, that he identifies himself most closely with the imagery of foulness and infection which defines the emotional world of the tragedy: 'they rain'd All kinds of sores and shames on my bare head' (iv.2.48); 'a cistern for foul toads To knot and gender in' (iv.2.61); 'as summer flies are in the shambles, That quicken even with blowing' (iv.2.66).

His acceptance of this language of corruption gives all the greater poignancy to the speech he makes before he puts Desdemona to death. It stands out with a beauty, very rare in the tragedy, and with a visual grace and sensory warmth employs the pleasing associations, elsewhere denied to us:

> I'll not shed her blood;
> Nor scar that whiter skin of hers than snow,
> And smooth as monumental alabaster.
>
> (v.2.3)

Once the deed is done, and he hears Emilia calling to him from without, his emotions are so perturbed that he breaks down again into brief phrases, abrupt, elliptical, the hurried utterances of a mind bewildered:

> Yes: 'tis Emilia. By and by. She's dead.
> 'Tis like she comes to speak of Cassio's death.—
> The noise was here. Ha! no more moving?
> Still as the grave. Shall she come in? were't good?—
> I think she stirs again:—no.
>
> (v.2.91)

There follow the painful concluding scenes in which Othello realises his tragic folly. To discover the answering language was a problem in the dramatic use of verse of the first order, and Shakespeare shows what resources he has in reserve. First he gives Othello a moving speech which opens quietly with his description that he will not struggle:

> I have another weapon in this chamber;
> It is a sword of Spain, the ice-brook's temper.
>
> (v.2.252)

The centre of the speech retains this quiet mood, but it is the quietness of an almost superhuman restraint:

> Here is my journey's end, here is my butt,
> And very sea-mark of my utmost sail.
> Do you go back dismay'd? 'tis a lost fear;
> Man but a rush against Othello's breast,
> And he retires.
>
> (v.2.267)

Then suddenly the weight of suppressed emotion is too much for
him, and he breaks out into a storm of rant, a language which
was more frequent in the early historical plays than in the mature
tragedies. It bursts forth in wild, crude phrases, ending in a
region beyond words in a cry of agony:

> Whip me, ye devils,
> From the possession of this heavenly sight!
> Blow me about in winds! roast me in sulphur!
> Wash me in steep-down gulfs of liquid fire!
> O Desdemona! Desdemona! dead!
> Oh! Oh! Oh!   (v.2.277)

There is a final speech, the most subtle, perhaps, in all the play,
for it gathers within itself an epitome of Othello's character before
the madness of jealousy had seized him. Quietly it opens, with
phrases of that same calm simplicity and firm but unarrogant
pride which he had used before the Duke. It moves into imagery
of the base Indian, who 'threw a pearl away Richer than all his
tribe' (v.2.347), and so reconstructs the memory of Othello as the
eastern figure, the noble honest figure among all the subtle and
curled darlings of Venice. Then it turns at the end into what
seems to be irrelevant reminiscence, and we are puzzled as were
those whom Othello addressed, only to discover that he has
deliberately engaged our attention so that the sentence may end—
'O bloody period!'—with his stabbing of himself. Seldom has
Shakespeare gathered into a single speech the epitome of a play
and of its main protagonist:

> Soft you; a word or two before you go   (v.2.338)

Such is the opening, easy, almost conversational, yet this is the
speech which is to end with 'the bloody period', that brilliant
narrative conclusion with which Othello holds his audience fascinated while he stabs himself:

> in Aleppo once,
> Where a malignant and a turban'd Turk
> Beat a Venetian and traduced the state,
> I took by the throat the circumcised dog,
> And smote him, thus. (*Stabs himself.*)   (v.2.352)

Between that opening of 'a word or two' and the conclusion the
whole movement of the play has passed. Othello has given that
brief and brilliant summary of his own character in words that by
their honest directness answer the character he is describing:

When you shall these unlucky deeds relate,
Speak of me as I am; nothing extenuate,
Nor set down aught in malice: then must you speak
Of one that loved not wisely but too well;
Of one not easily jealous, but being wrought
Perplex'd in the extreme.   (v.2.341)

It is F. P. Wilson who has commented on 'these unlucky deeds', and 'perplex'd in the extreme'. 'What colourless words, we are tempted to say,' he writes, 'and good critics have seen here the irony of understatement. But in Elizabethan English "unlucky" means or can mean ill-omened, disastrous; and "perplexed" means or can mean grieved, tortured, the mind on the rack. There is no hyperbole here but neither is there understatement. In the noble and simple magnificence of Othello's speech, the emotion is fully and exactly stated.'[1]

Then follow before the tragic conclusion the images of 'the base Indian' and the 'Arabian trees', which, though without geographical precision, define the eastern background to which Othello belonged.

I have defined Othello's language thus at length for seldom in the plays has Shakespeare made character and language fit with such precision, and the thesis could be maintained for all the major characters, and particularly for Iago. There are, of course, gestures in Othello's speech, which belong not so much to him personally, but to that common pool of language upon which all blank verse speakers in the plays can draw. But in Othello this is less apparent than in Macbeth or Lear. This close relevance and clarity, though brilliantly executed, must not too easily be assumed to give to the language here a superiority over that of the other tragedies. Indeed in many ways the contrary is true. Macbeth and Lear overleap the immediate scenes in which they find themselves and explore the universal implications of their actions. In the tragedy of Macbeth and Lear the whole universe is involved and they, knowing this, even if only in some intuitive way, anatomize all the ways of man under the heavens to seek an explanation or release from the situations in which they find themselves. But *Othello* remains a play of the private action, so that even when Othello calls upon the stars it remains a figure of speech, and not a union of his strange fate to the common destiny of man.

[1] *Shakespeare and The Diction of Common Life* (1941).

In contrast Macbeth sees his actions as so irreparable that they will rather corrupt the whole world than work out their own expiation:

> Will all great Neptune's ocean wash this blood
> Clean from my hand? No, this my hand will rather
> The multitudinous seas incarnadine,
> Making the green one red. (ii.2.60)

Later, when his mood is defiant rather than introspective, Macbeth utters a piece of wildly defiant rhetoric to the witches asserting that his own ends are more important than the whole of human existence. It is here when his passion is most compulsive that he has phantasms of insanity:

> I conjure you, by that which you profess,
> Howe'er you come to know it, answer me:
> Though you untie the winds and let them fight
> Against the churches; though the yesty waves
> Confound and swallow navigation up;
> Though bladed corn be lodged and trees blown down;
> Though castles topple on their warders' heads;
> Though palaces and pyramids do slope
> Their heads to their foundations; though the treasure
> Of nature's germens tumble all together,
> Even till destruction sicken; answer me
> To what I ask you. (iv.1.50)

The comparative narrowness of the theme in *Othello* is emphasised by the features which separate it from the theme of jealousy as ordinarily found in life. Othello is 'dusky' but marries a white woman and this in itself makes the theme exceptional, and further there is Iago with all his 'motiveless malignity'. As a consequence the language is less in range and more deliberate in its effects. It is for this very reason that some of the effects which become obscure in the other tragedies, because they are more complex, can be studied here with greater ease.

I have referred earlier to the comparative rareness of passages of positive beauty. This is deliberate, and gives an added poignancy to the few occasions where such pleasures are permitted. There is a keen and radiant beauty in one of Othello's earliest lines, where he faces Brabantio, Roderigo and the officers:

> Keep up your bright swords, for the dew will rust them. (i.2.59)

Again there is a moment when lines lovely in themselves are given to Desdemona for the song which she sings while Emilia prepares her for bed: there is tragic irony in the passage for it is death, not sleep, for which Desdemona is being prepared:

> The poor soul sat sighing by a sycamore tree,
>   Sing all a green willow;
> Her hand on her bosom, her head on her knee,
>   Sing willow, willow, willow.
>   (iv.3.41)

In Macbeth, as has already been suggested, Shakespeare created a character and a tragedy of a different order. For all the private motives and domestic relationships out of which tragedy is made in Othello he had no space here. Lady Macbeth's first greeting to her husband is of the crime that they are fated to commit·

> Thy letters have transported me beyond
> This ignorant present, and I feel now
> The future in the instant.
>   (i.5.57)

From that instant their association in murder is unremitting, excluding all thoughts that are kindly and normal, and then after Lady Macbeth has broken under the strain, Macbeth continues in desperate and evil loneliness. Such is the pressure that he has no time for Lady Macbeth's death: 'She should have died hereafter' (v.5.17). Macbeth's one reference to the normal kindliness of life, which, with an habitual clarity of vision, he admits to be outside his own experience, has a startling remoteness from the mood of the play:

> that which should accompany old age,
> As honour, love, obedience, troops of friends,
> I must not look to have.
>   (v.3.24)

In *Macbeth* with an abnormality and evil in experience Shakespeare presents the most poetical of his characters, who is sensitive to experience, who knows no element of self deception, whose nerves have been hardened from their early terror by a desperate course of ambition:

> The time has been, my senses would have cool'd
> To hear a night-shriek; and my fell of hair
> Would at a dismal treatise rouse and stir
> As life were in't.
>   (v.5.10)

In approaching this presentation of Macbeth, Shakespeare uses a great concentration of language: what had previously been an extended simile is now a metaphor, and what had been a phrase finds its condensation into a single word. An example which has frequently been quoted can be found in the lines spoken by Macbeth:

> my way of life
> Is fall'n into the sear, the yellow leaf.

(v.3.22)

The comparison had already been with him in his earlier verse but with greater diffuseness: in *Richard II* he had the lines:

> He that hath suffer'd this disorder'd spring
> Hath now himself met with the fall of leaf.

(iii.4.48)

and in Sonnet 73 he had written:

> That time of year thou mayst in me behold
> When yellow leaves, or none, or few do hang.

It was as if his earlier language was an armoury on which he could draw, and with these powers at his disposal he made the presentation of Macbeth the most fully poetical and yet most dramatic in all the tragedies.

His first speech, apart from a few brief comments, is to the weird sisters at the moment when they have 'melted As breath into the wind' (i.3.81). It is the last moment that he retains any contact with normal experience, and the tone is quiet, and the mood orderly and the language uncharged with emotion or phantasy:

> Stay, you imperfect speakers, tell me more:
> By Sinel's death I know I am thane of Glamis;
> But how of Cawdor? the thane of Cawdor lives,
> A prosperous gentleman; and to be king
> Stands not within the prospect of belief,
> No more than to be Cawdor.

(i.3.70)

Later in the same scene, when he has been told by Ross that he is Thane of Cawdor, a madness seizes him. His supreme quality is that at every moment of temptation and crime Macbeth stands ever wakeful to his own motives, and undeceived by his own corruptions, and armed with language to describe the sin he will commit and the horror that it should be committed. As Professor A. A.

Jack wrote: 'the huge conscience-stricken poet that is Macbeth overrides the actions of the dastard.'[1] So he passes from the 'happy prologues to the swelling act Of the imperial theme' (i.3.128):

> to that suggestion
> Whose horrid image doth unfix my hair
> And make my seated heart knock at my ribs,
> Against the use of nature? Present fears
> Are less than horrible imaginings:
> My thought, whose murder yet is but fantastical,
> Shakes so my single state of man that function
> Is smothered in surmise, and nothing is
> But what is not.
>
> (i.3.134)

Some of the elements can be easily distinguished and have a simple relation to the theme. Thus in the earlier scenes, while ambition is strongly with him Macbeth lays a continuous emphasis on *leaping*, and *vaulting* :

> that is a step
> On which I must fall down, or else o'erleap.
>
> (i.4.48)

and again:

> that but this blow
> Might be the be-all and the end-all here,
> But here, upon this bank and shoal of time,
> We'ld jump the life to come.
>
> (i.7.4)

and yet again:

> I have no spur
> To prick the sides of my intent, but only
> Vaulting ambition, which o'erleaps itself
> And falls on the other.
>
> (i.7.25)

In contrast there is the weariness of the final scenes:

> I have lived long enough: my way of life
> Is fall'n into the sear, the yellow leaf.
>
> (v.3.22)

Further Macbeth, always conscious of the evil to which fate is driving him, speaks of the kingship as a borrowed role, and the

[1] *Young Hamlet* (1950).

image is taken up by other characters so that it becomes one of
the most frequent in the whole tragedy. When he is attempting
to resist the temptation to murder Duncan he says to Lady
Macbeth:

> I have bought
> Golden opinions from all sorts of people,
> *Which would be worn now in their newest gloss,*
> Not cast aside so soon.
>
> (i.7.32)

When Ross and Angus first greet Macbeth as Thane of Cawdor,
it is through the image of borrowed clothes that he expresses his
perplexity:

> The thane of Cawdor lives: *why do you dress me*
> *In borrow'd robes?*
>
> (i.3.108)

A little later Banquo commenting how 'rapt' Macbeth is after he
has been told of the new honour returns to the same image:

> *New honours come upon him,*
> *Like our strange garments,* cleave not to their mould
> But with the aid of use.
>
> (i.3.144)

It was to Ross and Angus that Banquo addressed his remarks,
and it is almost as if Shakespeare had intended Angus to recall
them, when in one of the final scenes of the play he makes Angus
say:

> now does *he feel his title*
> *Hang loose about him, like a giant's robe*
> Upon a dwarfish thief.
>
> (v.2.20)

Macduff returns to the same image in suggesting that the old
robes, or the kingship of Duncan, may be happier than the new
robes of Macbeth's kingship:

> adieu!
> Lest our *old robes* sit easier than our new!
>
> (ii.4.37)

Once these more intelligible elements have been extracted there
remains the problem of defining the highly original quality of what
is most individual in Macbeth's language. I find above all the

element of concentration to which I have already referred. With this there is the creation of an imaginative language, no longer dependent on comparison with ordinary experience as simile and metaphor normally are, but with an independent symbolical pageantry of its own. In part it is made up of abstract figures, but these are made vivid and dramatic so that, as frequently in Shakespeare, the abstract and concrete are brought violently together. It is as if he had gone beyond experience and created a new world for Macbeth's fevered mind. One of the most brilliant examples follows Macbeth's address to an imaginary dagger before the murder of Duncan:

> Now o'er the one half-world
> Nature seems dead, and wicked dreams abuse
> The curtain'd sleep; witchcraft celebrates
> Pale Hecate's offerings, and wither'd murder,
> Alarm'd by his sentinel, the wolf,
> Whose howl's his watch, thus with his stealthy pace,
> With Tarquin's ravishing strides, towards his design
> Moves like a ghost. (ii.1.49)

The mind passes over these phrases of phantasy without realising fully how extraordinary they are. For here *wither'd* murder is warned by his guardian wolf that the hour for the performance of his crime has come, and is pictured moving towards his victim with a step as rapid as Tarquin's and as quiet as a ghost's. This is not a scene borrowed from experience but a sequence that exists in its own abstract life, yet caught with ample and rapid reference to the visible world. My paraphrase aims only at part of the original but it shows into what a new and original world Shakespeare's language has moved. The ultimate subtlety lies in the fact that this dread image of murder is created, at the very hour of the performance of the deed, by the murderer himself..

Another example occurs at the conclusion of the soliloquy which opens, 'If it were done when 'tis done' (i.7.1). Macbeth is reflecting on the virtues of Duncan and contemplating how unnatural an act his murder would be:

> Besides, this Duncan
> Hath borne his faculties so meek, hath been
> So clear in his great office, that his virtues
> Will plead like angels, trumpet-tongued, against
> The deep damnation of his taking-off;

And pity, like a naked new-born babe,
Striding the blast, or heaven's cherubim, horsed
Upon the sightless couriers of the air,
Shall blow the horrid deed in every eye,
That tears shall drown the wind.

(i.7.16)

This passage defies paraphrase, and no effort of the mind to follow the sequence of thought, or of the imagination to give it any visual shape is availing. It has something of the effect of the mounting imagery of the earlier plays, where one notion is left half developed while another crowds in upon it. But now the elements are not associated with experience, but arise again from a world of symbolical pageantry. The same power of personification, and then the endowment of the abstract with a vivid dramatic setting appears again in the famous 'Tomorrow, and tomorrow' speech (v.5.17) which is so familiar that the mind has been dulled to its obscurity.

While Macbeth has these speeches of a strange and formidable beauty to explore the journey of his conscience across the diseased territories of his mind, he employs elsewhere, and in most effective contrast, a language which is simple, and draws its associations from an everyday world. The most remarkable example occurs in his reply to the first Murderer who has pleaded: 'We are men, my liege.' Macbeth's speech reads:

Ay, in the catalogue ye go for men;
As hounds and greyhounds, mongrels, spaniels, curs,
Shoughs, water-rugs and demi-wolves are clept
All by the name of dogs: the valued file
Distinguishes the swift, the slow, the subtle,
The housekeeper, the hunter, every one
According to the gift which bounteous nature
Hath in him closed, whereby he does receive
Particular addition, from the bill
That writes them all alike: and so of men.

(iii.1.92)

The general intention of the comparison is obvious, and dramatically it is effective as an interval of emotional suspense between the first mention of Banquo in the scene, and the acceptance by the murderers of their assignment. For Macbeth himself this dog catalogue gives a notable contrast from the highly imaginative and symbolical language of his introspective passages. Even when all these considerations have been fully weighed the elaboration of the passage is extraordinary, though not commented on by critics. Possibly some memory led Shakespeare to expand the detail in the comparison. He may have had in mind *Of English Dogs* (1576) by A. Fleming, who promises 'to express and disclose in due order the grand and general of English Dogs, the difference of them, the use, the properties, and diverse natures of them.' Fleming has an attack on the spaniel whose servility Shakespeare so often emphasises, and he has an anecdote on the fawning quality of the greyhound. He has lists of dogs including mongrels and curs, the brache ('a bloodhound, but in English bitches belonging to the hunting kind of dogs'), and the lymemmer ('in smelling singular, and in swiftness incomparable'). But even if he knew Fleming his mind, as usual, went beyond any one source and ultimately, beyond any source at all. Fleming did not know of 'shoughs', or demi-wolves, or 'water-rugs' of which there is no recorded use either before or since. Shakespeare's mind had presumably made an image[1] of the water-spaniel which Fleming described as 'long, rough, and curled hair'.

Apart from Macbeth's own speeches much of the imaginative language of the tragedy is made out of simple elements. 'Nor heaven peep through the blanket of the dark' (i.5.54) is Lady Macbeth's plea before the murder of Duncan: it is made out of the same homely imagery as Macbeth's, 'Sleep that knits up the ravell'd sleave of care' (ii.2.37); 'nothing in his life Became him like the leaving it' (i.4.7) was Malcolm's account of the death of the Thane of Cawdor. 'Nought's had, all's spent, Where our desire is got without content' (iii.2.4) is Lady Macbeth in the scene before the murder of Banquo. Again Macbeth himself after ranging the hidden resources of language uses in his last desperation an image from the Elizabethan pastime of bear-baiting:

> They have tied me to a stake; I cannot fly,
> But, bear-like, I must fight the course.

> (v.7.1)

Added to these is the continuous use of the image of borrowed robes, to which reference has already been made, simple enough a comparison in itself, but made to illustrate the central theme of the tragedy.

---

[1] For Shakespeare 'rug' was a 'shaggy coat', not the modern floor rug.

From the simple, homely statements, used to illustrate profound conceptions, the language can with a sudden turn, within a single sentence, strike out to some strange territory where the highly metaphorical or even symbolical element is left in possession of the experience. Possibly the most striking instance is Macbeth's description to Banquo and others of his feelings after Duncan's death. Dramatically the speech may seem, at first sight, difficult to interpret, for Macbeth, the murderer, is expressing profound grief at the death of the king he has murdered. Yet when it is recalled how consciousness of evil is with Macbeth parallel with the pursuit of evil, the passage presents what may be interpreted as a sincere expression:

> Had I but died an hour before this chance,
> I had lived a blessed time; for, from this instant,
> There's nothing serious in mortality:
> All is but toys: renown and grace is dead;
> The wine of life is drawn, and the mere lees
> Is left this vault to brag of.
>
> (ii.3.96)

So from the simple statements, such as 'all is but toys' he stretches out to the complex image of the 'wine of life' which defies exact exposition, and yet seems completely to meet in meaning and in emotion Macbeth's needs at this moment.[1]

The frequent repetition of the same words and of the same images in this play increases its high poetical quality. The repetition in *Othello*, usually of elements that were repulsive, had the hard insistence of an argument. In *Macbeth* it is not so, for here, the associative suggestions, so rich and varied, and yet so closely interlinked, give to the play the power of a single symbol, as if it were some jewel, of many surfaces, and yet of one single structure. For the play, though so evil in its theme, far more so than *Othello*, has yet this strange poignancy that its language is so frequently beautiful. I have already suggested how this is possible by the tragic contrast of Macbeth's brutal and fated determination to evil and his deep introspection and self-analysis of his guilt. The images that seek into the sordid and the infected for their resources,

---

[1] *Vault* may be interpreted in several ways: either that Shakespeare has turned from thinking of a wine-vault to think of a burial-vault, or, and I think more probably, that he suggests that under the whole vault of the heavens, with renown and grace dead, nothing that is worth while remains.

so frequent on the lips of Iago, are not to be found in Macbeth until his last, wild outbursts in the final scenes:

> If thou couldst, doctor, cast
> The water of my land, find her disease,
> And purge it to a sound and pristine health,
> I would applaud thee to the very echo,
> That should applaud again.   (v.3.50)

Some of the permanent images, and the constantly used words and phrases in *Macbeth* have often been noted and indeed are inevitable in such a theme: 'thrones', 'blood', 'sleep' and 'night': it would have been difficult to escape these, even if the treatment had been in direct prose. Here they are all made to enhance the high poetical theme, and to them are added the strangely contrasting images of a 'babe', naked, unprotected and of a 'sightless' and uncontrollable force. With these is the frequent use of the word 'fear', and the still more insistent interpretation of this emotion through all its corrupting moods.[1]

The ultimate tragedy of Macbeth as, indeed, the tragedy of Othello is that the *reason* is overcome. Othello surrenders reason as an unwitting victim of Iago's intrigues; Macbeth is more profoundly tragic for he is aware, at each step, how his faculties are being undermined by passions so forceful, that they seem the result of necromancy. It is only natural, therefore, that this conception of the tragic surrender of reason should appear prominently in the language. Banquo makes the first suggestion, after the meeting with the witches: 'have we eaten on the insane root That takes the *reason* prisoner?' (i.3.84), and it is Banquo, again, in the same scene, who comments how,

> oftentimes, to win us to our harm,
> The instruments of darkness tell us truths.   (i.3.123)

Macbeth, in the same scene, on hearing that he is Thane of Cawdor, approaches once again the idea that his power of reason is suspended, so that his whole being concentrates on the murder that he may, one day, commit:

> My thought, whose murder yet is but fantastical,
> Shakes so my single state of man that function
> Is smother'd in surmise, and nothing is
> But what is not.   (i.3.139)

---

[1] See G. Wilson Knight, *The Wheel of Fire* (1930).

Samuel Johnson has defined the meaning of this complex passage: 'all powers of action are oppressed and crushed by one overwhelming image in the mind, and nothing is present to me but that which is really future. Of things now about me I have no perception, being intent wholly on that which has no existence'. The persistence of the idea can be seen in its incidental use by Lady Macbeth when she tells Macbeth how 'with wine and wassail' (i.7.64) she will drug the grooms. Her employment of the image works itself out in a precise and elaborate way, employing the old anatomical division of the brain:

> his two chamberlains
> Will I with wine and wassail so convince
> That memory, the warder of the brain,
> Shall be a fume, and the receipt of reason
> A limbeck only.

(i.7.63)

When in a speech which belongs to the rhetoric of emotional disguise, Macbeth defends before Macduff his action in killing Duncan's grooms, it is again to the conception of emotion as stronger than reason that he returns:

> The expedition of my violent love
> Outrun the pauser, *reason*.

(ii.3.116)

All these references belong to the earlier acts, where Macbeth is still able to see the road back to normality. Later he is sunk so deep in crime that he no longer considers 'the pauser, reason'.

No attempt to describe some of the more obvious and emphatic purposes of the language in *Macbeth* can do justice to all that is achieved. The creative imagination has an abundance, and employs it lavishly, yet never casually, but always in contribution to the main design. An example occurs when Ross enters after the murder of Duncan with an old man, who says that his memory stretches over seventy years and that he can remember many dreadful things but that 'this sore night Hath trifled former knowings'. Ross replies:

> Ah, good father,
> Thou seest, the heavens, as troubled with man's act,
> Threaten his bloody stage: by the clock, 'tis day,
> And yet dark night strangles the travelling lamp:

> Is't night's predominance, or the day's shame,
> That darkness does the face of earth entomb,
> When living light should kiss it?
>
> (ii.4.4)

From a factual point of view all that Ross is doing is to confirm the old man's description of the night. But the range of his imagery, giving to the natural event a supernatural implication, is fitting to the mood of the tragedy. Macbeth himself is given a great variety of imagery, even apart from the main trends which have already been discussed. So in a speech, describing his uncertainty while Banquo is still alive—'we have scotch'd the snake, not kill'd it' (iii.2.13)—he uses an image which brief though it is summarises all that there is in the afflicted moods of his mind:

> better be with the dead,
> Whom we, to gain our peace, have sent to peace,
> Than on the torture of the mind to lie
> In *restless ecstasy*.
>
> (iii.2.19)

CHAPTER XIII

KING LEAR

NOWHERE were Shakespeare's intentions in language more complex and his success more complete than in *King Lear*. All is subject to the dramatic design, and that is conceived in the terms of poetic drama, with the poetry solely at its service. No longer is the approach experimental, as in *Romeo and Juliet*, for the employment is now fully and consciously controlled, or, it may be, that the word, 'consciously', is inappropriate, for so wide are the resources held in command that it would seem here that the conscious mind is working in unity with the unconscious in a rare and rewarding way.

The poet has not the lively embarrassment of a Hamlet or a Polonius, of characters possessing an independent and intellectual interest in style, and so continuously precipitating their linguistic accomplishment in the action. Nor is there the complication of a protagonist such as Macbeth, introspective and self-questioning, exploring his own bewildered attachment to evil through a language highly endowed with poetic imagery. In moods ranging from sanity out to the regions of madness, and to the sane man's attempt to mock the deranged, Shakespeare has so contrived all answering linguistic patterns from plain and concentrated statement to the very phantasms of speech. He unites them all so that ultimately the tragedy rests in the mind as if it were a single poetic image.

Of the dominant or 'iterative' imagery in this tragedy comment has often been made. Violence of action is brought vividly to the audience and often by reference to the lower animals. There lies the central imaginative theme, the merciless cruelty of man, so fierce and unreasonable that only the savagery of beasts can give it an appropriate symbol. So Gloucester tells Regan that he has sent the king to Dover for:

> I would not see thy cruel nails
> Pluck out his poor old eyes; nor thy fierce sister
> *In his anointed flesh stick boarish fangs.* (iii.7.56)

Those who confine the effects of Shakespeare's language to imagery alone are in danger of exaggerating the importance of these dominant comparisons and of minimising the almost inexhaustible variety of the language in the tragedy. So Professor Spurgeon, in emphasising the element of violence, writes: 'the intensity of feeling and emotion in *King Lear* and the sharpness of its focus are revealed by the fact that in Shakespeare's imagination there runs throughout only one overpowering and dominating continuous image. So compelling is this that even well-marked different and subsidiary images are pressed into its service and used to augment and emphasise it.'[1] This is to confine Shakespeare's supreme achievement in poetic drama too narrowly, and, indeed, to miss some of its most original elements.

While the language as a whole is most rigorously employed for the main dramatic purpose there are some passages which seem to have detached themselves. Even here, where there is so much concentration, Shakespeare can, from time to time, fall back, even in an intense scene, into an essay material. For a moment a character explores, in a leisurely manner, inappropriate to his situation, all the possibilities of an idea which has occurred to him. An example can be found when Edgar is left alone upon the stage after Kent and Gloucester and the Fool have borne off the King. His speech is so flat in its sentiments, so thin in the phrasing and movement of its couplets, that some editors have doubted whether it was composed by Shakespeare. Yet a study of the plays shows that this explanation though possible is not essential, for such a type of writing can occur even in the most mature periods of his creation:

> When we our betters see bearing our woes,
> We scarcely think our miseries our foes.
> Who alone suffers suffers most i' the mind,
> Leaving free things and happy shows behind;
> But then the mind much sufferance doth o'er-skip,
> When grief hath mates, and bearing fellowship.

(iii.6.109)

Shakespeare further uses a heavy and unexciting language for passages of narration, a tradition which is common in his practice. It is as if he wished to separate out such speeches from the dramatic exchanges of the active characters. An example occurs when a Gentleman reports to Kent the way Cordelia received the news of her father's treatment by her sisters:

[1] Caroline F. Spurgeon, *Shakespeare's Imagery* (1935).

Ay, sir; she took them, read them in my presence;
And now and then an ample tear trill'd down
Her delicate cheek: it seem'd she was a queen
Over her passion; who, most rebel-like,
Sought to be king o'er her.

KENT. O, then it moved her.

GENT. Not to a rage: patience and sorrow strove
Who should express her goodliest. You have seen
Sunshine and rain at once: her smiles and tears
Were like a better way: those happy smilets,
That play'd on her ripe lip, seem'd not to know
What guests were in her eyes; which parted thence,
As pearls from diamonds dropp'd. In brief,
Sorrow would be a rarity most belov'd,
If all could so become it.

(iv.3.12)

Here is a leisurely, conceited style which Shakespeare had already employed, and at times surpassed, in the early histories. It sounds oddly immature now, amid the concentrated and original diction of this tragedy. Such writing occupies however a very small part of the whole.

It would seem to be within Shakespeare's intention to link the fate of Lear to the whole nature of human experience. This gives to the play an epic quality, and, in the poetic language, calls upon the uttermost resources of his powers of imaginative comparison, and endows, with a sharpened poetic significance, some of the passages which in the early plays might belong to the category of essay material. The following passage, spoken by Lear in the middle of the storm scene, might seem to belong to that generally reflective poetry in which Shakespeare indulges, but here there is concentration despite diversity, for Lear is throughout thinking of his own experience in relation to the general experience of humanity, as the last poignant and personal lines so amply show:

Let the great gods,
That keep this dreadful pother o'er our heads,
Find out their enemies now. Tremble, thou wretch,
That hast within thee undivulged crimes,
Unwhipp'd of justice: hide thee, thou bloody hand;
Thou perjured, and thou simular man of virtue
That art incestuous: caitiff, to pieces shake,

That under covert and convenient seeming
Hast practised on man's life: close pent-up guilts,
Rive your concealing continents, and cry
These dreadful summoners grace. I am a man
More sinn'd against than sinning.

(iii.2.49)

There remains, also, in this as in all the later plays, elements of the language whose contemporary significance cannot any longer be fully defined. Reference has already been made to the difficulty of discovering verbal borrowings in Shakespeare, on any extensive scale, outside the material from which his source is derived. Yet Edmund Blunden has discovered[1] some interesting borrowings by Lear, when he is distraught, from Horace. As Blunden writes: '"Riding over four-inched bridges" and other visions raised by poor Tom's autobiography have stirred Lear's recollection of a famous passage. "*Modo* he's call'd and Mahu" (iii.4.149) chances to chime with that. The next title he gives poor Tom is "learned Theban"[2] and after a little while that is changed for "good Athenian" (iii.4.185). In short, fascinated by Tom's amazements, Lear is all the time contemplating the position through the first Epistle of the second book of Horace, and particularly through these lines:

Ille per extentum funem mihi posse videtur
Ire poeta, meum qui pectus inaniter angit,
Irritat, mulcet, falsis terroribus implet,
Ut magus, et modo me Thebis, modo ponit Athenis.

So, there is a unity between the scattered eccentricities of Lear'. Blunden notes that later in the scene Shakespeare returns to the reminiscences of Horace. Poor Tom is ordered 'to find some better "garments"—he had only a blanket: "you will say they are Persian attire; but let them be changed".[3] This witty stroke is fully appreciated if we see that it plays on the last ode of Horace, Book First: Persicos odi, puer, apparatus ("My boy, Persian attire and I don't agree").'

This would seem derived from a wash of memory from some recent reading by Shakespeare, and now used in the tragedy, and this type of borrowing is unusual. As far as the auditor in the theatre can interpret, this is an additional or secret meaning, 'reserved by the author for his own delectation'. But yet there is

[1] *Shakespeare's Significances* (1929).   [2] iii.4.162.   [3] iii.6.85.

a crazy appropriateness in these phrases even if one has not detected the Horatian reference. It is as if Shakespeare had to give Lear some secret code sequence, and Horace was at hand, and was as good as any other.

The language of Lear and Edgar in this period of madness, presents a new element in Shakespeare's linguistic invention. He allowed Hamlet, who played with madness, to use a semi-free association, free enough to deceive Polonius, but orderly enough at the same time to have liberal admixtures of wit and the reasonable. Lear and Edgar go further, for in the storm scenes they speak in a way which must appear to the audience as disordered, though, in fact, Shakespeare has imported his own secret free-association of ideas to make the impression of disorder.

A notable example, which had puzzled the commentators, was explored some years ago by F. E. Budd.[1] He quotes the first remark made by Edgar, disguised as Tom of Bedlam, when with Lear, Kent, the Fool they have been given shelter by Gloucester from the raging of the storm:

> Frateretto calls me; and tells me Nero is an angler
> in the lake of darkness.

(iii.6.7)

Early commentators had been troubled to find Nero a fisherman but Budd tracked him down in Chaucer's *Monk's Tale*:

> Nettes of gold-thred hadde he gret plentie,
> To fisshe in Tybre, whan him liste pleye.[2]

Here is Nero firmly established as an angler yet as an angler in Tiber, rather than in the Lake of Darkness. Budd turning from Chaucer to Samuel Harsnett's *A Declaration of Egregious Popish Impostures* (1603), a book Shakespeare used for a number of names and phrases in *King Lear*,[3] found that Frateretto was one of

foure devils of the round, or Morrice, whom *Sara* in her fits tuned together, in measure and sweet cadence. At least you should conceive that the devils had no musicke in hell, especially that they would goe a maying without theyr musicke, the Fidler comes in with his Taber, and Pipe, and a whole Morrice after him, with motly visards for their better grace.

[1] *Review of English Studies*, Vol. II (1935), (No. 44, Oct. p. 421 et seq.)
[2] B.3665-6. [3] See below.

So at the very moment when Shakespeare first saw the name Frateretto he had with it the association of fiddling and in turn the fiddling led to Nero. But to stretch the association in a way that seemed crazy, but still had its secret order of reason, Frateretto and his association of fiddling called forth not Nero the fiddler but, via Chaucer, to Nero the angler, and then back to Frateretto again the angling becomes an angling in hell—in the Lake of Darkness—and the Lake of Darkness comes back to Chaucer again with the cruel description of how Nero killed his mother: 'For he her wombe slitte to biholde wher he conceived was.'

Samuel Harsnett's *A Declaration of Egregious Popish Impostures* which he had used in this passage left a trail of verbal memory across the play. There he found apart from Frateretto, the names of a number of other devils, and other references. As Harsnett's volume, published in 1603, is nearly contemporary with the play it is credible that members of the audience would realise the source of the references. If names of devils had not come conveniently from Harsnett, Shakespeare would have had to invent them. As it is the volume has no significant effect on his language in the play: it is an instance of borrowing but not of influence.

To the audience much of the mad language, whether it be by Lear or Edgar, seems just crazy, but Shakespeare, for some reason, gave it all a meaning, even if only a secret meaning. The reader in the study may extract some subtle motive from this, but in the theatre Lear's language will appear wildly distraught, and Edgar will seem to be a sane man feigning to speak nonsense. Blunden shows how in Lear's language, even at its wildest, the association of one thing with another can ultimately be traced. One of his most interesting examples is when Lear, after his escape to Dover, comes, with his crown of weeds, to the side of Gloucester and Edgar. Blunden has an acute observation on this passage: ' "No, they cannot touch me for coining" (iv.6.82); the metaphor echoes, and he changes it into actuality, "There's your press-money". He is "the king himself", preparing his army for the quarrel with France, inspecting recruits. "That fellow handles his bow like a crow-keeper" (iv.6.86). Again we must see not only the fantasy of Lear, but the bird-boy passing over the farm. "Look, look! a mouse"; apparently a reminiscence of the classical proverb, certainly a Falstaffian comment on a supposed recruit's usefulness, and clearly a remark brought on by his spying a field-mouse in the corn. "O! well flown, bird", by no great extension of this, is his enthusiasm for falconry bursting forth as he sees the hawk drop on that mouse . . . "Give the word", he finishes, like a sentry. "Sweet majoram" says Edgar. It sounds "aloof from the entire point": yet Lear says "Pass". And with good secret reason. "Sweet majoram" was accounted, according to Culpeper, a blessed remedy for diseases of the brain. Edgar was clearly a friend.'

Apart from the associations which Blunden has discussed in his brilliant paper it is clear that in this period Shakespeare was constantly turning to Philemon Holland's translation of Pliny's *Natural History*. The evidence for this is strong in *Othello*, and so it remains in *King Lear*. Some of the references are of no deep significance in the language. Thus Lear in defining 'Ingratitude' describes it as

> thou marble-hearted fiend,
> More hideous when thou show'st thee in a child
> Than the sea-monster! (i.4.281)

He may well have recalled Pliny's emphasis on the hideousness of the sea-monster but, on the other hand, there were plenty of other available sources.

The importance of Pliny lay not so much that he was an inexhaustible source for monsters, eclipses, and the stranger habits of all created things, but that in the pages of Philemon Holland's translation Shakespeare found that emphasis on Nature which he employed and re-interpreted in the tragedy. So Holland had written in his Introduction: 'And though Pliny and the rest were not able by Nature's light to search so far as to find out the God of Nature, who sitteth in the glorie of light which none attaineth, but contrariwise in the vanitie of their imagination bewrayed the ignorance of foolish hearts, some doting upon Nature herself, and others upon speciall creatures as their God.' This is the very language of Edmund:

> Thou, nature, art my goddess; to thy law
> My services are bound. (i.2.1)

I mention these examples to show that the language of the tragedy is a texture of reference and suggestion far too complex now to be fully defined, and the length of the text suggests that Shakespeare wrote out the play fully as he had conceived it though knowing that it would have to be 'cut'. Some of the subtlety of the language must have escaped even the contemporary audience, yet naturally they could follow, without effort, much that now remains obscure. So, in one of the most terrible passages, Lear addresses the blind Gloucester:

> I remember thine eyes well enough. Dost thou squiny at me?
> No, do thy worst, blind Cupid; I'll not love (iv.6.139).

The cruel force of the passage is far clearer with Edmund Blunden's note that 'blind Cupid' was 'the sign over a brothel', and this, presumably, the contemporary audience would have followed without the 'edification of the margent'. So this passage links up with Lear's attack on lechery and adultery, and builds up that unity in the thought and language of the tragedy which gives it ultimately an overpowering sense of unity, making it a work of inexhaustible suggestion.

While admitting that elements of the language and its intentions now rest in obscurity much remains where the intention is clear. While the language in *King Lear* is highly individualised, there are some words in the early Acts, used in *Othello*, and repeated here though employed nowhere else in Shakespeare. This would seem to confirm the use of Pliny in the two plays, to suggest that some of the imaginative stimulus of *Othello* remained with Shakespeare at the commencement of his composition of *King Lear*. A. C. Bradley lists the verbal identities in *Shakespearean Tragedy*:[1] *waterish* (*Lear* i.1.261 and *Othello* iii.3.15) and *fortune's alms* (*Lear* i.1.281 and *Othello* iii.4.122) are among the most striking.

The opening scene reveals some of the variety which Shakespeare here commanded, though the most subtle language is to appear later in the storm scenes. A precision marks the change of language from one character to another, and in its variety of employment by a single character to mark changes of mood. Lear's first main speech is formal, and expressed in that type of ceremonial language which Shakespeare normally used for this purpose, and is so employed by Claudius in the Court scene at the beginning of *Hamlet*. With such a regal ceremoniousness Lear addresses his Court:

> Meantime we shall express our darker purpose.
> Give me the map there. Know that we have divided
> In three our kingdom: and 'tis our fast intent
> To shake all cares and business from our age;

[1] pp. 441–442.

Conferring them on younger strengths, while we
Unburthen'd crawl toward death. Our son of Cornwall,
And you, our no less loving son of Albany,
We have this hour a constant will to publish
Our daughters' several dowers, that future strife
May be prevented now.

(i.1.37)

The only phrase to stand apart from this rhetorical usage is the
direct personal and imaginative phrasing of 'we Unburthen'd crawl
toward death'. It is as if in this phrase the old man for the first
time begins to gain supremacy over the King.

If Lear uses a tradition of formal rhetoric Goneril replies with
an essay on friendship in that opaque language which Shakespeare
consistently used when the speaker was trying to conceal his mind:

Sir, I love you more than words can wield the matter;
Dearer than eye-sight, space, and liberty;
Beyond what can be valued, rich or rare;
No less than life, with grace, health, beauty, honour;
As much as child e'er loved, or father found;
A love that makes breath poor, and speech unable;
Beyond all manner of so much I love you.

(i.1.56)

This is the language which Cordelia is later to describe as the
'glib and oily art' (i.1.227) and which Kent defines as the 'large
speeches' (i.1.187) of the two sisters. Goneril's language of deception here is very similar to the formal language in which Edmund
conceals his mind from his father:

Persuade me to the murder of your lordship;
But that I told him, the revenging gods
'Gainst parricides did all their thunders bend;
Spoke, with how manifold and strong a bond
The child was bound to the father.

(ii.1.46)

In contrast is Cordelia's simplicity where the statements are
direct, and as far as possible, monosyllabic, though the triple
movement adds a slight decorative or rhetorical gesture:

You have begot me, bred me, loved me: I
Return those duties back as are right fit,
Obey you, love you, and most honour you.
Why have my sisters husbands, if they say
They love you all?   (i 1.98)

A different type of language is given to the King of France, who is presented as the gracious and romantic suitor, and he, alone, speaks the phrases of the sonneteers. He comes, as it were from an earlier mood of Shakespearian composition, more proper to the comedies, or to *Romeo and Juliet*.

> Fairest Cordelia, that art most rich, being poor;
> Most choice, forsaken; and most loved, despised!
> Thee and thy virtues here I seize upon:
> Be it lawful, I take up what's cast away.
> Gods, gods! 'tis strange that from their cold'st neglect
> My love should kindle to inflamed respect.
> Thy dowerless daughter, king, thrown to my chance,
> Is queen of us, of ours, and our fair France:
> Not all the dukes of waterish Burgundy
> Can buy this unprized precious maid of me.
>
> (i.1.253)

Kent, the honest follower, is at once defined by his language in the appropriate and unqualified phrases with which he rebukes the King:

> be Kent unmannerly,
> When Lear is mad. What wilt thou do, old man?
> Think'st thou that duty shall have dread to speak,
> When power to flattery bows? To plainness honour's bound,
> When majesty stoops to folly.
>
> (i.1.147)

An outstanding feature is the sinister reasonableness of the language of the evil characters. From time to time they are given those vivid and imaginative phrases such as Shakespeare distributes to all characters throughout the plays irrespective of their moral worth. So Goneril in speaking to Cordelia uses the brilliant compactness of 'fortune's alms' in advising her of what should be her relations with the King of France:

> Let your study
> Be to content your lord, who hath received you
> *At fortune's alms*. You have obedience scanted,
> And well are worth the want that you have wanted.
>
> (i.1.279)

More often these evil characters in speaking to each other use a rigidly compact and businesslike expression. A typical example occurs when Goneril and Regan make arrangements for housing their father:

GONERIL. Sister, it is not a little I have to say of what most nearly
appertains to us both. I think our father will hence tonight.

REGAN. That's most certain, and with you; next month with us.

GONERIL. You see how full of changes his age is; the observation we
have made of it hath not been little: he always loved our sister
most; and with what poor judgement he hath now cast her off
appears too grossly.

REGAN. 'Tis the infirmity of his age: yet he hath ever but slenderly
known himself.

(i.1.286)

They speak with all the abrupt and matter-of-fact tones of two
sisters making family arrangements by telephone.

A similar compression in the language of Edmund, especially
when he is concerned with action, leads to one of the most concentrated speeches in any one of the plays:

> I hear my father coming: pardon me;
> In cunning I must draw my sword upon you:
> Draw; seem to defend yourself; now quit you well.
> Yield: come before my father. Light, ho, here!
> Fly, brother. Torches, torches! So, farewell.
> Some blood drawn on me would beget opinion
> Of my more fierce endeavours: I have seen drunkards
> Do more than this in sport. Father, father!
> Stop, stop! No help?

(ii.1.30)

These are not isolated examples, for throughout, the evil characters, when they are concerned with their actions, have no room
for sentiment or contemplation or rhetoric. In contrast one may
note that Albany, who is of a softer grain, is given speeches of a
more poetical and imaginative quality:

> O Goneril!
> You are not worth the dust which the rude wind
> Blows in your face. I fear your disposition:
> That nature, which contemns its origin,
> Cannot be border'd certain in itself;
> She that herself will sliver and disbranch
> From her material sap, perforce must wither
> And come to deadly use.

(iv.2.29)

One of the major effects is the contrast between this raw compression of the evil characters and the range and variety of Lear's

speeches. We have seen how he began with the formal rhetoric of a king, and this breaks down only when he is challenged by Cordelia. The early movements of his anger are expressed through a highly formal language, in which he has the command of a wide ranging imagery. It is different from the language of Macbeth which is introspective, for Lear, in his dilemma, looks out upon the world rather than in upon himself, and challenges that outside world as being the cause of his own distemper. Some of the most moving speeches are those when the early impassioned rhetoric breaks down into the awareness of his own weakness, and of the coming on of insanity. In the speech which follows, the last lines, which are personal and true, follow upon a mood of wild anger:

> Detested kite! thou liest:
> My train are men of choice and rarest parts,
> That all particulars of duty know,
> And in the most exact regard support
> The worships of their name. O most small fault,
> How ugly didst thou in Cordelia show!
> That, like an engine, wrench'd my frame of nature
> From the fix'd place; drew from my heart all love,
> And added to the gall. O Lear, Lear, Lear!
> Beat at this gate, that let thy folly in,
> And thy dear judgement out!
>
> (i.4.284)

From such speeches Lear develops into a language of a mind, broken and disordered. Shakespeare uses his mature powers to represent these states. One can see anger affecting the ordered arrangement of the speech when Lear addresses Gloucester:

> The king would speak with Cornwall; the dear father
> Would with his daughter speak, commands her service:
> Are they inform'd of this? My breath and blood!
> Fiery? the fiery duke? Tell the hot duke that—
> No, but not yet: may be he is not well:
> Infirmity doth still neglect all office
> Whereto our health is bound; we are not ourselves
> When nature, being oppress'd, commands the mind
> To suffer with the body.
>
> (ii.4.102)

It is later, in the storm scenes, that this wild and disordered speech is most fully used, and here Shakespeare allows a great variety of subtle suggestion to enter in. So Lear to Edgar in one of the mad scenes:

> Nature's above art in that respect. There's your press-money. That fellow handles his bow like a crow-keeper: draw me a clothier's yard. Look, look, a mouse! Peace, peace; this piece of toasted cheese will do't. There's my gauntlet; I'll prove it on a giant. Bring up the brown bills. O, well flown, bird! i' the clout, i' the clout: hewgh! Give the word (iv.6.86).

As I have already shown, with the aid of a quotation from Edmund Blunden, these passages are not meaningless; a desperate attempt to pursue one association with another exists in Lear's mind, so that while reason no longer commands, something short of chaos has taken its place. All this makes language in the storm scenes unending in its suggestion, and its hidden unities.

Lear's language is not a regular progress from the wild rhetoric to the complex but distraught speech. Part of his pathos is to be found in the moments of a return to sanity, or at least to an anger which is controlled. So in the heath scene one has the most imaginative expression of a wild and self-consuming rage:

> Blow, winds, and crack your cheeks! rage! blow!
> You cataracts and hurricanoes, spout
> Till you have drench'd our steeples, drown'd the cocks!
> You sulphurous and thought-executing fires,
> Vaunt-couriers to oak-cleaving thunderbolts,
> Singe my white head! And thou, all-shaking thunder,
> Smite flat the thick rotundity o' the world!
> Crack nature's moulds, all germens spill at once,
> That make ingrateful man!
>
> (iii.2.1)

In contrast to all this there appears later the gentle pathos and the considerate quality of the famous speech:

> Poor naked wretches, wheresoe'er you are,
> That bide the pelting of this pitiless storm,
> How shall your houseless heads and unfed sides,
> Your loop'd and window'd raggedness, defend you
> From seasons such as these? O, I have ta'en
> Too little care of this! Take physic, pomp;
> Expose thyself to feel what wretches feel,
> That thou mayst shake the superflux to them,
> And show the heavens more just.
>
> (iii.4.28)

Often there is a pressure and violence in keeping with the dread theme of the tragedy, contrasting, and indeed adding to the pathos of the simpler passages. Thus one of the most scarifying speeches in the whole of Shakespearian tragedy is to be found in Lear's lines to Gloucester:

> I pardon that man's life. What was thy cause?
> Adultery?
> Thou shalt not die: die for adultery! No:
> The wren goes to't, and the small gilded fly
> Does lecher in my sight.

(iv.6.111)

In complete and supremely pathetic contrast is Lear's mono-syllabic tenderness and sincerity as he recognises Cordelia on his return to sanity:

> Pray, do not mock me:
> I am a very foolish fond old man,
> Fourscore and upward, not an hour more nor less;
> And, to deal plainly,
> I fear I am not in my perfect mind.

(iv.7.59)

The kindliness is made all the more moving by the other and cruel moods which pursue it.

Ultimately the greatness of the tragedies is that each has a language, individual and proper to itself, gathering its theme, the atmosphere of the time in which the action is set and its values, along with the spiritual idea in which the tragic conception centres, into a single, unified poetic image. Despite all its diversity the sense of that unity is never greater than in *Lear*. Some of the other tragedies may give greater pleasure, but the knowledge remains that in *Lear* no presentation on the stage, no close study of the text can reveal the whole. Yet the more detailed the examination the more unified becomes the creative purpose.

CHAPTER XIV

THE ROMAN PLAYS:

Julius Caesar; *Antony and Cleopatra*; *Coriolanus*

THESE three plays stand apart, for they all owe their themes to a single source, namely *The Lives of the Noble Grecians and Romanes*, translated into English by Sir Thomas North. This was a work which Shakespeare followed closely for his plots, and further, dipped into for his diction in a way unparalleled by any other source. In all three plays single words, phrases, whole passages will be rendered into blank verse out of North's direct and coloured prose. The most notable and often quoted example of Shakespeare's respect and employment of North's language occurs in the famous description by Enobarbus of Cleopatra's barge:

> The barge she sat in, like a burnish'd throne,
> Burn'd on the water: the poop was beaten gold;
> Purple the sails, and so perfumed that
> The winds were love-sick with them; the oars were silver,
> Which to the tune of flutes kept stroke, and made
> The water which they beat to follow faster,
> As amorous of their strokes. For her own person,
> It beggar'd all description: she did lie
> In her pavilion—cloth-of-gold of tissue—
> O'er-picturing that Venus where we see
> The fancy outwork nature: on each side her
> Stood pretty dimpled boys, like smiling Cupids,
> With divers-colour'd fans, whose wind did seem
> To glow the delicate cheeks which they did cool,
> And what they undid did.

(ii.2.196)

In North the description reads: 'to take her barge in the river of Cydnus, the poop whereof was of gold, the sails of purple, and the oars of silver, which kept stroke in rowing after the sound of the music of flutes, oboes, cytherns, viols, and such other instruments as they played upon the barge. And now for the person of herself: she was laid under a pavilion of cloth of gold of tissue, apparelled

7

and attired like the goddess Venus, commonly drawn in picture; and hard by her on either hand of her, pretty fair boys apparelled as painters do set forth god Cupid, with little fans in their hands, with which they fanned wind upon her.'

The indebtedness is closer than the comparison of these two passages would suggest, for Shakespeare's

> Purple the sails, and so perfumed that
> The winds were love-sick with them

is based on the passage in North which follows that already quoted: 'Her Ladies and gentlemen also, the fairest of them were apparelled like the nymphs, *Nereides* (which are the mermaids of the waters) and like *Graces*, some steering the helm, others tending the tackle and ropes of the barge, out of which there *came a wonderful passing sweet savour of perfumes*, that perfumed the wharf's side, pestered with innumerable multitudes of people.'

This close reliance on North's diction is more marked, as far as extended passages are concerned, in *Antony and Cleopatra* and in *Coriolanus* than in *Julius Caesar*, but throughout North enters linguistically into the plays in a way permitted to no other source. The result is that although the Roman plays belong to different periods in Shakespeare's work, and in that way naturally differ from each other, they are, further, distinct from the plays of the period to which they belong. Thus *Julius Caesar*, presumably, precedes *Hamlet*, and some of the critics of character have found a prefiguring of Hamlet in Brutus, yet the lucid and well-defined purposes of the language of *Julius Caesar* are far removed from the complex and analytical brilliance of *Hamlet*. *Antony and Cleopatra* probably follows soon after *Macbeth*, and it has those great resources of imagery which Shakespeare employed in the great tragedies in a way that almost overwhelms the imagination. Yet it has its own methods by which the poetic language governs the spaciousness of the action, though it could be urged that something of the graver accents of *King Lear* and *Macbeth* have disappeared. *Coriolanus*, which possibly followed *Antony and Cleopatra*, is a tragedy from which the splendour of language has been drained, either, as some have thought, by creative exhaustion or, as is suggested below, from a deliberate attempt to show a political and intellectual argument without the intrusion of other, and possibly more decorative and entertaining matters.

Julius Caesar, one of the most lucid of all the plays, and one which marks a stage in Shakespeare's control of language in drama, cannot be justly estimated through any narrow consideration of its imagery alone. Professor Spurgeon, approaching its language in this way, leaves one with the impression only of negative achievement: '*Julius Caesar* is straight-forward, slow-moving, restrained, almost bare in style; it has relatively few images (less than half those in *Coriolanus* and less than one-third those in *Antony and Cleopatra*), and a characteristic of these is that they are clear, definite, and worked out in a full and leisurely way. . . . There is no leading or floating image in the play; one feels it was not written under the particular stress of emotion or excitement which gives rise to a dominant image.'[1] Yet the close effectiveness of the language in relation to the action shows that much more than this has been achieved. Some of the speeches are among the best-known in Shakespeare, lines and passages linger in the memory, and the poetic language is at the service of the theatre for the adequate presentation of the tragic theme.

How then has this been achieved? Admirably served by North, not only with the plot but by the main sequence of incident, Shakespeare approaches the presentation with a self-confident assurance of intention. He had worked his way through the earlier modes of rhetoric and the high resounding language, which dominated, and in a way adorned, a great part of the English history plays. With North's orderly and finely composed narrative before him he aimed at effects, less excessive and dependent rather upon the structure of the sentences and the speeches than upon imagery. It is an achievement that cannot be assessed by any counting of images, but its influence on the movement of the action is almost everywhere apparent. So Marullus, in his speech to the citizens in the opening scene, seems, at first sight, to be employing a simple language. In fact his speech has a pattern in its structure which leads to an emphasis and beauty. So, for instance, the old rule of triplicity, found in its earliest form in *Love's Labour's Lost* appears here in a new guise:

> And do you now put on your best attire?
> And do you now cull out a holiday?
> And do you now strew flowers in his way
> That comes in triumph over Pompey's blood?
>
> (*Julius Caesar*, i.1.53)

---

[1] *Shakespeare's Imagery.*

If the citizens are reprimanded for *three* grievous errors so are
they indicated *three* ways of repentance:

> Run to your houses, fall upon your knees,
> Pray to the gods to intermit the plague
> That needs must light on this ingratitude.

$$(i.1.58)$$

These are only two examples of the formal, but pleasing patterns
of rhetoric with which the speech has been constructed. Yet the
formality adds to the ease of presentation instead of drawing attention upon itself. Marullus is making the first of those lucid, public
statements, where the strength is in the displacement of the
material. He has eliminated the passages of conceited and aggressive brilliance which insist on intruding themselves in between
the auditor and the argument. On a succession of such speeches,
varied of course in strength and in *tempo*, the play and its action
depend. Such is Cassius's speech to Brutus (i.2), where he first
accuses Caesar of ambition; Cassius's to Casca, when he brings
him into the conspiracy (i.3); Brutus's soliloquy (ii.1.10). 'It must
be by his death'; and his later speeches to the conspirators in the
same scene, and so to the famous, funeral speeches of Brutus and
Antony (iii.2). In no other play does this phenomenon occur.
Partly it is that the action is so completely a public action: more
so than either of the other Roman plays, or, indeed any of the
English history plays, and so, in consequence, Shakespeare has
experimented, and successfully, with what he described as a *public*
diction. This has come when he has worked his way through the
brilliant but obtrusive elements of his earlier style.

It is for the sake of this lucidity of public diction, made moving
and emphatic by the pattern of the sentences, that imagery, where
employed, is brought, in a disciplined way, to the service of the
argument. So in Cassius's first discussion with Brutus, the image
of the mirror ('for the eye sees not itself, But by reflection, by
some other things')[1] is worked out with all elements of detail and
decoration subdued so that the argument may be maintained. To
achieve this swift development of the action, and the necessary
discussion, along with a liveliness in the diction, every device of
balance in phrase, of assonance, and of alliteration is used. An
example, one of many, can be seen in Cassius's famous comment
on Caesar:

[1] 1.2.52.

> Why, man, he doth bestride the narrow world
> Like a Colossus, and we petty men
> Walk under his huge legs and peep about
> To find ourselves dishonourable graves.
> Men at some time are masters of their fates:
> The fault, dear Brutus, is not in our stars,
> But in ourselves, that we are underlings.   (i.2.135)

Once again the effective image is caught into the argument, and not permitted to draw attention to itself: alliteration helps the pattern with 'petty men' who 'peep about', and the 'men' who are 'masters of their fates', accompanied by other numerous, though less obvious, supporting effects of assonance, concluding with the open vowel alliteration of 'in ourselves, that we are underlings'.

The triumph of language in *Julius Caesar* is in the way in which, given this singleness of aim, Shakespeare has avoided monotony. For, unlike *Hamlet*, where the diction varies with character and mood, and from soliloquy to public speech, here from public oration to the secret thoughts of the lonely meditating mind all is gathered into one cumulative surge of ordered and formal narration. So in the remarkable soliloquy of Brutus (ii.1) where the main argument begins with the lucid and concentrated phrase:

> The abuse of greatness is, when it disjoins
> Remorse from power.   (ii.1.18)

Brutus follows this passage with the image of the 'ladder', elaborate possibly, but not in the way of a narrative simile, where the detail seems to take a life of its own, but with every phrase on the descriptive side, firmly answering a step in the argument:

> But 'tis a common proof,
> That lowliness is young ambition's ladder,
> Whereto the climber-upward turns his face;
> But when he once attains the upmost round,
> He then unto the ladder turns his back,
> Looks in the clouds, scorning the base degrees
> By which he did ascend.   (ii.1.21)

It is this control of language which distinguishes *Julius Caesar* most clearly from the preceding plays, and it is this very discipline which helps to give a unity of design where the plot and its early catastrophe present difficulties to the dramatist. For while dramatically the natural climax of the tragedy is to be found in Caesar's death, the most moving speeches occur in the later acts, with the orations of Brutus and Antony and the quarrel scene of Brutus and Cassius. Again the strength lies not in the imagery, but rather in the structure of the speeches themselves. Antony, it is true, in viewing the body of Caesar, in the presence of the conspirators is allowed to expand the image of the stricken hart:

> Here wast thou bay'd, brave hart;
> Here didst thou fall; and here thy hunters stand,
> Sign'd in thy spoil, and crimson'd in thy lethe.
> O world, thou wast the forest to this hart;
> And this, indeed, O world, the heart of thee.
> How like a deer, strucken by many princes,
> Dost thou here lie!   (iii.1.204)

This seems at first sight a return to an earlier manner, yet the scene as a whole shows that Antony is deliberately allowed to expand the image, to be unable as it were to extricate himself from its detail, so as to indicate that he is so carried away by the sight of Caesar's body that he forgets the presence of the conspirators:

CASSIUS. Mark Antony,—
ANTONY. Pardon me, Caius Cassius:
> The enemies of Caesar shall say this;
> Then, in a friend, it is cold modesty.   (iii.1.211)

And a few lines later Antony adds that he was, 'Sway'd from the point, by looking down on Caesar.'

In *Julius Caesar* there is evidence that Shakespeare had learned more fully than at any previous period the effectiveness, especially by way of contrast, of direct statement. Wherever the situation itself conveys the emotion he makes no attempt here to restate the effect in a rhetorical and conceited language. It is as if he had learned by the speeches of Arthur in *King John*, and was now applying the lesson of that experience. So Portia by straightforward statements tells Brutus of the anxiety which his demeanour has caused her:

> You've ungently, Brutus,
> Stole from my bed: and yesternight, at supper,
> You suddenly arose, and walk'd about,
> Musing and sighing, with your arms across,
> And when I ask'd you what the matter was,
> You stared upon me with ungentle looks.
>   (ii.1.237)

This same simplicity enters into the public scenes in the final, almost elegiac note with which the tragedy concludes. Such is Brutus's farewell to Cassius:

> No, Cassius, no: think not, thou noble Roman,
> That ever Brutus will go bound to Rome;
> He bears too great a mind. But this same day
> Must end that work the ides of March begun;
> And whether we shall meet again I know not.
> Therefore our everlasting farewell take:
> For ever, and for ever, farewell, Cassius!
> If we do meet again, why, we shall smile;
> If not, why then, this parting was well made.   (v.i.iii)

Such is the language of this play, where Shakespeare, assisted by a source which he trusted, and reaching a stage in his own linguistic development, unembarrassed by any over-subtle characters, controlled those resources of language which sometimes seemed ready to dominate him.

In *Antony and Cleopatra* all is changed. Though it has not the supreme poetic identity of theme and poetry of *Macbeth*, or the unmatched originality of the storm scenes of *King Lear*, it has beauty, splendour and brilliance, unparalleled elsewhere, and the whole great variety of the theme, and its scenes, geographically so widely stretched, are somehow brought together by the individual *personality* of the language. Not always has its greatness been appreciated, nor its loveliness, and above all its contribution to bringing unity in the audacious diversity of the action. Goethe noted and commented on this last feature: 'Be another remark here made: it will be difficult to find a second poet in whose separate works there is always a different conception operative and throughout effective, as can be demonstrated in Shakespeare's plays. . . . In *Antony and Cleopatra*, it is proclaimed with a thousand tongues that self-indulgence and achievement are incompatible.'[1]

In confirmation of Goethe's criticism one can turn to the brilliant and sudden opening which fixes the theme:

> Nay, but this *dotage* of our general's
> O'erflows the measure.   (i.i.i)

This very word 'dotage' is taken up again by Antony in the second scene, so emphasising the central motive:

[1] Quoted from H. H. Furness New Variorum *Anthonie and Cleopatra*, 1907.

> These strong Egyptian fetters I must break,
> Or lose myself in *dotage*.
>
> (i.2.120)

Against this central theme, frequently re-emphasised, there is Antony's language of magnificence when he accepts the passion that captivates him:

> Let Rome in Tiber melt, and the wide arch
> Of the ranged empire fall! Here is my space.
>
> (i.1.33)

Against the contrast of those two moods the whole of the tragedy exists, from Cleopatra's romantic magnificence:

> Eternity was in our lips and eyes,
> Bliss in our brows' bent; none our parts so poor,
> But was a race of heaven.
>
> (i.3.35)

to her more realistic account of passion in her talk with Charmian:

> I laugh'd him out of patience; and that night
> I laugh'd him into patience: and next morn,
> Ere the ninth hour, I drunk him to his bed;
> Then put my tires and mantles on him, whilst
> I wore his sword Philippan.
>
> (ii.5.19)

In the contrast of extremes, it is there that the distinctive and brilliant feature of the language lies! It extends from the romantic to the sordid. An example occurs in the passage in the first Act in which Caesar describes the vigour of Antony as a soldier before his days with Cleopatra:

> at thy heel
> Did famine follow; whom thou fought'st against,
> Though daintily brought up, with patience more
> Than savages could suffer: thou didst drink
> The stale of horses, and the gilded puddle
> Which beasts would cough at: thy palate then did deign
> The roughest berry on the rudest hedge.
>
> (i.4.58)

On this Hazlitt commented: 'It is worth while to observe that Shakespeare has contrasted the extreme magnificence of the descriptions in this play with pictures of extreme suffering and physical horror, not less striking—partly perhaps to excuse the effeminacy of Mark Antony of whom they are related as having happened, but more to preserve a certain balance of feeling in the mind.' Incidentally Shakespeare's passage, which is based on Plutarch, emphasises and adds to the realistic details in the original.

The variety is greater, more brilliant than in any of the other tragedies. There is not the spiritual depth, and, ultimately, not the originality. Hamlet, Macbeth, and Lear are driven on by something outside any possible control, while Antony is a study of the decay of will, which for moments is arrested, and could conceivably be controlled. Lear's mind is governed by the increasing success of senility in its struggle with power. Antony is always aware of his own disintegration; his is a sacrifice, romantically justifiable perhaps, but of something which could be salvaged. These very circumstances, along with the wide extension of the action are exploited in the range of the verse.

There is, first, the verse of a luxuriant beauty present throughout the play, coming as a recurring motive whenever the magnificence of Cleopatra and the high valour of Antony are remembered, or whenever their passion is sympathetically recalled:

> Or does he walk? or is he on his horse?
> O happy horse, to bear the weight of Antony!
> Do bravely, horse! for wot'st thou whom thou movest?
> The demi-Atlas of this earth, the arm
> And burgonet of men.
>
> (i.5.20)

It is Enobarbus who brings this language of romantic excess into contact with reality, recognising all the charm of Cleopatra and yet conscious of its danger:

> Age cannot wither her, nor custom stale
> Her infinite variety: other women cloy
> The appetites they feed; but she makes hungry
> Where most she satisfies: for vilest things
> Become themselves in her; that the holy priests
> Bless her when she is riggish.
>
> (ii.2.240)

The variety lies not only in mood but in the style of the language itself. Much of what is most effective in the tragedy rests in the simplicity of direct statement. It can be found in the soldier's appeal to Antony:

> O noble emperor, do not fight by sea;
> Trust not to rotten planks: do you misdoubt
> This sword and these my wounds? Let the Egyptians
> And the Phoenicians go a-ducking: we
> Have used to conquer, standing on the earth,
> And fighting foot to foot.   (iii.7.62)

Caesar is permitted a direct language which contrasts with the richer, though more dangerously expansive speech of Antony:

> He calls me boy and chides, as he had power
> To beat me out of Egypt; my messenger
> He hath whipp'd with rods; dares me to personal combat,
> Caesar to Antony: let the old ruffian know
> I have many other ways to die; meantime
> Laugh at his challenge.   (iv.1.1)

Antony's speech, though often seeking an imagery of emphasis and excess, can also be simple, especially in its moods of pathos:

> Unarm, Eros; the long day's task is done,
> And we must sleep.   (iv.14.35)

Before the end of the speech he breaks through from statement to that larger gesture of magnificence and of imagination, so frequent in the play:

> Eros!—I come, my queen:—Eros!—Stay for me:
> Where souls do couch on flowers, we'll hand in hand,
> And with our sprightly port make the ghosts gaze:
> Dido and her Aeneas shall want troops,
> And all the haunt be ours.   (iv.14.50)

While much of the most effective language is thus restrained within simple and direct statement, Shakespeare develops a number of more complex variations.

Nowhere is Shakespeare bolder in the invention that leads him to use nouns as verbs and so create a concentrated effect in the diction:[1] 'a hand that kings Have lipp'd' (ii.5.29); 'I'll unhair thy head' (ii.5.64); 'Julius Caesar, Who at Philippi the good Brutus ghosted' (ii.6.12); 'Had our great palace the capacity To camp this host' (iv.8.32); and

> Wouldst thou be window'd in great Rome and see
> Thy master . . . . bending down
> His corrigible neck.   (iv.14.72)

[1] These examples are cited by Sister Joseph in *Shakespeare's Use of the Arts of Language* (1947).

They show how pliable the instruments of language had become in his hand. He seems ready to try each word in a new context, or a new function, to introduce it to a new meaning, or a fresh association. Here lies, in part, his devotion to puns, though this is an interest shared by his contemporaries and belonging to a common renaissance tradition. This alertness of his mind with vocabulary is seen also in his skill in inventing the negative for a word as in 'I'll unhair thy head'. So frequently did he introduce these invented negatives that A. Hart suggests that this element alone helps to distinguish his plays from those of his contemporaries.[1] They are confirmed by other invented forms of the negative as in *King Lear* (i.4.270): 'a little to disquantity your train'.

The language of Antony himself is vivid and compressed, with images caught and captured in single words. So, when, feeling himself betrayed by Cleopatra and her followers, he says:

> The hearts
> That spaniel'd[2] me at heels, to whom I gave
> Their wishes, do discandy, melt their sweets
> On blossoming Caesar.   (iv.12.20)

This concentrated language is made possible because Shakespeare is re-exploring a cluster of images which he had used at least three times before.[3] The closest is in Hamlet's speech to Horatio:

> Why should the poor be flatter'd?
> No, let the candied tongue lick absurd pomp,
> And crook the pregnant hinges of the knee
> Where thrift may follow fawning.

It was to culminate, as George Rylands has shown, in an elaborate passage in *Timon of Athens*.[4] Much of all this had been noted as early as 1794 by W. Whiter in *A Specimen of a Commentary on Shakespeare*.[5] Shakespeare through returning to one group of associations has come to write, in a manner so compressed, that intelligibility, when the lines are first heard in the theatre, must be difficult.

In many other speeches the concentration is equally great with-

---

[1] A. Hart, *Shakespeare and the Homilies* (1934).
[2] The Folios read *pannelled*: *spaniel'd* first introduced by Hanmer is an emendation, on which Johnson commented that 'it was reasonable to expect that even rival commentators would be satisfied.'
[3] *Julius Caesar*, iii.1.39. *Hamlet* iii.2.64. 1 *Henry IV* i.3.251.
[4] *Timon of Athens* iv.3.250, see G. Rylands *Words and Poetry* (1928).
[5] See also p. 10.

out the same degree of obscurity. Enobarbus, in commenting on Antony's challenge to Caesar for a single combat, speaks with a combination of direct statement and compact yet clear imagery:

> Yes, like enough, high-battled Caesar will
> Unstate his happiness, and be staged to the show,
> Against a sworder! I see men's judgements are
> A parcel of their fortunes; and things outward
> Do draw the inward quality after them,
> To suffer all alike. That he should dream,
> Knowing all measures, the full Caesar will
> Answer his emptiness! Caesar, thou hast subdued
> His judgement too.   (iii.13.29)

In watching Antony die, Cleopatra uses a similar language, beautiful, compressed, and yet not complex or involved:

> The crown o' the earth doth melt. My lord!
> O, wither'd is the garland of the war,
> The soldier's pole is fall'n: young boys and girls
> Are level now with men; the odds is gone,
> And there is nothing left remarkable
> Beneath the visiting moon.   (iv.15.63)

'Pole' as Johnson explained is: 'he at whom the soldiers pointed, as a pageant held high for observation', and once this image is discovered, the 'garland of the war' is clear, and the 'boys and girls' have been caught into Shakespeare's mind by linking the 'garland' and the 'pole' to the festivities of a village.

In few of the plays are there so many obviously beautiful passages, in none so various an imagery or style in language. Shakespeare, who will permit a phrase of irony, or even humour into tragedy, enters here in what is to my mind the boldest example in all the plays. Cleopatra and her ladies are hoisting the dying Antony on to the monument. It is the supreme moment in the play. Cleopatra's comment is:

> Here's sport indeed! How heavy weighs my lord!
>   (iv.15.32)

The commentators have been troubled by the phrase, yet here is the very mood of the play, the contrast of pleasure and tragedy, caught now and remembered in a single word, as Cleopatra recalls how often and in other ways she had held Antony in her arms. One speech by Enobarbus seems to capture the peculiar charm of this tragedy, which steps so easily from realism to magnificence:

                               I saw her once
        Hop forty paces through the public street;
        And having lost her breath, she spoke, and panted,
        That she did make defect perfection,
        And, breathless, power breathe forth.

                                                          (ii.2.233)

    The contrast of the language of *Coriolanus* with that of *Antony and Cleopatra* is striking. Instead of magnificence and variety unending, there is what seems at first sight a flatness or aridity. The easiest explanation would be to suggest some creative exhaustion, as if Shakespeare had used up the resources of his imaginative association in *Antony and Cleopatra*, and now moved, with a drab bareness, through the later play. To judge thus would be to consider too severely, for the theme of *Coriolanus* is itself more intellectual, and constitutes a continual argument, into which the personal elements are allowed to intrude only to the extent to which they can modify the political theme. It would be as false to condemn the language of *Coriolanus* as being something left over from *Antony and Cleopatra*, as negative and inadequate, as it would be to condemn the later poetry of W. B. Yeats because it did not possess the obviously melodious qualities of his earlier lyrics. *Antony and Cleopatra* is based on a personal theme, made supremely more impressive because the whole of the world depends on the private actions and passions of the protagonists, but *Coriolanus* is a political theme and the personal relations intrude only to define and emphasise the nature of the political characters. Out of that contrast arises the difference in the language of the two plays.

    Once this allowance has been made there does remain some sense of harshness in the language of *Coriolanus*, and there are some suggestions that Shakespeare himself was not as completely absorbed in the theme poetically as elsewhere. The language does not discover its own identity, as does the language of the other great tragedies, and there is a very liberal use of prose, not only in the more pedestrian passages, but in major and important discussions. It is as if Shakespeare had left part of the tragedy half-worked, or as if he had composed some sections in a mood where his interest had been distracted. For instance the whole of the first part of Act II, Scene I, is in prose, where Menenius discusses with Sicinius and Brutus. In other moods Shakespeare would most certainly have written in verse a passage such as Menenius's speech:

> I am known to be a humorous patrician, and one that loves a cup of hot wine with not a drop of allaying Tiber in 't; said to be something imperfect in favouring the first complaint; hasty and tinderlike upon too trivial motion; one that converses more with the buttock of the night than with the forehead of the morning (ii.1.51).

A similar impression is gained by Shakespeare's dependence upon North's Plutarch, in incident and language. It is surprising to find that this the last of the Roman plays is far more dependent upon the source than either of its predecessors. In some passages Shakespeare changes the prose of Plutarch into blank verse with a minimum of modification:

> My name is Caius Marcius, who hath done
> To thee particularly and to all the Volsces
> Great hurt and mischief; thereto witness may
> My surname, Coriolanus: the painful service,
> The extreme dangers and the drops of blood
> Shed for my thankless country are requited
> But with that surname; a good memory,
> And witness of the malice and displeasure
> Which thou shouldst bear me: only that name remains;
> The cruelty and envy of the people,
> Permitted by our dastard nobles, who
> Have all forsook me, hath devour'd the rest;
> And suffer'd me by the voice of slaves to be
> Whoop'd out of Rome.   (iv.5.71)

The corresponding passage in North's Plutarch reads:

> I am Caius Martius, who hath done to thy self particularly, and to all the Volsces generally, great hurte and mischief, which I cannot denie for my surname of Coriolanus that I beare. For I never had other benefit nor recompence, of all the true and paynefull service I have done and the extreme daunger I have bene in, but this only surname: a good memorie and witnes, of the malice and displeasure thou showldest beare me. In deede the name only remaineth with me: for the rest, the envie and crueltie of the people of Rome have taken from me, by the sufferance of the dastardly nobilitie and magistrates, who have forsaken me, and let me be banished by the people.

These impressions are emphasised by the absence of those many passages of moving and beautiful language which adorn and give magnificence to *Antony and Cleopatra*. The mood, as I have suggested, is illustrative of the theme of the play, but in the language it seems incompletely realised. At times there is a harshness and a stridency, and ever the inevitable economy:

> See here these movers that do prize their hours
> At a crack'd drachma! Cushions, leaden spoons,
> Irons of a doit, doublets that hangmen would
> Bury with those that wore them, these base slaves,
> Ere yet the fight be done, pack up: down with them!
>
> (i.5.5)

So strong is this dominating impression that the few passages which have their own comeliness stand out in vivid contrast. Coriolanus is given one such example in a speech where as is typical of the play he has been complaining 'Why in this woolvish toge' he should 'beg of Hob and Dick' (ii.3.122). He suddenly turns to a sentence which has that illimitable suggestion which recurs again and again in the language of *Hamlet*, *Macbeth* or *Antony and Cleopatra*, though now the effect is more concentrated:

> Custom calls me to 't:
> What custom wills, in all things should we do 't,
> The dust on antique time would lie unswept,
> And mountainous error be too highly heapt
> For truth to o'erpeer.
>
> (ii.3.124)

It has been sometimes urged that the unadorned language of the tragedy is accompanied by elements which are even tedious. The charge is however unjust, for on the only occasions where Shakespeare permits a slow elaboration of the diction, he is deliberately defining a character by the style of the language. In Menenius's account of the fable of the 'body's members' he is deliberately tedious in order to bring out that an old man is speaking. More often, when Shakespeare's interest is fully aroused, the tragedy shows the packed, concentrated, and elusive language which he uses frequently in these later plays, although often as if he were afraid that it might pass the bounds of reason and break down into unintelligibility. Examples are numerous, particularly in the speeches of the Tribunes, and so for instance in the comment of Brutus on Coriolanus:

All tongues speak of him, and the bleared sights
Are spectacled to see him: your prattling nurse
Into a rapture lets her baby cry
While she chats him: the kitchen malkin pins
Her richest lockram 'bout her reechy neck,
Clambering the walls to eye him: stalls, bulks, windows,
Are smother'd up, leads fill'd, and ridges horsed
With variable complexions, all agreeing
In earnestness to see him: seld-shown flamens
Do press among the popular throngs and puff
To win a vulgar station: our veil'd dames
Commit the war of white and damask in
Their nicely-gawded cheeks to the wanton spoil
Of Phoebus' burning kisses.

(ii.1.221)

Unattractive the language in *Coriolanus* may be at times and on occasion incompletely realised, but on the whole it has been made most purposefully to serve the action.

CHAPTER XV

CYMBELINE; *THE WINTER'S TALE*; *THE TEMPEST*

THOUGH the language of these three plays cannot be treated as one, they are all different, except for the early scenes of *The Winter's Tale*, from the tragedies that precede them. This contrast is very marked in *Cymbeline*, where if one looks for highly metaphorical language, crowded phrase, and bold personification, that by a dramatic setting has stepped into a lively symbolism, one will suffer inevitable disappointment. In comparison with the tragedies the language has on the whole a quietness, a thinness, an absence of overtones or subtle associations. It serves the complex action with complete adequacy but it does not in its passage explore the depths of human experience, any more than does the action itself.

It is almost as if something had been given up and resigned. The tumults and the high passions are excluded and instead there is a gentleness and easy intelligibility. This distinguishing quality can be found in Guiderius's address to Imogen, who lies as if dead in the arms of Arviragus:

> O sweetest, fairest lily!
> My brother wears thee not the one half so well
> As when thou grew'st thyself.

(iv.2.201)

It occurs again, a little later, in the same scene where Arviragus addresses the seemingly dead Imogen in lines which have a quiet lyrical and elegiac quality:

> With fairest flowers
> Whilst summer lasts and I live here, Fidele,
> I'll sweeten thy sad grave: thou shalt not lack
> The flower that's like thy face, pale primrose, nor
> The azured harebell, like thy veins, no, nor
> The leaf of eglantine, whom not to slander,
> Out-sweeten'd not thy breath: the ruddock would,
> With charitable bill—O bill, sore-shaming
> Those rich-left heirs that let their fathers lie
> Without a monument!

(iv.2.218)

There is no urgency in this, no compelling emotion, for all is constructed as if it were the faded memory of a feeling rather than the feeling itself. This is a view which, I know, will not be accepted by those who have found elaborate and symbolical meanings for these plays. No part of Shakespeare's work makes theory so obvious a temptation but it is a temptation easily avoided if the plays are taken back to the theatre and valued for the effect they have there.

At first it might seem that much in the language was a return to that of the earlier plays, yet this is not so. The only real similarity is that the compression has disappeared and nature has returned as one of the main motives into the imagery. As one comes from the tragedies the most striking change is the more diffuse displacement of the language, the leisurely way in which comparisons are developed. So Imogen says, in a typical passage:

> ere I could
> Give him that parting kiss which I had set
> Betwixt two charming words, comes in my father
> And *like the tyrannous breathing of the north*
> *Shakes all our buds from growing.*   (i.3.33)

Nature occupies the major place in the language and Professor Spurgeon, following her usual statistical methods, records: 'The country atmosphere of the play is very marked, and this is as true of the scenes laid in Rome or the king's palace in Britain as of those in the mountains of Wales. This atmosphere is largely created and sustained by the very large proportion of country images, unusually large even for Shakespeare, amounting to about forty per cent of the total number.'[1]

Despite these major parallels with the early language Shakespeare writes in *Cymbeline* as one who has mastered the greatest powers of speech and now chooses to write quietly, and without emphasis. There are some moments when a sentence by some alertness or poignancy reminds one of the powers that for the moment are dormant. Arviragus employs such a phrase when he enters carrying in his arms Imogen who is believed to be dead. In its moving simplicity it may be claimed that this is the most beautiful phrase in the whole play:

> The bird is dead
> That we have made so much on.   (iv.2.197)

[1] *Shakespeare's Imagery.*

Much of the most effective verse has this same quality of the elegiac. In its subdued atmosphere it carries a gesture of resignation, as if the great things had passed, and that their pressure and passion could not be endured again. Such is the mood that enters the song of Arviragus and Guiderius, which is one of the most moving of all Shakespeare's lyrics:

> Fear no more the heat o' the sun,
>   Nor the furious winter's rages;
> Thou thy worldly task hast done,
>   Home art gone, and ta'en thy wages:
> Golden lads and girls all must,
>   As chimney-sweepers, come to dust.

(iv.2.258)

Not all the play is of the dominant atmosphere. The intrigue is so elaborate and sustained that much of the language is called into its service, though without any distinctive quality. Only occasionally does Shakespeare quicken into something that resembles the complex and highly charged language he has abandoned. Once only does he strike out into that hot, distempered diction which came so often into the dark comedies and into *Hamlet*. Iachimo has such a speech on his first meeting with Imogen: 'What makes your admiration?' Imogen asks, and Iachimo replies:

> It cannot be i' the eye, for apes and monkeys
> 'Twixt two such shes would chatter this way and
> Contemn with mows the other; nor i' the judgement,
> For idiots in this case of favour would
> Be wisely definite; nor i' the appetite;
> Sluttery to such neat excellence opposed
> Should make desire vomit emptiness,
> Not so allured to feed.

(i.6.39)

Language as abrupt and strident as this, with such violence of questing, strikes like a blow across the soft movement of most of the play. The language of Belarius has a certain liveliness, and the pace quickens as he calls his sons to stoop and pray at the entrance to the cave:

> the gates of monarchs
> Are arch'd so high that giants may jet through
> And keep their impious turbans on, without
> Good morrow to the sun.

(iii.3.4)

But much of Belarius's language despite its vigour answers the mood already identified as one of resignation, the memory of things passed:

> O, this life
> Is nobler than attending for a check,
> Richer than doing nothing for a bauble,
> Prouder than rustling in unpaid-for silk.   (iii.3.21)

The language has, at times, its own individuality. Shakespeare employs one effect in this play which as far as I can discover he had not used before. He introduces a number of speeches made of quick, short phrases. Such a method would be monotonous if the pause came at the end of each line of blank verse, but with the skill of a practised hand he avoids this. The pause is played skilfully at various places within the line. Imogen is given such a language in her soliloquy when she stands in boy's clothes before the cave of Belarius:

> Two beggars told me
> I could not miss my way: will poor folks lie,
> That have afflictions on them, knowing 'tis
> A punishment or trial? Yes; no wonder,
> When rich ones scarce tell true. To lapse in fulness
> Is sorer than to lie for need, and falsehood
> Is worse in kings than beggars.
>
>   (iii.6.8)

Shakespeare has stretched the ordinary line of blank verse until the pattern is almost broken, as for instance in the following lines later in Imogen's speech:

> But what is this?
> Here is a path to't: 'tis some savage hold:
> I were best not call; I dare not call: yet famine,
> Ere clean it o'erthrow nature, makes it valiant.
>
>   (iii.6.17)

This effect of breaking-up the verse, while bold and original, is used with no easily definable dramatic purpose. It is as if Shakespeare, knowing that he had tried blank verse in every other shape now experimented with this fragmented manner which was ever in danger of destroying the shape altogether. If now he uses it only because the freshness pleases him, he is to return in the early scenes of *The Winter's Tale* to this same way of writing and employ it with great dramatic effect.

For the early scenes of *The Winter's Tale* seem to be recapturing the motives for action, and the language of the tragedies. Leontes' jealousy of Hermione is a return to the *Othello* theme, except that now, jealousy springs into life, without the promptings of an Iago. In a quick, broken, urgent language Shakespeare strikes out the picture of this sudden distempered passion in Leontes:

> Too hot, too hot!
> To mingle friendship far is mingling bloods.
> I have tremor cordis on me: my heart dances;
> But not for joy; not joy. This entertainment
> May a free face put on, derive a liberty
> From heartiness, from bounty, fertile bosom,
> And well become the agent; 't may, I grant;
> But to be paddling palms and pinching fingers,
> As now they are, and making practised smiles,
> As in a looking-glass, and then to sigh, as 'twere
> The mort o' the deer; O, that is entertainment
> My bosom likes not, nor my brows!
>
> (i.2.108)

The passage is made up of short statements, usually less than a line in length with a cumulative effect that seems deliberately to be breaking down the melody, and the more elaborate rhythmical effects of which he has proved blank verse capable. Imagery on the whole has been set aside. The language comes up to meet one in spurts, an effect at which Shakespeare had not aimed before *Cymbeline*. What in *Cymbeline* was incidental becomes here one of the dominant forms of language for this is the type of speech used by Leontes throughout these early scenes. The more extreme example is in Leontes' address to Mamillius:

> Thou want'st a rough pash and the shoots that I have,
> To be full like me: yet they say we are
> Almost as like as eggs; women say so,
> That will say any thing: but were they false
> As o'er-dyed blacks, as wind, as waters, false
> As dice are to be wish'd by one that fixes
> No bourn 'twixt his and mine, yet were it true
> To say this boy were like me. Come, sir page,
> Look on me with your welkin eye: sweet villain!
> Most dear'st! my collop! Can thy dam?—may't be?
>
> (i.2.128)

Here is his new manner used with mature intention. The rough and abrupt phrases, which huddle upon one another so as almost to break the texture of the line, represent the mind of Leontes maddened by his distemper of jealousy. There is a bold use of the colloquial—'women say so, That will say any thing'—so that the whole passage has an atmosphere of conversation. Yet the effect is more subtle than a direct realism, for the meaning is enlivened and explored by images, such as the over-dyed black clothes, and the falsely played dice: these are thrown into the argument, to be used and rejected with a rapidity that answers the fevered quickness of the whole passage.

Urgent and moving as is the language of these early scenes it lacks the dramatic and imaginative strength of the great tragedies. There is some sense of withdrawal, of some imaginative exhaustion, though of great technical skill. It is as if the storehouse of memory had been ransacked so often that its stores were, at length, a little depleted. This appears clearly in a remarkable passage where Leontes considers how much happier he would have been if he had remained ignorant of the adultery of which he believes his wife guilty. He takes hold of the image of the spider in a glass of wine and works his way through it, not dully, as in some of the early, narrative images, but with a heavy persistence:

> Alack, for lesser knowledge! how accursed
> In being so blest! There may be in the cup
> A spider steep'd, and one may drink, depart,
> And yet partake no venom, for his knowledge
> Is not infected: but if one present
> The abhorr'd ingredient to his eye, make known
> How he hath drunk, he cracks his gorge, his sides,
> With violent hefts. I have drunk, and seen the spider.
>
> (ii.1.38)

With this one may compare Othello's moving plea, expressed in simple language, but with a full *dramatic* exploration of the idea:

> What sense had I of her stol'n hours of lust?
> I saw 't not, thought it not, it harm'd not me:
> I slept the next night well, was free and merry;
> I found not Cassio's kisses on her lips:
> He that is robb'd, not wanting what is stol'n,
> Let him not know't, and he's not robb'd at all.
> IAGO. I am sorry to hear this.

OTHELLO. I had been happy, if the general camp,
　　Pioneers and all, had tasted her sweet body,
　　So I had nothing known.

(iii.3.338)

The language of *The Winter's Tale* changes, abruptly, in the middle of Act III, Scene 3. There at line 58 Shakespeare disposes of Antigonus—'Exit, pursued by a bear'—in what Sir Walter Raleigh described as 'the most unprincipled and reckless fashion'. In the next line there enters a Shepherd. We move from the memory of tragedy, still strong in the first scenes, to the gentleness of the close, and there is no turning back, for never again was Shakespeare to attempt the complex, allusive language of Leontes. I do not mean that the later scenes are without the concentrated phrase, newly minted. Leontes provides one in his address to Florizel:

> 　　　　　The blessed gods
> Purge all infection from our air whilst you
> Do *climate* here!

(v.1.168)

But the power of compression is no longer used for intensity of thought and introspection as in the tragedies. What has entered is beautiful, but it has hidden within it the memory of something abandoned. It is as if he had tried in the early scenes to work his way back from the unstrenuous and artificial beauty of *Cymbeline* and now he had given up the attempt. The surrender to the mood of *Cymbeline* can be found most exactly in Perdita's flower speech which parallels so closely Arviragus's speech over the seemingly dead Imogen. After addressing the disguised Polixenes and Camillo:

> 　　　　Here's flowers for you;
> Hot lavender, mints, savory, marjoram;
> The marigold.

(iv.4.103)

she turns to Florizel:

> 　　　　　O Proserpina,
> For the flowers now, that frighted thou let'st fall
> From Dis's waggon! daffodils,
> That come before the swallow dares, and take
> The winds of March with beauty; violets dim,
> But sweeter than the lids of Juno's eyes
> Or Cytherea's breath; pale primroses,

> That die unmarried, ere they can behold
> Bright Phoebus in his strength—a malady
> Most incident to maids; bold oxlips and
> The crown imperial; lilies of all kinds,
> The flower-de-luce being one!   (iv.4.116)

This is no longer the fresh rural nature of the early plays but a more sophisticated and elaborate movement. It is nature used to make an elegant pattern, as if it were being consciously displayed for the courtier's eye. It has been suggested that Shakespeare is using this language to create a myth, and to show Perdita as a Spring Goddess. The intention would thus be anthropological rather than courtly. But I fail to see that an audience in the theatre could reach such a conclusion, and it is with the audience in the theatre that drama is concerned.

He seldom uses now the sustained passages of argument which were so notable in the 'dark' comedies and the tragedies, where the lines were welded into large and elaborately constructed sentences, in which each clause added without confusion to the strength of the whole. Yet, the power remains, although so seldom employed. Perdita, for instance, tells Polixenes that she will not grow 'streak'd gillyvors, Which some call nature's bastards' (iv.4.82).

> For I have heard it said
> There is an art which in their piedness shares
> With great creating nature.   (iv.4.86)

To this Polixenes replies in a well-known passage, which though it has a dramatic irony, constitutes one of the most sustained and moving passages in the play:

> Yet nature is made better by no mean
> But nature makes that mean: so, over that art
> Which you say adds to nature, is an art
> That nature makes. You see, sweet maid, we marry
> A gentler scion to the wildest stock,
> And make conceive a bark of baser kind
> By bud of nobler race: this is an art
> Which does mend nature, change it rather, but
> The art itself is nature.   (iv.4.89)

There is the cunning boldly, even audaciously used, but the skill is not gathered up and defined to any new purpose.

The Tempest, though commonly grouped with these romances of the last period, and similar to them, in that it has little in common with the tragedies, is very distinct in its language. After the boisterous prose of the storm scene—'What cares these roarers for the name of king?' (i.1.18)—the action moves to the deliberately quiet, and brilliantly concentrated retrospective speech by Prospero. Whether or not this constitutes a revision of the play, by the reduction of a number of scenes in an earlier version into a single recapitulatory speech, happily does not concern the present argument. Shakespeare, in one of the longest speeches in the plays, using an unemphatic style, creates the mood of the island and, at the same time, in a most concentrated manner, reveals Prospero's previous history. Such is the concentration that in a single sentence he encompasses the whole plot of his brother and the King of Naples:

> This King of Naples, being an enemy
> To me inveterate, hearkens my brother's suit;
> Which was, that he, in lieu o' the premises
> Of homage and I know not how much tribute,
> Should presently extirpate me and mine
> Out of the dukedom and confer fair Milan
> With all the honours on my brother: whereon,
> A treacherous army levied, one midnight
> Fated to the purpose did Antonio open
> The gates of Milan, and, i' the dead of darkness,
> The ministers for the purpose hurried thence
> Me and thy crying self.   (i.2.121)

Seldom had there been so much said in the plays in so few words since Hamlet described his adventures with the pirates.

In studied contrast is the language of Caliban, where the expression is always in the most simple statements, and where all depends not on the imagination but on statements of fact, and on sensory impressions. This is brilliantly achieved in Caliban's famous speech to Stephano:

> the isle is full of noises,
> Sounds and sweet airs, that give delight and hurt not.
>   (iii.2.144)

The spirit of this primitive creature, struggling with intelligence, covetous, sensual, pathetic is all conveyed in the description of his dream later in the same speech:

> in dreaming,
> The clouds methought would open and show riches
> Ready to drop upon me, that, when I waked,
> I cried to dream again.
>
> (iii.2.149)

His comparisons and his imagery, are restrained, with very few exceptions, within the range of experience which has been possible for him. So he describes the torments that Prospero's spirits have placed on him:

> Sometime like apes that mow and chatter at me
> And after bite me, then like hedgehogs which
> Lie tumbling in my barefoot way and mount
> Their pricks at my football.
>
> (ii.2.9)

It is through Caliban that we come to know the scenery and life of the island, in the vivid, simple statements that he makes of what has come within his sphere of knowledge: he tells Stephano:

> I'll show thee the best springs; I'll pluck thee berries;
> I'll fish for thee and get thee wood enough.
>
> (ii.2.164)

and later:

> I prithee, let me bring thee where crabs grow;
> And I with my long nails will dig thee pig-nuts;
> Show thee a jay's nest and instruct thee how
> To snare the nimble marmoset; I'll bring thee
> To clustering filberts and sometimes I'll get thee
> Young scamels from the rock.
>
> (ii.2.171)

The language of Ferdinand is in direct contrast to Caliban's: its movement is graciously elaborate and the syntax involved though never obscure. It is the language of one who can play with the pattern of his sentences, yet any strong sensory and factual background is missing in this young prince puzzled by a strange and fantastical experience:

> Where should this music be? i' the air or the earth?
> It sounds no more: and, sure, it waits upon
> Some god o' the island. Sitting on a bank,
> Weeping again the king my father's wreck,
> This music crept by me upon the waters,
> Allaying both their fury and my passion
> With its sweet air.
>
> (i.2.387)

In the disposition of his phrases he has the balance and pretty
skill of a courtier, yet his imagery is limited, as of one whose
mind is new to the world, and as if his innocence were but little
touched·with experience. As he carries his logs, which he elegantly
describes as 'This wooden slavery' (iii.1.62), he speaks in his light
but well-patterned periods:

> This my mean task
> Would be as heavy to me as odious, but
> The mistress which I serve quickens what's dead
> And makes my labours pleasures: O, she is
> Ten times more gentle than her father's crabbed,
> And he's composed of harshness.

(iii.1.4)

On the whole the play has few of those general reflections on
life, which marked the tragedies, and especially the speeches of
Hamlet and Macbeth, where the mind sought out from the
immediate experience to its universal significance. There are,
however, two notable exceptions: Gonzalo is given a speech based
on Montaigne's *Des Cannibales*, in which he describes his ideal of
a state:

> I' the commonwealth I would by contraries
> Execute all things; for no kind of traffic
> Would I admit; no name of magistrate;
> Letters should not be known; riches, poverty,
> And use of service, none; contract, succession,
> Bourn, bound of land, tilth, vineyard, none;
> No use of metal, corn, or wine, or oil;
> No occupation; all men idle, all;
> And women too, but innocent and pure;
> No sovereignty.

(ii.1.147)

At first this seems a piece of gratuitous reflection by Gonzalo, but
in fact it does constitute something of the spiritual quality from
which the play arises and it is possible that it was out of Montaigne
that Shakespeare took the presiding idea of his island.

The other passage is the still more famous comment of Prospero
after the Masque:

> These our actors,
> As I foretold you, were all spirits and
> Are melted into air, into thin air:
> And, like the baseless fabric of this vision,

> The cloud-capp'd towers, the gorgeous palaces,
> The solemn temples, the great globe itself,
> Yea, all which it inherit, shall dissolve
> And, like this insubstantial pageant faded,
> Leave not a rack behind. We are such stuff
> As dreams are made on, and our little life
> Is rounded with a sleep.   (iv.1.148)

Even if, as has been suggested, the passage owes something to a stanza from the Earl of Sterling's *Tragedie of Darius* (1603), the structure of the passage is Shakespeare's own. Sterling's lines read:

> Let greatnesse of her glascie sceptres vaunt;
>   Not scepters, no, but reeds, soone brus'd, soone broken:
> And let this worldie pomp our wits inchant,
>   All fades, and scarclie leaves behind a token
> Those golden pallaces, those gorgeous halles,
>   With fourniture superfluouslie faire!
> Those statlie courts, those sky-encountering walles
>   Evanish up like vapours in the aire.

The thought itself is a commonplace of classical literature which has here been emblazoned into one of the most moving imaginative passages in all the plays. It symbolises not only the mood of this play but the whole quiescent sense that grows with the last plays. In the tragedies when a character had seized upon a cosmic vision it had been in a mood of destructive violence. Nothing could be further removed from Prospero's speech than Lear's outbursts against the ordering of the world.

It is a more philosophical and spiritual conception that Prospero finds in his own 'insubstantial pageant' (iv.1.155), a mood where again gentleness touches resignation knowing that the great actions and the high passions are passed. As Prospero himself says in the next few lines:

> Bear with my weakness; my old brain is troubled:
> Be not disturb'd with my infirmity.   (iv.1.159)

One other passage stands out both for its own brilliance and its place in the interpretation of the play. After he has commanded Ariel to release 'the king and's followers' (v.1.7) Prospero utters his well-known soliloquy which opens

> Ye elves of hills, brooks, standing lakes and groves (v.1.33)

Here Shakespeare closely follows a passage in Ovid's *Metamorphoses* (vii.197-219) which Arthur Golding translated. As E. I. Fripp has shown[1] Shakespeare knew Ovid in the original and indeed had the Latin text in mind in this passage. This did not prevent him from also using Arthur Golding's translation and I have thought Fripp ungenerous in referring to Golding's work as 'clownish'.

The break with Golding comes in the personal passage with which Prospero concludes:

> But this rough magic
> I here abjure, and, when I have required
> Some heavenly music, which even now I do,
> To work mine end upon their senses that
> This airy charm is for, I'll break my staff,
> Bury it certain fathoms in the earth,
> And deeper than did ever plummet sound
> I'll drown my book.   (v.1.50)

This moving passage has again, and somehow more profoundly than in the actual situation in which it is found, the sense of resignation and acceptance. I know that the play has been interpreted autobiographically, and also in a Christian and mystical way. It may be. There are intuitions of experience beyond and more powerful than the situations and characters of a romantic entertainment. It is as if *A Midsummer-Night's Dream* had been re-conceived in a profounder mood. Throughout *The Tempest* one cannot escape the feeling that this is a final mood, something which follows the early riches, and the later ardours and endurances. There is a great strength and ingenuity, but an absence of emphasis, a sense that the end of the road has been reached.

[1] *Shakespeare Studies* (1930).

INDEX

Date Due